# Glory Jays

## *Canada's World Series Champions*

Rosie DiManno

Sagamore Publishing

Production supervision
    and book design: Brian J. Moore
Cover design: Michelle R. Dressen
Editor: Russ Lake
Proofreader: Phyllis L. Bannon


Library of Congress Catalog Card Number: 92-63137
ISBN: 0-915611-68-6

Printed and bound in Canada by John Deyell Company Limited.

*For Patrick, who prefers hockey*
♦♦♦♦♦♦

# Contents

# Acknowledgments

If I'd known a year ago that I was going to write a book about the Toronto Blue Jays, I would have kept better notes. As it is, some of what appears within these pages was published originally in the *Toronto Star*, the newspaper that indulged my fondness for baseball in '92, from spring training to the World Series.

I am indebted, most particularly, to the *Star's real* baseball writers, who allowed me to plunder their copy and appropriate whatever I needed from their day-to-day dispatches from the front. They are beat writers Tom Slater, Allan Ryan, Jim Byers, and columnist Dave Perkins. Other writers have been acknowledged in the text.

I would also like to thank Kevin Boland, a connoisseur of baseball and my benevolent tutor. Kevin's supervision of this manuscript, in-progress, saved me from much embarrassment.

Whatever inaccuracies remain are totally my own.

Rosie DiManno

# Glory Jays

## *Alpha and Omega* 1

It was a bacchanal of baseball.

A revel that stretched from the Grapefruit League to the World Series, from the giggly encounters of Dunedin to the heart-thumping dramatics in Atlanta, from the vernal hopes of spring to the triumphant denouement of autumn.

A season in the sun and the wind and the rain. But mostly in the hermetically sealed comfort of the SkyDome in Toronto, the most vainglorious playpen ever built by man, with a synthetic carpet underfoot and a steel-strutted carapace overhead. The lid shunted open like the aperture of a camera, letting in light and air, but only at the whim of timid custodians, a kind of wussy weather synod that convened prior to every home game. It was a futuristic robodome for a team that was trying to bury its past.

It had been only a tiny past at that, the blink of an eye in cosmic terms. But for the Toronto Blue Jays it hung heavy on their souls, a great weight of opportunities squandered and roads not taken, of dead ends and detours and the cul-de-sac where also-rans resided. The Blue Jays pined to move up in the world, way up, all the way to the high-rent district of the World Series.

They're living there now: World Series Champions of 1992.

What a wild, strange trip it's been. For Winfield, and Morris, and Alomar, and White; for Carter and Olerud and Gruber and Borders; for Henke and Stieb and Key and Guzman; for Wells and Stottlemyre and Maldonado and Ward (D.); for Bell and Lee and Timlin and Sprague, for Griffin and Tabler and Mulliniks and Ward (T.); for Eichhorn and Cone and Hentgen and Knorr; for Maksudian and Quinlan and Weathers and Kent. For all the transient Jays who came up and were sent down. For the ones

who started somewhere else and the ones who ended somewhere else. For Beeston, and Gillick, and Gaston, and Ash. For the
more than four million fans who spun through the turnstiles at
the SkyDome in '92, setting another major league attendance
record.

It had begun 15 years earlier, in the snow and chill of Exhibition Stadium, with a blizzard whipping off Lake Ontario and
players strapping shin guards to their shoes so they could schuss
around the infield. We wiped our noses with our mittens and
greeted the game of summer in our winter wretchedness. The
Jays won that first encounter in 1977, as they did their last in 1992.
In between, we taught ourselves baseball. And sometimes it
seemed like any schlemiel belching beer fumes in the stands
could play at least as adequately as some of the woeful pretend-
ers down below.

But we were patient. We survived the seasons where we lost
100 games and the seasons where we lost the division by only
two. That which did not kill us made us strong. We fantasized
about what could be and what should have been. We were wise
enough to laugh when the alternative was to sob. We loved them,
scolded them, and forgave them. They were dimwits and dolts.
They were darlings.

Three times they had sauntered off to the American League
playoffs. Three times they had succumbed. It was getting tire-
some. Ten-cent wits christened them the Blow Jays and Americans reassured themselves that no Canadian upstart franchise
really knew how to play this game. The Montreal Expos had
titillated too, before fading into a decade of futility. God was in
His Heaven, the World Series trophy was in the United States,
and all was well with the world.

Look again.

A Canadian team in the White House. Lordy-lordy.

There was a sense of destiny to this season, as there had never
been before. Of course nothing is ever pre-ordained in sports and
there were no short-cuts from meaningless baseball in March to
meaningful baseball in October. But the Jays were the team that
set the pace in the AL East through the marathon foreplay of a
162-game campaign. Their tympany dictated the tempo and the
rhythm of the dance.

The team felt like a winner, right from those lazy days in
Dunedin, as the players drifted into camp still shaking the winter

lethargy out of their bones. There was new blood in the old bodies that general manager Pat Gillick had secured over the wheeling-dealing months, while baseball fans hibernated. Dave Winfield and Jack Morris, aged 40 and 36 respectively, brought a wizened grit to the Toronto mixture that had fallen so disastrously short the year before.

Dunedin is a slow-poke little town, a hiccup on the highway north of Tampa. It's a place of geriatric diversions and funeral parlors on Main Street — retirees account for more than 40 percent of the population. But Dunedin was as proprietary about its Jays as Toronto, with team bunting strung from light standards and a "Welcome Back" message blinking from the digital signboard at the intersection where Highway 19 traffic decanted into local streets.

It's a town of modest clapboard bungalows with no basements and screened-in porches in whose shadowy recesses Blue Jay hats could be spotted hanging from a hook. But there are also estates of fading elegance along the waterfront, with wrap-around verandahs and filigreed latticework and stone steps that disappear into the bay. It is one of the oldest settlements in the state, founded in 1870 by two Scottish pioneers who christened it Dunedin: Castle on the Rock. The Jays had been training there since the beginning of their days.

Spring training is the season of baseball bigamy. The Jays blow into town, have a six-week fling with the locals, then sneak back north to the receptive arms of another city. Leaving $12 million or so on the night table as they head for the door, with the familiar parting promise: same time next year. Dunedin is a baseball Brigadoon, bestirring itself for sojourning athletes and the noisy fans who flock after them, then settling down to another long slumber.

Joe Carter showed up early. So did Todd Stottlemyre, and Pat Borders, and Robbie Alomar and many more. It was as if they couldn't wait to get on with it, to *play*. It was that time again and baseball beckoned. When Alfredo Griffin, still recovering from an injured knee, arrived in mid-March as a last-minute free agent signing (shortstop prospect Eddy Zosky heard the news and blanched), Manny Lee gave him back his old number 4 jersey. It was a sweet gesture because that's the number Griffin had worn in his halcyon days as a Blue Jay — he had shared rookie of the year accolades in 1979 — before moving on to the Oakland Athletics and the Los Angeles Dodgers.

Lee's thoughtfulness also said something about this reconstituted Blue Jay squad. It was a team, and it would behave like a team, not a collection of individual egos working at cross-purposes. They had tried it that way before and it hadn't worked. A world championship required a common will: veterans and scrubeenies, the new and the old, rowing together. "This team's close," observed Winfield, meaning close to winning it all. "I got a feeling."

Manager Cito Gaston, who had been publicly rebuked (but not by his masters) in the fall, when the Jays bowed out of the American League playoffs in just five games against the Minnesota Twins, was smiling again. There had been mostly frowns and grimaces the year before when agonizing back problems had driven him from the dugout to the hospital. His easy-going disposition had crumbled in the process, making him cross and cranky. In the off-season, he had finally submitted to surgery and now he lifted his sweater to show off his scar. "Sometimes I look back and I wonder how I ever made it through the season," he said, assuming the familiar skipper stance — hands jammed down the front of his pants. "That was the kind of pain I wouldn't wish on my worst enemy." And who might that be? "Hopefully, I don't even have a worst enemy."

Gaston was impressed with what he saw as he surveyed the Blue Jay hands, who were groaning and grumbling under the perverse tutelage of conditioning coordinator Rick Knox. The manager liked this early phase of spring training when he could just watch and think. It was still too soon for even early cuts. "I've always enjoyed spring training. 'Course, I used to enjoy it a lot more when I was a player and didn't have to worry about going to all these damn meetings. Then you could get in a little golf, a little fishing." But he could recall the trepidation some athletes felt coming into camp, especially the ones at either end of their careers — the kids trying to break in and the veterans trying to hang on.

"I remember my first training camp in San Diego. I was so dumb back then. But I had a heck of a spring training. Hit something like .370. Then, once the season started, I couldn't hit the side of a barn. One time, later in the season, we were on a plane, flying over the place that we had trained. And this guy says to me, 'Hey Cito, go on down there and get your stroke back from where you left it.'"

There is a faithfulness, a comfort, in the easy rhythms and languorous days of spring training. It's a good-natured charade, this mini-season under a molten sun (in fact, it rained for much of the time last year): six weeks of gestation at the end of which would emerge a team that Gaston had no doubt envisioned months earlier. In baseball's babyhood, when players spent the off-season working at real jobs, spring training was a conditioning necessity. Now, most spend the off-season pursuing juicy contract renewals. Yet the *mise-en-scene* of spring training continues. Baseball is in love with its own past and, like other monolithic religions, it does not take kindly to change. Six weeks it is, and probably ever shall be.

Baseball in the spring is the rumble of lumber as bats are spilled on the field. It's the crack of fungos and the sharp pop of a ball in a glove. It's outfielders shagging flies, infielders chasing grounders, pitchers throwing cautiously on the side. It's bum-slapping and rude banter. It's reminiscing. "Remember the time I came up to bat in the bottom of the ninth with the score tied and..." It's the whoosh and snap of the automated pitching machine, the pinging of the metal stays that hold down the netting around the backfield batting cage, the wind that rustles through the palm trees beyond centre field, the early morning rain beating a tattoo on the roof of the batting tunnel. It's soft earth under your feet and the smell of wet grass.

"I remember spring training as a young kid," Morris recollected one morning. "You're out there trying to impress, you're rushing things, never want to tell anybody when you're hurting. Obviously, I don't go about it like that anymore. Basically, I'm working at staying alive, staying healthy and not taking any line drives off my face."

Metaphorically speaking, the same could be said for this Toronto Blue Jay squad as it broke camp in early April. Were they good enough, this time? Would they still be standing on the last day of baseball in 1992?

Sure, everybody knows the answer now. It all seems so clear, so inevitable in retrospect. Already the harsher memories recede in a flash of World Series diamonds. But it wasn't as pretty as all that, nor as painless.

This is the story of how the Toronto Blue Jays got from there to here. And the men who made it happen.

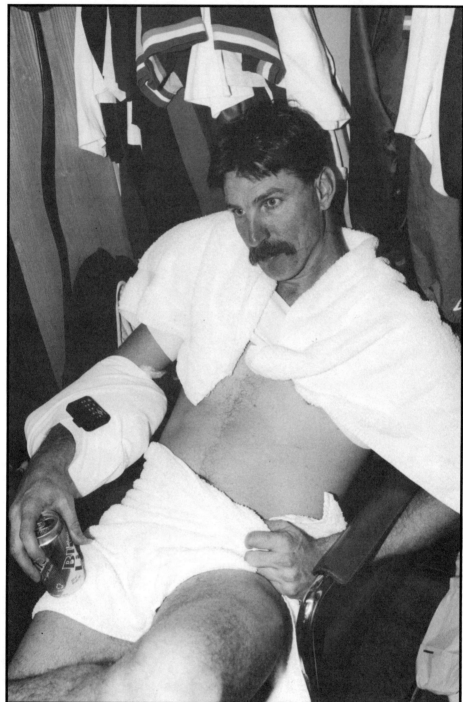

# Gl🔴ry Jays

## *Cactus Jack* 2

Jack Morris arrived at spring training 22 minutes late.

He had a Minnesota Twins duffel bag slung over his shoulder and a ready excuse for his tardiness. "It took me an hour to find this place," he grumbled. "Somebody gave me bad directions."

It is doubtful whether Morris has ever taken much direction from another human being. Here is a man who plots his own progress and draws his own road maps in life. It is this self-reliance, this faith in his own instincts, that had brought the 36-year-old pitcher to the Toronto Blue Jays as a latter-day messiah of baseball. He was the one who would lead the team out of the wilderness of post-season deficiency and into the inner sanctum of the World Series. He knew his way and, in their previous trips towards the October classic, the Jays had always managed to lose theirs.

Just four months earlier, Morris had been the sneering obstacle in Toronto's path when the Twins had dumped the Jays in a shocking five-game dismissal during the American League Championship Series. He had stiffed them twice during that debacle, further entrenching Toronto's reputation as a club that staggered and gagged in the rarefied atmosphere of autumn baseball. They could not take the heat, it was said, or the pressure, or the brilliance of the spotlight. They did not have the character, a fabled, if ill-defined quality in sporting circles. They did not have the *cojones*.

Morris had *cojones*.

The veteran with the corrugated face and the prickly personality — Sparky Anderson had astutely nicknamed him Cactus early in his career — had demonstrated that, yet again, in Game

7 of the 1991 World Series against the gallant Atlanta Braves. It was a game he refused to lose, inning after inning after inning. In what many claim may have been the most thrilling championship encounter of all, the tireless Morris had persisted for a 10-frame 1-0 victory that earned him a second World Series ring and Most Valuable Player laurels. He had wept, on that glorious night of celebration, so overcome had he been with joy and relief.

But that, as he would say from Day 1 as a Blue Jay, was ancient history.

The seduction of Jack Morris had begun shortly after the roar of the crowd had subsided in Minnesota and all the other places where people love baseball. The rest of us may have settled into winter hibernation, snuggling up for warmth to our memories of the season just past, as we looked forward to the coming of spring and the opening of the baseball bivouacs in Florida and Arizona. But Jack had his sights set elsewhere, on something far more immediate.

He was a free agent, as he had been one year earlier, when he left the Detroit Tigers after 14 seasons and returned to what he called home — the playing fields of Minnesota, the state of his birth. He had grown up in St. Paul, had tossed balls as a seven-year-old in the shadow of old Metropolitan Stadium, and he made much of this return sojourn. There was symmetry in this voyage as he hurried homeward. The boy who had made good, who had willed himself to be the best, was going back to the womb of his baseball genesis, to the team he had cheered on as a 10-year-old at school when the teacher had rolled a TV set into the classroom so the kids could root for the Minnesota Twins in their first World Series.

The same team, alas, which had passed on the homegrown prospect at the 1976 June draft and that had shown suspicious indifference a decade later when Morris criss-crossed the country in a sometimes comical, ultimately futile attempt to peddle his wares as an unencumbered free market athlete. He re-signed with Detroit, reluctantly, as he did again the following year, though his belittling experiences would provide a key piece of evidence in the players' collusion grievances that so shamed the owners in the late '80s.

Yet here he was, scanning the horizons again for greener pastures. But the green that lured him away from the Twins was the color of money. Lots of money. He was a free agent and the financially bloated Jays had made him an offer he saw no reason to refuse: $10.85 million guaranteed over two years, $14.85 million if he pitched a third year. So he bolted and became the highest paid Blue Jay ever. "Plain and simple, loyalty is a two-way street," Morris said. "The Minnesota Twins made a business decision and Jack Morris made a business decision. That's all there is to it."

Suddenly, it was okay to love Jack Morris in Toronto. With the signing at the SkyDome consecrated over the clinking of champagne glasses, Morris was instantly transformed into a local hero, no longer the despised enemy who had engendered so much loathing, had inflicted so much pain on a populace grown weary from the inevitability of failure at the ballpark. Loyalty is a tenuous terrain in the world of professional sports. The geography of personal attachment is forever shifting. Players come and go and the heart is constantly squeezed, held hostage to the vicissitudes of hard baseball decisions made with the head, in the executive suites of the power brokers.

Yes, Jack Morris was still a scoundrel, one of the baddest scoundrels in baseball. But now he was Toronto's scoundrel.

The proprietary interest in Morris, whose reputation had by now achieved legendary proportions, began on that day and would work itself into a low-grade fever until the morning that he arrived at the Cecil P. Englebert Recreational Complex in Dunedin, Florida, to start earning all those beautiful American dollars. The iconoclastic pitcher, the winningest moundperson in the game throughout the '80s, was greeted by an expectant Greek chorus of scribblers and scrutineers who had assembled to record the event for posterity. It's a long straight-ahead walk from the parking lot to the clubhouse at that particular training facility and Morris had spotted the media welcoming committee before the reporters had spotted him.

He was no novice to the ways of the fourth and fifth estates. The relationship between Morris and the media had always been a fractious one, especially in his days as a Tiger, when he had managed to annoy and alienate the working stiffs who were paid to document his life, within and without the white lines. He had become most notorious for a comment he made to a female reporting intern who had ventured into the Detroit clubhouse.

He opined that he didn't talk to women when he was naked, unless they were lying on top of him at the time.

But this was a whole new ballgame and a whole new rabble of pontificators. And Jack Morris had learned from his mistakes. He had matured. So he smiled and he shook the hands that were tentatively offered to him. He acknowledged the faces that he recognized, then set about making himself accessible to strangers with notebooks. Morris was prepared to make nice on the first day of school.

It was a claustrophobic experience as Morris stepped into the clubhouse where most of his new teammates had already assembled. Though only pitchers and catchers were compelled to report this early in spring training, many of the position players had already gravitated to the Blue Jay mothership in Florida. One couldn't help but feel a little sorry for Morris as the reporters, and the photographers, and the television cameras trailed in his wake. His presence was The Event.

Morris was eyed warily at first by his new comrades-in-arms, some of whom looked hastily away as he met their gaze. It was an awkward scene until David "Boomer" Wells, a fellow pitcher, gallumphed over and stuck out his paw. Then, still hampered by the jostling journalists, Morris submitted to the annual spring-training regimen of medical testing.

He remained good-natured enough as the galaxy of reporters spun in a tight orbit around him, but the determined grin lapsed into an occasional grimace as the chroniclers pressed and probed while his blood pressure was monitored and a needle was jabbed in his arm and a finger was poked into his mouth. The only eventuality that wasn't recorded was the rectal exam that took place behind closed doors. "That would have made a helluva picture," Morris snorted.

Morris was ushered into another cubicle to have his eyes inspected. He took a seat next to Dave Stieb — the very same Stieb that Morris had once contemptuously dismissed as a quitter for taking himself out of a game in the sixth inning, a game which Morris would go on to lose. Stieb, by the by, also happens to be the second-most winning pitcher of the 80s. They had been bitter combatants and now suddenly they were fraternal colleagues.

The two men stared hard at each other. Then they cackled.

It would be a long day and by the end of it, after lobbing a few balls and huffing a few laps around the field, the preternaturally pale Morris was drenched with perspiration, almost quivering with exhaustion. At 36, he was renowned for his toughness and his physical conditioning but all this exertion under a withering Florida sun had taken its toll.

It had been a hectic, mentally stressful winter for Morris, with little time to concentrate on the body that had provided him with such a lucrative livelihood. Not only did he turn his back on the Minnesota Twins, only months after propelling them to an exhilarating World Series championship, and not only did he have to withstand the avalanche of criticism that followed what many considered a carpetbagger act of unforgivable dimensions, but he had also finally concluded a lingering, acrimonious divorce settlement with his wife, the mother of his two sons.

Now the hard part was about to begin.

The expectations for Morris the Blue Jay were gargantuan. In spite of his age and in spite of the fact that no mortal could possibly hope to duplicate the delicious exploits of the season before, Morris was, in fact, being told to do just that. Repeat. Do it again mister, if you're so damn hot.

"No man can do everything," he insisted, as he rested on a bench and picked at his toes. "It is a team sport. Everybody has to do his part. My approach has never really changed. I give it all I've got. When I go to bed at night, if I know I've given 100 percent, I can sleep."

He had nerves of steel and he exulted in pressure, in carrying the load. "I know there's pressure, I know there's stress. I know all those crazy words that try to describe what we do. But if you have confidence in your ability, you don't have to deal with the outside pressures. It's still a simple game. You throw a baseball 60 feet six inches and hope the guy misses it. It doesn't get too complicated, really."

Along with his muscled arm and his work-ethic, the imperious Jack Morris brought to the Toronto Blue Jays his prominence as a nervy fellow, someone noted for an abrasive personality and a smart-ass mouth. On the plus side of the ledger, at least he was never boring. Individualism and cockiness are not always appreciated in a team sport that too often cloaks itself in goody-goody altruism, in spite of the warts and scandals that have increasingly become a part of baseball. But in those first few days, Morris continued to claim that he had been unfairly castigated as a difficult person. He said it was a bum rap and one that had been perpetuated by a disgruntled media, back in Detroit. "In general, the writing press has tremendous power. And they don't really even know the person they're writing about. I can't control that. I realize that now, at this point in my career. I'd like people to get to know me but it's impossible. I just don't have enough time. The most important thing for me is to do my job. That's Number One.

"Players are never really known for who they are individually. They're known for what they've done on the field or what they might say at certain times in the heat of battle. What I've done on the field speaks for itself. And I'm not running for any political office so it doesn't really make a hell of a lot of difference what my opinion is."

In those salad days of spring training, Jack Morris charmed the scribes. He made himself available. He was gregarious. He gave good quote. And those who were recording his pearls of wisdom did not know then how familiar some of these observations would become over the ensuing months, did not yet realize that Jack Morris — while an occasionally brilliant wit — was a polished performer, delivering platitudes that would echo down through the season, right up until his own reckoning in the World Series. His moment of hubris.

But that was later.

"You give 100 percent, you feel good about yourself, ultimately it rubs off on each other and the whole team starts believing positive thoughts," he mused, when asked to discuss his perceived role on the team. "You know, this game is so mental. It's such a grind, from this first day at spring training to the last game of the season. The way you get through it is positive thinking, having fun, encouraging your teammates to be the best they can be. It's fun for me to do that."

The game, that was the most fun part of all.

"The game is the greatest," he enthused. "It's pure. You can't hide when you're on the mound or in the batter's box or out on the field. There's nowhere to hide. You gotta do it. It's so black and white."

As black and white, and sometimes as flinty, as the decisions he had made about his own career, which had put him now into a Blue Jay uniform. "I don't know anyone in my position who would not have done the same thing. I loved the year I had in Minnesota. It's going to go down as one of the most fun times I've had in baseball. It was enjoyable for all of us, the players and the fans. So, how do I deal with it? All I can say is thanks, it was a great ride."

Still, he had chosen to dismount.

"When you're a veteran player, people know what you've done in the past, so that speaks for itself. Going to a new club, you have to earn their respect. But I'm looking forward to it. I'm excited about this team. See, it has to be enjoyable. That's why it's important to be on a winning team. You like coming to the ballpark. You look forward to every day." The future, he said back then, would take care of itself. "You're only as good as your last game. Fortunately, my last game was a good one but it was a long time ago. I got to spend the whole winter with that feeling. But when I pitch my first game here this spring, that will all be in the past. And I have to look at it that way. The past doesn't mean a heck of a lot."

Manager Cito Gaston didn't wait long to announce that Jack Morris would be his starting pitcher on opening day which, fatefully, would be at Tiger Stadium in Detroit. It would mark his 13th consecutive opening day appearance, a major league record. Robin Roberts had 12 in a row for the Phillies (1950-1961) and Tom Seaver had a dozen with the New York Mets and Cincinnati Reds (1968-1979). "It says that I am able to stay in the Number One spot in the rotation in all those years," observed Morris, who expected no less.

He had done no throwing in the off-season, and it showed as the Grapefruit League got underway, but Morris was unperturbed. He was concerned with his legs anyway, not his arm. "That's what carries you," he explained. "You can't take all that running lightly. As an older pitcher, you've got to concentrate on getting the work to get the legs strong. If the legs aren't there, the arm will never stay strong. Spring training is all about getting your work in."

Heading into Detroit, Morris knew what to expect, because there is a certain class of athletes who have earned a kind of anti-respect that is certain to elicit boos from the fans. This universal acknowledgment is an honor.

There was pride at stake for Morris, in keeping his opening game streak intact, but he was practical enough to recognize that this particular record would serve him in good stead in the future, when there might be something else at stake — Hall of Fame balloting, perchance. "Three hundred wins is automatic for the Hall of Fame but I don't know if I'm going to get them," he admitted. (He has 237 Ws going into 1993). "So you have to do other things to get the attention of the voters."

Of equal significance to Morris was finishing what he started. He is pathologically reluctant to come out of a game, whether it appears that he's got the victory in the bag or whether he is being mortar-shelled. "Early in my career, I lost a couple of games late. That's when I learned to turn it up, to find what works to get you through it. Durable pitchers can smell the finish line."

The old horse took the mound that bright April afternoon in Detroit, with the hisses and raspberries cascading from the rafters. He began it and, 144 pitches later, he ended it. A 4-2 triumph, marred only slightly by the second-deck homer he delivered to Cecil Fielder to open the ninth inning and, two outs later, the dinger that Rob Deer — thrice struck out by Morris in the game — deposited in the upper deck in left. Apart from that, Morris conceded just three singles and three walks. Nobody realized it then but this performance would provide an interesting blueprint for the redoubtable pitcher's first year as a Jay. He would continue to be victimized by the long ball though it would rarely hurt him, until post-season rolled around and then it would hurt him most of all. He would also continue to forfeit walks at a generous rate. But this debut was a minor gem in its own right because Morris showed his public something about himself, about his stamina even as he approached the avuncular stage of his career; and about his impertinence, his self-mocking humor. When he gave up the round-tripper to Fielder, he grinned, as if he had just imparted a gift. One lion saluting another.

Said Dave Winfield afterwards: "That was something to watch. I know Jack's not going to go 145 pitches all the time because that takes it out of you, but he was pumped and I think he wanted to put a few things in our guys' minds. That this is what he's all about. He's in the game on every pitch. Not just every inning or even every batter, but every pitch."

Morris, too, appreciated that he had passed his first test. Perhaps it was a different test than the one the rest of us had witnessed. "I feel accepted with these guys," he said, nodding towards his teammates. "It's only been one and a half months we've been together, but I think they understand what I'm about. What I'm about is giving my best every time out there. Sometimes it's not good enough. Sometimes you have to accept that, that your best is not good enough, but there is no reason to hang your head. I think they are finding that out about me."

Morris would be the master again his next outing, against Baltimore. From there he labored through eight innings and gave up six earned runs — including three homers — in a contest against the New York Yankees in which the Jays prevailed, though the W would go to reliever Duane Ward. On April 21, Morris became a 30-game winner, of sorts, when the Jays nosed out the Indians 2-1 at the SkyDome. That would be 30 wins all-time against the Tribe for Morris, versus just 10 losses. That marked the most impressive dominance over any team for any active major league pitcher. All of this augured well for the club, off to one of its finest starts ever, and for Morris personally, who could reasonably be assured of reaching more landmark achievements.

Five days later, reality set in, when the Jays were pasted 9-0 by the Kansas City Royals. Morris lasted six innings and gave up five runs. On that evening, he also heard a scattering of boos in the SkyDome. He lost again his next turn in the rotation, in Milwaukee, 5-4. That diamond tango featured a two-run homer by Greg Vaughn to tie the game in the fifth and Franklin Stubbs' winning four-bagger in the eighth. "A couple of inches, a couple of feet, the game of baseball," Morris reasoned with a shrug. "You play 162 of them and all this crap evens out."

But a troubling pattern was setting in for Morris. Balls were zooming out of the ballpark at an alarming pace: eight homers in six starts or, roughly, one every six innings. Someone asked Morris for the specifics on one of those long balls. The pitcher reverted to the crabby competitor of yore. "I can guarantee you nobody back in Toronto is gonna give a shit where those pitches were, other than where they landed. I threw them right where I wanted but nobody gives a damn about that, including the guy that threw 'em."

A few days later, Morris took a break from the team — a hiatus sanctioned by Gaston — to conduct a real estate transaction in Montana, where he had purchased a ranch. (As well as a neighboring farmhouse for his mother, who had told him since he was a child that she wanted to live in a house on a hill.) Rejoining the club in Seattle, he was yanked with one gone in the fifth. By then the Jays were in a 7-1 hole. In his abbreviated appearance, Morris had walked four batters, thrown two wild pitches and allowed three home runs. In a stunning reversal of fortune, however, the Jays would go on to reclaim the game 8-7 courtesy of a grand slam off the mighty bat of Dave Winfield with two out in the ninth. There was chest-beating in the Jays clubhouse afterwards but Morris sat slumped in a corner. "I stunk," he snapped. "They pounded me."

He was in a more appealing groove next time out, against Oakland, dealing with 15 base runners over 6 2/3 frames. His share of the line score read: seven hits, five walks, two errors and a hit batsman but he still got away with just a solitary run against him as the Jays ended up 4-3 winners. Even that one run was unearned. "Man, he battled out there," observed an admiring Pat Borders, the catcher. "It seems like bases loaded or nobody on, doesn't matter to him. He's still coming at you with the same stuff."

Morris talked about the "rough patches" that all athletes go through over the long haul of a long season. "Every year there's a time, maybe two times, sometimes three, where things just aren't going very well. It's little bitty flaws, little bitty things that you just have to fight through to correct. Pitching's a game of adjusting."

But, again, Morris showed another side of his multi-faceted baseball persona. Pitching Rickey Henderson carefully, he tired of the cocky outfielder's game-delaying shenanigans at the plate. After he had stepped out once too often, Morris just threw the ball. It clipped Henderson on the back of the hand. Deliberate? Who's to say? But it did suggest that when he's pitching, Jack Morris is the boss.

In a May series against his former club, the Twins, Morris would demonstrate that he can also influence the course of a game when he's just sitting on the bench. It was his bellowing from the Blue Jays' dugout, abetted by some heckling from the Twins, that prompted a bench-clearing incident at the SkyDome. The teams were tied 2-2 when shortstop Greg Gagne smashed a two-run homer to right field. Earlier, Morris had been babbling at home plate umpire Larry Young that Gagne was using a corked bat. He was miffed at the way the Twins kept asking Young to check the balls that were being thrown by starter Todd Stottlemyre. Gagne, naturally, denied that he was using a tampered instrument. Twins' manager Tom Kelly took an offended tone: "He's our chapel leader. He wouldn't know how to cork one to start with."

Whatever the case, the game eventually exploded with players pouring onto the field to do something, anything, in a silly display of testosterone overdrive. However, the dust-up proved cathartic for the Jays who would rally for an 8-7 final. "It's one of those days when everybody was instigating," Morris allowed.

It was the only contest the Jays would win in that three-game series against the Twins. That prompted Morris to utter some cleverly timed comments about the inherent dangers of playing passive. "We've got to realize that you don't win by putting bodies out on the field. As a team, we have to play harder every day. We have so much talent here that maybe we don't always remember that."

Having said his piece, though, Morris immediately went out and got rocked in Chicago: eight hits and six runs over 2 2/3 innings, on a miserably cold and damp day at Comiskey. "First time in my career, I never even broke a sweat. When you're not sweating, you've got no feeling...no chance to grip the ball. Every pitch was a new experience." When the two clubs faced off again, back in Toronto a week later, Morris delivered a complete game and held the White Sox to three hits in what he called "my best game in a month." Jays prevailed 3-2.

For Morris, there was a shock in store just around the corner. In Minneapolis, in early June, he was approached by someone he assumed was looking for an autograph. Instead, Morris was handed an envelope. Turns out he'd been subpoenaed to testify on behalf of the National Football League in an upcoming federal case brought by several NFL players over what they claimed was restricted free agency.

According to a motion filed with the court, the NFL could call on Morris and use snippets of three videotapes. The videos would show: a tearful Morris signing with the Twins in February

1991; a jubilant Morris after winning Game 7 of the World Series; a satisfied Morris announcing he'd signed a deal with the Jays the previous December. "I'm not really sure what these people are trying to do," Morris complained. "And I don't even like football."

Only momentarily distracted, Morris put his possible courtroom appearance aside and dumped the Baltimore Orioles 4-3 at Camden Yards. As was becoming customary, he had to escape a wobbly first inning, wherein he threw 32 pitches and walked the bases loaded. But he bore down and the Jays edged their fellow avians 4-3. It was Morris' sixth victory of the season. He followed that up with a stellar effort in Boston, going toe-to-toe and hardnose-to-hardnose with Roger Clemens. Morris blanked the Red Sox 4-0 and served up another nine-inning offering. It may, in fact, have been Morris' finest game of the season.

From then on, Morris put on an entertaining show that ran more or less uninterrupted until late summer. He could do no wrong, at least none that mattered. The fates were kind to him. On nights when he stunk out the joint, like the time in Cleveland when he gave up 10 hits in seven wretched innings, he still somehow managed to wriggle off the hook. Either a reliever would take over, and get nailed for the ultimate loss, or the batters would come through to rescue Morris with a fusillade of hits. There was always a feeling, when Morris took the mound, that the Jays could not, would not, lose—no matter how lopsided the score. By the All-Star break, he had a record of 10 and 3. In Anaheim, on July 21, he gave up eight hits in seven innings including six in the wild and crazy fifth and still he managed to pull out his eighth straight win.

Teammate Rance Mulliniks, who'd played against Morris for years, offered some perspective. "He was always a tough pitcher. You always knew, going out there, that Jack was gonna be around for eight, nine innings. He was gonna battle you all the way. The thing I remember about Jack, even before he came here, was that no matter how bad it got for him on a particular day, if he was getting knocked around, having trouble making good pitches or putting the ball where he wanted it, he always stayed aggressive and kept coming at you. A lot of pitchers, they start getting knocked around a bit, they get real gun-shy. With some pitchers, they give up three or four runs early, they have an attitude that they can't win that game that given day. Jack's attitude is always, if I give up three or four early, that's all right. I'm gonna settle down and not allow the other team to score from this point on and I'll still give my team a chance to win the game. Everybody says, oh, he has a high ERA. But he's never actually been a guy that had a great ERA. What you've got to understand about Jack, compared to other pitchers, is that Jack was out there a lot in the eighth or ninth innings to suck up some earned runs that other pitchers couldn't take because in the sixth or seventh innings they were pretty much gassed and out of the game. When Jack pitches, that's the day the bullpen gets the night off.

"You know the other thing I like about Jack? You never have a problem telling how Jack feels about what is going on out there on the mound 'cause he always shows his emotions. He shows how he feels."

Dave Winfield had walloped his first American League home run off Morris. Now they were mates. "Ah, Jack can be grumpy sometimes. He'll groan and grumble in the clubhouse but he also keeps a lot of people loose. He exudes so much confidence. He has a real upbeat nature. That's probably why players get so many runs for him. He won't allow you to lose. And he has no fear."

In fact, Morris did not lose another game until July 26 when the Jays were upended 9-1 in Oakland. It was his first defeat in nine starts. At that point, the stat sheet showed that opponents had been hitting .330 against him in the first inning — 22 of the 76 runs he had conceded had come in the initial frame. But with a record that stood at 12-4, who was going to worry about the peripheral numbers, including an ERA of 4.54? By August, he was back winning games with scores such as 15-11 (over the Tigers). It was in Detroit that Morris picked up a newspaper clipping that he taped over his locker back at SkyDome. That printed piece of mischief predicted the Jays would choke, as usual, and blow the division — just as they had in 1987 when they lost seven down the stretch, including the last three to Detroit, which made the Tigers American League East champions.

Verily, the standings in the East were closer by the end of August than most baseball prognosticators had expected. Typically, the Jays went into a "dog days of summer" swoon that reincarnated old ghosts. During these anxious times, it was most often Morris who strode out to the rescue. There was always a feeling deep in the gut that Morris would put things right, that he would halt losing streaks, that he would perform baseball alchemy. He became a kind of amulet for good fortune, as the demi-pennant sweepstakes rounded the final turn.

On August 22, back in the Metrodome, he stopped the bleeding again, backboning the Jays to a 4-2 decision, all the while jawing at the hostile fans and his former teammates. "We haven't exactly been tearing up baseball the way we could be," he understated. "I think tonight we needed a contribution from a pitcher."

"Huge," offered Winfield. "We had to have it." The win gained the Jays a length over the on-rushing Orioles who didn't seem to understand that they were supposed to roll over and play dead. Neither did the Milwaukee Brewers. On August 27, Morris climbed to 17 and 5 on the season when he presided over a 5-4 engagement against those same tenacious Brewers. (The score was 5-1 when he left after seven innings.) That loss dropped Milwaukee 5 1/2 games off the pace and gave the Jays a much needed respite from the rigors of the race.

Now Morris could sniff something else — another 20-game season, his third, the first two having come as a Tiger. He was dogged in his pursuit of that goal even as he downplayed its significance. In Arlington, Texas, on September 12, he became the first Blue Jay pitcher to reach the 19-victory plateau. In establishing that franchise record, he had to claw and scratch his way through a potent Rangers attack, which now included Jose Canseco. He did it all while suffering from what he called "the worst cold of my life."

The big two-oh, however, was elusive. On September 17, Morris ambled to the mound at the SkyDome in that dull-footed, pigeon-toed way of his, with nothing between him and 20 wins except the Cleveland Indians. In his locker, a bottle of champagne waited to be uncorked. But the Indians were not sticking to the script. Morris threw 116 pitches, lasted nine innings, and exited this affair with no decision. One inning later, John Olerud slammed a two-run homer to beat the Tribe 7-5 but by then

Morris was in the showers and Duane Ward had taken over the hill. Morris accepted it with aplomb. "Personal goals are wonderful but 20 wins...that's a number you guys (media types) put more emphasis on than I do. Besides, I've already done it twice. The thing I want is to just get to the dance. It's what I cherish most. I've been very lucky to have won twice already (World Championships) but I'd like to win three, four, however many."

Morris didn't get over the hump the next time out either, in Baltimore, where he pitched a complete game that ended in a 4-1 loss, his first in eight starts. Baltimore was back within five of the Jays.

That set the stage for the ridiculous encounter in New York City on September 27. Perhaps, in retrospect, this was a fitting way and an appropriate place for Jack Morris to bag his score of victories for 1992. One week left in the pennant race, leading 9-0 in Yankee Stadium, the deranged inmates hurling abuse, and in the fifth inning the skies burst open and a thunderous downpour halted the proceedings. (This in spite of some stupid at-bat tricks by Toronto, most particularly a slapstick swing by Alfredo Griffin on a pitch that sailed to the backstop, a good seven feet off the plate. The homeplate umpire was not amused by the hurry-up offence play. He called for the tarp.)

There it stood, for two hours. Only a fraction of the Bronx patrons withstood the drenching and few of those expected Morris to return to his chores after the delay, what with the arm tightening up. But that's exactly what he did, hanging in for one more inning, then leaving the Jays to finish it off 12-2. Unfortunately, fans back in Toronto didn't get to see Morris' little piece of Blue Jay history; the Canadian television broadcaster gambled that the rain would keep falling and switched to other programming.

"I'm just happy that the people concerned with these numbers are relieved," Morris aw-shucked after his shiftwork assignment. "It was more important we get the win. I'd be a fool to sit here and say it doesn't mean anything but I'd also be a fool not to compliment my teammates. They more than did the job offensively for me."

There would be one more Morris victory in the year's campaign, an 8-7 contest against the Tigers in Toronto. That clinched no worse than a tie for the title of American League East champions. Afterwards, most of the players congregated at a nearby saloon where they cheered on the Oakland Athletics over the Milwaukee Brewers (to no avail). But Morris was not among the Blue Jay rabble. Who would have believed, on that night, that this would be the last personal triumph for Morris to savor in 1992?

The next morning Morris met with a reporter. It was early yet, hours till game-time, and he folded his body into a seat in the stands behind third base. The lights were dim, the air was still and there was no one around to cheer. Just one man and his ballpark. Communing. As if this were an act of intimacy.

He enjoyed coming to the park early, he said. He'd always done it. "I'm not sitting here having any deep thoughts. It just helps me to relax. I get out here, look at things going on, watch the other people involved outside the game do their thing, look up in the restaurants, see the people preparing for their rush." Morris is a bit of a voyeur. He likes to watch the world when it's not watching him. And that doesn't happen too often. As he spoke, he pounded his fist into his glove.

By now, we knew all about him as a tough-guy pitcher. But there are a lot of people inside Jack Morris, the man: athlete, philanthropist, rake, sassy-tongued devil, sly interview, leader, loner. On this day, he seemed tired, introspective. There was little evidence of the bad boy, though one suspected the brat was lurking just beneath the surface. He was courteous, even kindly.

This was a major transformation: From Black Jack to Mellow Morris. But he had passed his 37th birthday by then and even rogues grow up eventually. As his former manager, Sparky Anderson, had observed a few days earlier: "I think Jack is finally satisfied with the person he has become." Then, after casually revealing that Morris has donated extensively (and anonymously) to a children's hospital in Detroit, Anderson added: "He's a man at peace with himself. But he's sacrificed a lot along the way."

Morris was the first to agree with that. "I have thrown a lot of my life into this game. It's pretty much been my early adult life. But the only way to succeed in this game is to throw yourself into it. On the other hand, I'm learning to appreciate other things and, probably, in the long run, that will make my job easier. If I can be honest, I think it's the success that I've had that has made me finally relax. I say to myself, even on bad days, I have nothing to prove to anybody else. As selfish as that may sound, that's my attitude now. Because, if God forbid I should get injured tomorrow and was out of the game, I could walk away knowing I did the best I could, I gave it the best I had.

"As you grow through the game of baseball, if your confidence doesn't grow with you, you're going to fail before you succeed. In this job, if you don't believe in yourself, you're done."

He analyzed, once again, his abandonment of the Minnesota Twins. "Go ahead and call me a mercenary. I don't care. I'm a paid athlete in a short career. I will do the very best I can for whomever is paying me. It's not sick and it's not disloyal."

He was a contented man nearing the end of another successful season. This was, ultimately, what defined him. Baseball. It was baseball that comforted and soothed, too, when his life seemed to be disintegrating only a year earlier. That was while he was resisting his wife's efforts to get a divorce. His comments from those days were drenched in heartache. It seemed, oftentimes, that he was trying to speak to his estranged spouse through the media, even though he denied it. "I was hoping there would be ways to work things out. But we finally both realized that there wasn't any way to work it out. The only thing to do was to part ways. I considered myself a failure then, but I don't anymore."

It was a humbling experience and, more than anything else, was responsible for the kinder, gentler Jack Morris of '92. A wounded man is a more compassionate man. "I think it has made me more mellow because of a lot of reasons I don't necessarily understand. But you realize that life isn't perfect and that there is no ideal. And to live life, you have to be able to roll with the punches, learn from the mistakes to make today a better day. I think that's what's happening to me. Time heals."

The lingering sadness came from not being able to see more of his sons, 9-year-old Erik and 11-year-old Austin, who still lived in Detroit with their mother. "It's so hard. I love them more than anything and I know they love me. I call them as much as I can and our time together is quality time. As long as they know that both their parents love them, they're going to be healthy kids."

It was a good life, he said, and it would be even finer when he got back home to his ranch in Montana and the boys would come to visit. In the meantime, baseball was a grand way to make a living. It wasn't just a job, it was a vocation. And, in its finer moments, it was still a lovely game.

"People always ask me, what was the best part? And they expect me to say, oh, the no-hitter or the World Series. And those were all terrific, of course. But the sweetest part, for me, has been all those special times shared with teammates. The camaraderie and the fun.

"And even some of the pain."

Bernard Weil—*Toronto Star*

# Glory Jays

## Papa Joe 3

It is mid-morning on a sultry Friday in Chicago. Shoppers on Michigan Avenue jostle with office workers who have spilled out early to luxuriate in the warmth of a May heat wave that will revert to a wintry chill before the weekend is out. For the moment, though, there is a summer languor in the air and perspiration on the brow. It is a day for lolling and people-watching.

Lolling is something baseball players, bored after a few turista trips around the horn, do well. They loll in their hotel rooms, they loll in the lobby, they loll at the park for hours before the games get underway. They sleep and they eat, they play cards and hand-held video games. They watch soap operas on TV and they shop in malls. The continent is a connect-the-dots tapestry of ballyards and shopping malls.

But on this morning, the side door of the Westin Hotel flies open and out charges a man wearing jeans and a polo shirt. He is pushing a toddler in a stroller. Two little girls, their hair in ribbons, grasp tightly onto either side of the baby carriage. The man steers the vehicle across the street, holds up for a moment as if to gather the troops, then strides purposefully northwards. He may even have a real destination in mind, but that is hardly the point of this exercise. The only thing that matters is that he is here with his kids, and these shared moments of familial pleasure — moments that so many parents take for granted — do not come frequently for professional athletes.

This is life on the road with Dad.

The dad in this case is Joe Carter. And the small brood is composed of daughters Kia Kionne and Ebony Shante and son Jordan Alexander. But this cozy domestic scene is also an appro-

priate metaphor for Joe Carter the Toronto Blue Jay. He is the big
daddy in a clubhouse that had historically been rudderless and
fatherless. He is the pater familias of the Blue Jay clan, even as
Dave Winfield would come along later to assume the role of
village elder.

Late one evening, in a Toronto reggae nightclub, a couple of
rookies were drinking wine coolers and acting silly as young
women sent waiters over with their telephone numbers scribbled
on napkins. One of the rooks grabbed a pack of cigarettes from a
woman and proceeded to light up. The other rookie's eyes
widened in shock. "What are you doing?" he demanded. "You
don't even smoke." His teammate, perhaps trying to look older
with a ciggie between his fingers, responded: "Well I do now."
The two argued for a bit, back and forth. Finally, the non-
smoking part of the tandem announced, "If you don't put that out
right now, I'M TELLING JOE!" That was the end of that.

On another day, at spring training, damp-behind-the-ears
Derek Bell was chattering with a female reporter next to the
batting cage, or "talking trash" as he put it. Engrossed in this idle
conversation he had neglected his turn at bat. From practically
halfway across the field, Carter marched over and (metaphorically) grabbed Bell by his ears. "Get your butt in there," he
ordered. Bell, properly contrite, skedaddled.

These may seem like inconsequential anecdotes, but they say
something about Carter's role on the club. He is the heart of the
order. (Not to mention resident barber.) This is not by mere
happenstance either. It is one reason why the Jays went out and
traded for him in December of 1990, bringing Carter to Toronto
from the San Diego Padres  along with Roberto Alomar in
exchange for Tony Fernandez and Fred McGriff. It was a block-
buster deal, as these things go, although the record would
indicate that the Jays got the better part of the bargain. The arrival
of Carter and Alomar would forever change the complexion of
the ballclub. They had entered a new era, they were growing up.
And in Carter they had a grown-up who could help settle down
not only the kids but the sophomores in the organization who
were still apt to act, well, sophomoric.

The autumn before, the Blue Jays were overtaken at the wire
by the Boston Red Sox. Individually and collectively they had
disintegrated as the season concluded, had slipped behind the

Beantowners during the penultimate series of the '90 campaign, in Fenway Park, and then failed to undo the damage they had wrought as the curtain came down in Baltimore. The year, and Toronto's aspirations, were over.

This kind of thing could not be allowed to continue. General manager Pat Gillick would shortly set about revamping his ballclub, searching for a new mix, a better mix, of professionals. The main ingredient in that stew was Joe Carter.

He was then, at 30 years of age, a most curious sort of journeyman if that term could be used in its strictest sense: someone who's been around the block in major league baseball. A first round pick of the Chicago Cubs in the June 1981 free agent draft (second overall) Carter had led a peripatetic existence in recent years, not what one might have expected for a player who consistently posted unobjectionable numbers. The Cubs had dealt him to the lowly Cleveland Indians in 1984. As possessor of the most emphatic pop in the Tribe's otherwise mewling line-up, Carter had surpassed the century mark for ribbies in 1986 (121) and 1987 (106). The next year he fell just short with 98 although that figure was nicely bracketed with 27 home runs and 27 stolen bases. The following season he climbed back up to 105 RBIs and 35 homers. So what does a guy get for that kind of production? Traded.

In San Diego, his next destination, Carter continued to do what was expected of him in 1990. This time his hard numbers read: 22 round-trippers and 115 RBIs, though his batting average withered to .232. Still, he could be forgiven for thinking that he had some kind of security out on the sunny coast where they were yet again trying to build a contender. Joke was on him, or rather, the Padres, as it ultimately turned out. (McGriff would continue to execute towering single-shot home runs; the sullen Fernandez would eventually wind his way to the New York Mets, probably the most ill-suited venue for his gloomy temperament.)

And Carter? He would get himself a World Series ring. But there was a lot of swat and a whole lot of Carter-induced high spirit in the Blue Jay clubhouse between then and now.

He was versatile in that he could play left and right field, as well as fill in at first base or, when a rest was required, slip into the designated hitter slot. Nor did he make demands on where he preferred to take his position. Just an "Ordinary Joe" is the image he wanted to cultivate.

As a teenager at his Oklahoma City high school, Carter had turned no heads and was not included in the draft of future prospects. When he graduated to Wichita State on a football scholarship, all he could offer was raw talent and enthusiasm. His college coach would later tell the Toronto Star that Carter "couldn't throw a lick; he didn't know how to play a position other than by sheer athletic ability."

As a youth, he had set his sights on an athletic career, any kind of athletic career. Under his father's tutelage, he was playing basketball, football and baseball. His dad, Joe Sr., was fond of telling how there used to be 12 fruit trees in the back of the family home: peaches, apples, pears and plums. But within a few years, only one remained. The rest had been slain in sporting accidents involving his 11 children. Joe, the fourth-youngest, was particularly fond of using the plums for batting practice.

At college, he was just a skinny 6-foot-3 beanpole — albeit an athletically gifted one — not the powerful broad-shouldered, slim-hipped physical specimen he would become after embarking on a weight-training program, a regimen undertaken largely in preparation as the school's back-up quarterback. Until his father interceded, Joe was riding the bench as a freshman on the baseball squad. Joe Sr. talked the coach into putting Joe Jr. into the line-up. He came flying off the bench and has never returned to it. Years later, when Carter signed a $9.2 million contract with the San Diego Padres, he bought his folks a car and a boat. He also gave them enough money to retire.

By the time he was re-invented as a Blue Jay, Carter was being referred to by the media as "Joltin' Joe." Carter was slotted into the number four spot in the batting order, where he was expected to provide some much needed offensive oomph. But the organizational paladins also looked to him to lead by example, on the field and off. At Dunedin, he immediately brought a sense of fun to the proceedings by initiating what would become the annual Pizza Contest — a game of situational hitting where the batters are divided into two squads and the coaches tabulate the results on a points basis. Losers bought the pizza. (Carter and company had to pick up the inaugural tab of $140.) He also introduced bridge to the clubhouse, where in past seasons the card-playing ran along the lines of cribbage, hearts and pluck. But, with reporters, he downplayed his perceived leadership role. "New team, new people for me. Same thing last spring, too, remember. But the transition here has been pretty nice so far. Looks like a great bunch of guys."

Carter kept up his end of the bargain but the "great bunch of guys" were still missing key elements. As an individual component, Carter would finish the season with a .273 average, 33 home runs and 108 RBIs, which meant he had surpassed the century mark five of six seasons. In the process, he also accomplished a historical feat: no one in the annals of baseball had ever before turned in three consecutive 100-RBI seasons with three different teams. Interestingly, this bit of statistical trivia did not necessarily reflect well on Carter. If he was so damn reliable, then why had he bounced around both leagues like an itinerant also-ran? Why had he elicited boos in Cleveland? Why did the power-hitter have little staying power with any organization?

So too were there grumblings, in some media quarters, about his much-vaunted bonhomie. The suspicion grew that perhaps he was something of a fraud, a shuck 'n' jive jester whose reputation as a leader had been seriously exaggerated. After all, his production had waned in the closing weeks of the '91 campaign, even though it was his RBI that shoved Robbie Alomar across the plate in the game that clinched the American League East title for the Jays. Still, he was no Mr. September and the evidence suggested that perhaps he was just tired. He was now 31 years old and he was playing on the punishing artificial turf of the SkyDome.

As odd as it sounds, there was an aura of mediocrity to Carter's annual RBI triumphs, perhaps only because it had become so routine for him. It was expected, and he himself expected no less. Achieving the century mark, he said, was not his personal yard-stick of accomplishment. He measured his own efforts by the numbers of RBIs that he racked up *over* 100. "I always know I'm going to get the 100," he told *Toronto Star* columnist Dave Perkins. "It's how many over 100 I get that determines how good a year it is." He was actually perturbed, when he attained the mark in September '91, at how long it had taken him to get there. "I should have been there a while ago. You know how many runners I've left at third base the last while?"

The previous year, when he drove in 115 runs while hitting .267 with runners in scoring position, meant he had cashed in 30.7 percent of the runners available to him. That suggested he was only so-so in terms of taking advantage of the opportunities as he came to the plate with men on base. "I've heard the arguments," he admitted to Perkins. "People try to make 115 RBIs not mean anything."

On the personal front, he also demonstrated a frustrating inconsistency. The fans, and most journalists, were fond of Carter, who would usually make himself available for interviews, charitable events, whatever was required, and not necessarily by the fine print in his contract. But Carter could also be cool and aloof. He certainly had his moods.

And he had guts, that much could not be denied. In game three of the American League championships against the Minnesota Twins, Carter climbed the wall in right field to chase a Shane Mack wannabe homer in the fifth inning. He stuck his right foot into the padded outfield wall and his ankle twisted grotesquely. The 51,454 SkyDome patrons gasped as Carter hobbled, in obvious anguish, to retrieve the ball (it turned into a triple for Mack) and flung it haphazardly back to the infield. Then he collapsed in a writhing heap.

"I thought I'd broken it as soon as it happened," said Carter, who credited his high-top shoes for the fact he had suffered a severe sprain and not a break. The ankle was heavily taped and Carter persisted for two more innings "playing on guts" as manager Cito Gaston put it. The Jays lost that game, as they would the next two — a sweep at home that bounced them out of the playoffs — but Carter, in his first career playoffs, would not be denied. He continued to play. After all, while appearing in 505 consecutive games (second only to Cal Ripken among active players), he had persevered through an assortment of injuries that had included a broken toe, nose and hand. As a DH, though, his contributions were minimal. Between his at-bats, he could not bear to sit idly on the bench as a spectator. Instead, he played table tennis with the clubhouse boys while keeping an eye on the TV set. "I'm terrible on the bench," he admitted. "My teammates don't like me there either, 'cause I make too much noise."

His courage did not appear to inspire his teammates, as they meekly bowed out of the playoffs. Observed Mookie Wilson: "If a man had been in a car wreck and had both his arms broken and was standing on the field clapping, now that might've been uplifting."

In the aftermath of that lousy conclusion to the season, there was familiar talk of the Blue Jays' lack of character, that they were unable to rise to the occasion when it mattered most. Carter, who hadn't been with Toronto for the previous disappointments, wasn't buying it. "It's not always us," he insisted. "It has to do with the opposition also."

The next morning, at 8 a.m., Carter cleaned out his locker for the year and was gone, long before reporters appeared to record the leave-taking. Four months later, at the Cecil P. Englebert complex in Dunedin, he was putting everything back in its place. He had arrived one day early and all thoughts of the Jays' abrupt dismissal the previous autumn had been thrown onto the trashheap of history. Carter was his usual personable self, yakking it up with one player after another. One afternoon, he threw batting practice, while a crowd of about 300 fans urged him to deliver the knuckleball. He accommodated the request by letting loose a flutter pitch that dove into the ground about five feet in front of the plate. "Any other requests?" A few days later, his pizza squad again lost their annual match to Kelly Gruber's contingent. Meanwhile, he made time to offer advice and encouragement to the baby Jays.

"We're looking for one thing, and that's to come home with the world championship," he told reporters. "There's no ifs, ands, or buts. That is our goal." And he liked the team's chances. "If you can't get excited about this ballclub, you need your heart checked. This is going to be a great ballclub."

In late March, Carter was scratched from the line-up for a Grapefruit League game against the Kansas City Royals because of back spasms. Spring training, of course, doesn't count, so his consecutive game streak was still intact. "Nothing serious. I might have sprained a ligament. I'd have played if we were in the regular season, but down here, you don't push it." He came back and immediately settled into a hitting slump. Not to worry, he insisted. "I don't want to leave all my hits down here. I don't get too excited about my average in spring training. Knowing you have a job, you can take your time." The spasms crept from his lower back to his upper back.

On April 6, in Detroit, Joe Carter was in left field with Derek Bell roaming in right. Three days later, his 507 consecutive game streak did finally come to an end. His ailing back made it impossible for Carter to even assume DH duties. "It's not a relief," he said of his streak's interruption. "Even if I didn't have the streak, I'd want to play. I don't like to come to the ballpark and not play but I've got to act rational. This is the third game of the season, we have 159 to go. I'm not going to go out there and risk hurting myself. This team has enough horses to carry it without someone going out there desperately hurt." But the streak, while it lasted, was a source of pride. "It shows I go out and can be counted on every day to help my ballclub."

He missed only the one game. On April 12, in the SkyDome against the Baltimore Orioles, Carter smashed his first home run of the regular season, a two-out solo in the opening frame against Jose Mesa. It would be number one of 34, as it turned out, in a year that, for Carter, could be related as a six-month-long tale of the tape. But there were other interesting chapters, too, like the sacrifice flies that would score runners at key moments. On April 16, against the New York Yankees, he had two of them. (Greg Myers added another, equaling a team record for one game.) Two days later, Carter suffered a slight groin pull but this time he did not miss any action. Against the Boston Red Sox on April 20, it was Carter who drove in the insurance run in the 13th inning for a 6-4 Toronto victory. Now he was in the middle of a hitting streak that would extend to 16 games before he was thwarted by the Royals back in Toronto on April 24. This in spite of still being hampered by the groin pull.

Against the Milwaukee Brewers on May 3, Carter enjoyed a splendid outing. The Toronto offence, which had sputtered in recent days, was jump-started by his third and fourth homers of the year. The first one tied the game, the second one snapped a tie in the eighth. He rounded out the affair with a double and even his single out was a rocket to third. In the process, Carter continued his domination of starter Bill Wegman, running his numbers to 15 for 35 (.429) with four doubles, two triples and four homers. "I know I've had a lot of success against him but my secret is no secret. I just seem to see the ball." Responded Wegman: "Next time, I'm gonna walk him four times."

There was a two-run dinger for Carter a couple of days later, against the Oakland Athletics and, just 24 hours after that, another two-run homer against Seattle. By May 10, in the middle of a 1-for-12 slump, Carter atoned by knocking in three runs with a four-bagger and a single as the Jays dumped the California Angels 4-1. The fourth-inning home run just kept carrying, finally leaving the park at the 404-foot sign. It was obvious the big-bopper was enjoying his third-spot position in the batting line-up, between Alomar and Dave Winfield, which ensured that he saw better pitches than he ever had in the past. The opposition could not minimize the damage by trying to pitch around him, the way Gaston had designed his offensive package. But it sometimes appeared that pitchers were throwing right at him instead.

In a May game against the Brewers, Carter blew his stack when he was thwacked on the arm by starter Jaime Navarro. In part, his discontent stemmed from the memory that he had been bonked on the previous evening by Rick Bones. Could this have anything to do with the fact that he had hit those two homers against this same Brew Crew less than a month earlier? As far as Carter was concerned, the answer to that question was clear. He charged the mound and was tossed from the game for initiating the fracas that ensued. That ejection spoiled his wife's birthday. Only moments before the melee, she had been presented with balloons and a birthday cake in the stands. A guy in a gorilla suit had even serenaded her. Her husband had arranged it.

Navarro, naturally, begged off any culpability. "I didn't come after him, he came after me. He was screaming at me, 'That's the second time.' We were ahead 5-0, and I had him 0-2 in the count. I wasn't trying to hit him. I've got pretty good control but I hit somebody once in a while. I'm sorry but that's part of the game."

A year earlier, Carter had won player-of-the-month honors for June. In 1992, he looked good to repeat. June 1, against the Twins, Carter accounted for three hits, including a two-run homer that tied things at 3-3 in the sixth, in a game in which the Jays would prevail 5-3. The next night he singled in the 10th, after Devon White's home run, then added a big insurance run on a Dave Winfield double as Toronto won its fourth straight — all in the final at-bat. Just over a week later, Carter's two-run homer in the third — his second in as many nights — provided the decisive clout as the Jays blanked the Red Sox 4-0 in Toronto.

June continued to bloom prettily for Carter. Tangling again with the Sox, Carter homered off Canadian starter Mike Gardiner with two-out in the first. The solo blast was his third home run of the four-game series and extended his most recent hitting streak to seven games as the Jays dumped Boston 6-2. For those numbers, Carter was named American League player of the week. He was now leading the AL with 14 hits, six runs, four doubles, eight RBIs, 32 total bases and a 1.103 slugging percentage. And, oh, he had hit four homers in those seven days. This was all the more important because six Blue Jay regulars were hitting under .250. Carter, along with Alomar and Winfield, were carrying the load offensively. "So far, it's been a Carter and Winfield show," said Gaston. "Sometimes, though, that's not enough, not with them hitting right back of each other." Carter would finish the month in the same vein, with a three-run homer at the SkyDome, though the Jays were overpowered by the Texas Rangers in a 16-13 shootout. He concluded the month with eight homers and 23 RBIs. Those numbers were team highs for June. He also had a .330 batting average and a .651 slugging percentage over the 26 games.

July proved to be more of the same though Carter was modest about his success. After whacking a 418-foot shot off the scoreboard in left at the SkyDome, as the Jays cruised past the California Angels 6-2, Carter paid tribute to Winfield: "Now I've got a bona fide hall of famer behind me. I've played eight years and I've never had anyone hitting behind me before."

The slugger was putting up the kind of numbers that would seem to guarantee him a call to the All-Star game that was to be played in San Diego, his former home. The year before, Carter had made his All-Star debut, right at the SkyDome and had gone 1-for-1. He had basked in the glow, especially since he had been overlooked so many times in the past; he wanted to repeat the experience. On July 8, he slammed his 19th home run of the season, a three-run drive that catapulted the Jays to a 5-0 lead over the Mariners. His sac fly in the seventh drove in Toronto's sixth run.

In the All-Star balloting, Carter finished fifth among outfielders, directly behind Winfield. Jose Canseco was the fan favorite, but he was also on the disabled list. Twins skipper Tom Kelly, who was managing the American League contingent, named

Carter to the team ahead of Winfield anyway. Carter, while delighted with his selection, said his teammate should have been there, if not instead, then at least as well. "I think he deserved to go. He's been there all year for us but I've only been hot for a month and a half." But there was more good news for Carter — Kelly had named him to start the All-Star game, in lieu of the ailing Canseco.

He was one of the first players to arrive at Jack Murphy Stadium on the morning before the spectacle. Told that he would be starting in right field and batting cleanup, Carter could barely contain himself. "All right! There's a lot of good things happening here. That's awesome. To have my first two All-Star games in Toronto and now San Diego is tremendous, unbelievable. It couldn't have worked out any better."

Ditto for the game itself. The American League annihilated the National League 13-6 and Carter had two hits, an RBI and scored a run while improving his all-star batting average to .750. He was involved in the loony first-inning outburst, at the expense of starter Tom Glavine, cracking the third single in a string of seven consecutive hits. Carter's blooper filled the bases for Mark McGwire, who rapped a two-run single to centre.

Returning to his regular day-job, Carter poked a solo home run against the Angels at Anaheim in a game the Jays would lose 5-4. It was his 20th of the season, but he also doubled and scored as the Jays tied it briefly at 3-3. The rest of the month was not as bounteous. In fact, he finally broke out of an 0-for-20 slump on the last day of July with a long two-run homer as the Jays vanquished the New York Yankees 13-2 at SkyDome. The next day, after fouling off a surprise bunt attempt, Carter lofted the next pitch to the bottom of the fence in left-centre to cash in all the runs the Jays would need to beat the Yankees 3-1, their eighth straight win over the Bronx bunch. Carter was nailed trying for three on the play but it didn't matter. His two-run two-out homer the next afternoon, part of a dramatic four-run outburst in the seventh, helped the Jays nip the Yankees 7-6 for the three-game sweep.

Against the Tigers in Detroit, Carter scored three runs and drove in four with one round-tripper, as the hometowners went down 15-11. Then the Jays dropped the next three against the Tigers. Carter went 0-for-13 and stranded 12 runners. Back in Toronto, against the Baltimore Orioles, he cranked out a two-run homer as the Jays prevailed 8-4, further diminishing the fellow avians' ambitions of a division title. Carter liked it at the SkyDome and his numbers showed that. His 43 RBIs on home turf led the team, as did his 14 home runs. His 25th four-bagger came at the SkyDome too, though the Jays succumbed to the Orioles this time, 11-4, and the race for the partial pennant heated up again. Facing off against the Orioles the next night, Carter took over duties at first base for the third time in '92 while John Olerud was given a rest. This was an occasional assignment that he didn't mind in the least. "I guess I enjoy it on a part-time basis." This time around, it had even been his idea. Anticipating a trip to the World Series, which would mean leaving the designated hitter bat at home for road games, Carter had suggested to Gaston that the team try him at first and put Winfield in the outfield, thereby keeping the latter's power in the line-up. Agreed, said the skipper.

The other unusual occurrence about the August 13th 4-2 victory over the Orioles — the teams split the series — was that Carter lay down a sac bunt for the first time since his days as a Cleveland Indian. That moved Alomar to third from whence he scored the insurance run on a Candy Maldonado single. Again Carter was named American League player of the week. During that stretch, he had batted .407 (11 for 27) with five RBIs and nine runs scored. In addition to three homers against Baltimore, he had crunched out four doubles and produced an .889 slugging percentage from a total of 24 bases. He also had tremendous .484 on-base average during the seven-game span.

In Milwaukee on August 18, trying to hold off the surging Brewers, the Jays went on a 12-1 rampage. Carter contributed a three-run shot and starter Jimmy Key began the process of righting himself after a disastrous 1-4 mark (and 7.71 ERA) since the All-Star break. "It was much needed from a team stand-point," said Carter, as Milwaukee remained 6 1/2 lengths behind. "We definitely need Jimmy to come around." Later in the month, facing the Brewers again at the SkyDome, Carter was glad to see his friend Bill Wegman on the mound. He bopped another homer off him and the Jays finished 5-3 on the scoreboard.

Now rolling into September, Carter showed no signs of slowing down or wearing down. In a 9-3 encounter with the Chicago White Sox, he secured three of Toronto's 11 hits, getting the sixth-inning fireworks started with a leadoff double into the left corner, then stealing third. On Sept. 4, with the Twins in town, Carter connected for his 30th homer of the season as the Jays dispatched the visitors 16-5. That marked the fourth time in his career that Carter had hit for 30 or more homers in a season. But it was also a fine all-around effort as he struck for three hits, including the three-run homer, and an RBI triple that made 99 on the year. Number 100 came the next night in a 7-3 contest over the Twins but the experience had become too familiar to induce much celebrating. "The only target I ever set for myself is to play 162 games," he told reporters as they hovered around his locker. "I wouldn't call it boasting but I know I'm going to drive in 100 runs. I feel like I'm going to do it every year but the main thing for me is to stay healthy. I can't really explain it but (driving in runs) is just something I do."

He was asked, then, if he resented the fact that his accomplishments had not brought him the kind of big-league celebrity accorded the likes of Jose Canseco or Mark McGwire. He shrugged it off. "I haven't got the recognition that guys like Canseco or McGwire get because I'm not a flamboyant-type player. I'm just a laid-back kind of guy." There was much to be said, he added, about his obscurity. In some cities, successful ballplayers "can't walk down the street without getting mobbed. Toronto's a very good baseball town but fans give you your privacy. They let you eat, and then they attack you."

In Kansas City, just down the road from the town he had made his off-season home for many years, Carter redirected a Luis Aquino pitch far over the wall for his 31st home run of the year. That gave the Jays a 4-0 lead (they would add one more run before it was over) and marked only his second lifetime four-bagger at Royal Stadium. The blast nearly carried into one of the fountains far beyond the 385-foot mark in left-centre field. "I just thought it was going to be in the gap but I saw it go out and went, Wow!"

On September 24, against the Orioles in Baltimore, Carter fouled a pitch off his own knee and curled up in a fetal position at the plate. His condition, with just a week left in the regular campaign and nothing settled in the AL East, was listed as day-to-day. He sat out the next night and appeared as a pinch hitter the game after that, popping to centre for the final out in New

York as the Yankees held on for a 2-1 victory. "I spent one more day as a cheerleader but tomorrow, one way or another, I'll be there."

He was, in right field. He made a lot of noise, too, especially with his bat, as he powered the Jays to a 12-2 final on a four-hit, four RBI afternoon. He launched his attack with a triple that disappeared into the mist at Yankee Stadium, on the first pitch he saw, then added RBI singles in the second and third.

On the second-to-last day of the 162-game season, Carter notched his final dinger of the regular campaign, a two-run homer courtesy of Detroit starter David Haas as the Jays polished off the Tigers 3-1 and clinched the American League East. In the clubhouse, hours after the game was over, the celebrations continued. That's when Carter, by now soaking from the ritual champagne showers, strode purposefully out of the video room and, in his continuing role as Daddy, called a halt to the festivities. "Get dressed and go home!" he bellowed to the troops. They did.

And on the next day, the final day, Joe Carter rested.

# Gl⚾ry Jays

## *Sir David*              **4**

In baseball, as in everything else, there is no real present tense. There is only the past and the future. The moment at hand cannot truly be quantified because it exists purely on a conceptual level. It is an illusion.

What has gone before is divine for the purposes of nostalgia, which has fueled a renaissance in a game that more than any other exults in the margins of memory. Old men who played for peanuts are making more money now at conventions and card shows than they ever pulled in as youthful athletes. Sometimes it feels as if the characters of memorabilia are more real than the professionals we encounter at the ballpark and certainly more admirable. But what has come before, for those players who are still active, is also the hard currency of contract negotiations. The arbitrageurs of baseball, when they are not busy projecting the prospects of a greenhorn, are casting a cold eye on the recent history of those who are seeking only to continue their employment. In the vernacular of baseball, this translates as: What have you done for me lately?

Dave Stieb, more than any other player, was a man with a Blue Jay history. But as last season began, the question was, did he have any future with the only major league ballclub he had ever known? This was uppermost on his mind, and management's, when he arrived at Dunedin after a 10-month layoff precipitated by injuries, a chronic back problem and finally, reluctantly, surgery.

He was 34 years old and had been a Jay since 1979, long before the team had acquired any competitive respectability around the league. He and the club had come of age together though the gaining of wisdom seemed to benefit the franchise more than it did their ace pitcher. There was a part of Stieb that never grew up, and we are not talking here about youthful exuberance or the sweetness of men who will always be boys as they make a grown-up career out of a child's pastime.

Stieb's immaturity was evidenced in his inability to control his emotions on the field — he wore his passions and his resentments on his sleeve. He upbraided himself on the mound, he glared at his teammates when they didn't perform up to his exacting standards; he fussed with umpires and tangled with the opposition. He let the game get under his skin, which was thin. His disposition was neither warm nor endearing and he was not well-liked. But he was Sir David and he had earned the right to his idiosyncrasies after 13 years as the prince of the pitching staff.

He had worn the uniform longer than any player in team history, arriving in June of 1979, only a year after he'd been selected in the free agent draft out of Southern Illinois University. He had started four season openers, had seven times been selected to represent the Blue Jays in the annual All-Star game. He laid claim to every pitching record of note with the franchise and in 1985 had signed a long-term contract that suggested he would play out his entire career with Toronto. In early '91, the Jays voluntarily increased his salary to $3 million for the season instead of the $1.6 million he was to be paid under terms of the original contract. It was an act of faith and fairness on behalf of the club. He had embarked on his 13th campaign without ever suffering an injury that required a stint on the disabled list. He was reliable even as he was star-crossed.

He had never managed a 20-win season though he held the franchise's single-season mark of 18 as well as the record for most career victories with 170. He threw hard, had good stuff, and possessed a wicked slider, acknowledged by his opponents as probably the best in baseball.

It felt sometimes as if he had been with the team forever. There was the youthful and cocksure Stieb of the early '80s, a Tom Selleck look-alike whose brashness and irritability seemed like a natural concomitant to the awesome skills he brought to the mound. There was the forlorn and woebegone Dave Stieb who watched helplessly as a windblown flyball caromed off the right field fence on a starless night at Exhibition Stadium in the autumn of 1985 — Game 7 of the American League Championship Series. There was the Dave Stieb of any given night in any given year who would claw at himself emotionally on the mound; fretting and twitching, tugging this and worrying that, bouncing the ball off his protective cup, shooting daggers at the batters, at his own teammates, verbally admonishing himself and the whole world. Making a spectacle of himself. Losing it.

There were those two consecutive starts of near-genius pitching prowess when Stieb carried no-hitters into the bottom of the ninth inning with two outs, only to be wretchedly denied. Then, in Cleveland in 1990, there was a wonderfully joyous Stieb finally nailing that elusive no-hitter and being carried off the field on his teammates' shoulders. Curiously, he doesn't remember that game as a thing of beauty. "I had four walks, that's what I remember." But he was delighted enough with the accomplishment that he had the Cleveland organization send him 65 ticket stubs from the game, which he had mounted and then distributed to friends and teammates.

But there is one haunting image that lingers in memory. It is of Dave Stieb standing on the mound in Arlington Stadium early last summer. Storm clouds are fulminating on the horizon and the wind is whipping up dust devils that churn across the field. The sky is like an angry purple bruise. An oppressive gloom smothers the ballpark and the only relief is the sudden glare of jagged lightning bolts. Thunder crackles in their wake as the blink of illumination fades to gray.

It is a gothic night. A Wagnerian night. A Stephen King night.

Debris swirls in a funnel about the pitcher's shoulders as the thunderhead scuds violently towards the mound. It is as if Dave Stieb himself is the object of all this sound and fury. It is also a fitting metaphor for all the days and nights of Dave Stieb's professional life: Sound and fury.

There had never been anything serene about the way Stieb played, not even in the halcyon days when the pitching was easy. From the beginning and through to the closing chapters as a Jay, there had been an edge of impending melodrama to his performances, be it on the field or in the clubhouse. He was a skittish moundsman and a sometimes peevish human being. Between the lines, he had been compared to an overbred racehorse. He occasionally spooked himself. In the dressing room, reporters treaded softly around his locker. He was not so much volatile as icily cutting, a shiv between the ribs.

Dave Stieb was not lovable. But, as he would be the first to point out, he had never asked to be loved either. If anything, he had deliberately and willfully resisted the masses. He had spurned the peculiar intimacy that can develop between athlete and fan. And, if there is one sad postscript to his tenure as a Blue Jay, it may be that, in the end, a little bit of lovin' would have been a comfort. But there was little reservoir of goodwill for Stieb to draw from in his hours of need last season.

"Sure, I'd like to have everybody love me," he admitted one day. "But I don't like the small talk that goes along with being in this position. Most of the time I just want to be left alone. I don't like interacting with people I do not know. I don't like having to make myself available to everyone. There are a lot of days when I definitely don't want to talk to anyone at all."

When Stieb arrived at spring training last February, earlier than was necessary, he was not at all sure that he was still Dave Stieb, pitcher, or Dave Stieb, former pitcher. This confusion went back to a game against the Oakland Athletics on May 22 of the previous year. He had developed a sore shoulder after striking out eight opponents in that defeat. The discomfort was attributed at first to a collision between the pitcher and a runner at first base. In Baltimore 2 1/2 weeks later, Stieb began complaining that his lower back was sore but extensive testing didn't reveal the true cause, a herniated disk, until late in June. When it became increasingly clear that he would be out for the season, general manager Pat Gillick had to do some quick card-shuffling to procure the services of Cleveland's Tom Candiotti. It was a brief stay. The knuckleballer, after a pitiful performance against the Minnesota Twins in the five-game American League Championship Series, vamoosed to the Los Angeles Dodgers as a free agent.

Stieb had flown back to be with the team during the playoffs, even if all he could offer was encouragement from the bench. His recovery routine at that stage, after trying papaya juice injections and cortisone shots, consisted of daily exercises and light therapy. But shagging flies and showering with his teammates was about as close as he could get to the experience of his third American League playoffs.

He had spent most of the summer at his home in California, laying flat, hoping the pains shooting through his back and down his right leg would subside. He was in constant agony, unable to walk, unable to get behind the wheel of a car, unable to play with his kids. At times, he felt as if he was the babe in arms and not his infant daughter. But the bulging disk — the damage was on the fifth lumbar and first sacrial vertebrae — did not improve and the anguish did not cease. As 1991 ended, Stieb finally agreed that the only route to take was surgery. On December 4 he went under the knife in Setton Hospital at Daly City, California. Performing the honors was Dr. Arthur White, who had executed the same procedure on Joe Montana of the San Francisco 49ers. The open-incision procedure lasted only 45 minutes and Dr. White speculated that Stieb could be back in training within two weeks, throwing full-out in ten. The disk had been ruptured so the doctor had trimmed it and scraped inside the spinal column, which took the pressure off the nerve that extended into the leg. Stieb started his convalescence period by walking one-eighth of a mile a day. Nine days after going under the knife, he began working out. It looked like a long uphill climb back to the major leagues but he was determined to be there when spring training opened.

He was.

His natural physical conditioning had made that possible, as well as the light training that he had maintained during his nearly year-long absence from baseball. Stieb was so eager to get going, he reported in advance of the official starting date for pitchers and catchers. One day, he compared scars with manager Cito Gaston, who had also finally submitted to surgery for a persistent back problem. "His looks much better than mine," said Stieb. "Cito's is just this little line. Mine's maybe a quarter-inch wide."

He told reporters he was pain-free but nobody was willing to hazard a guess as to how long it would take before Stieb could cut loose and throw hard. Gaston and his staff privately estimated that the pitcher would likely remain in Florida for extended rehabilitation when the team flew north to begin the season. Stieb had other plans. "My only goal is to start one of the first five games of the season. Right now, the key's going to be getting the shoulder back in shape. I'm going to take that slowly but I think in three weeks or so I can have the arm ready. I hope to be pitching in games in mid-March."

He tossed softly off the mound at first, flat-footed. Then he went full motion and half-speed. The coaching staff was impressed with these baby steps from a major league pitcher who used to zing fastballs and snap sliders. In late March he threw to live hitters for the first time in batting practice. In a simulated game, his first serious work of the spring, Stieb's offerings were pounded out of the park beyond the left field fence at Dunedin Stadium. "I threw some tree trimmers," Stieb observed, shaking his head. "I was horrible but I'm not unhappy with the way I felt physically." It was all trial and error, he explained. "But I do feel that as long as my arm doesn't hurt, it'll all fall in line. The question is when."

Not in time to start the season with the Jays, as it turned out. Stieb, along with reliever Mike Timlin, also on a rehab assignment, was put on the disabled list and lingered in Dunedin as the rest of the team packed up for opening day at Tiger Stadium. He found himself pitching against Class A players while his big-league colleagues were going full-tilt in The Show. And even the kids were making reasonable contact on his offerings.

Finally, Stieb got the green light. He was ready to play with the grownups again. His debut was scheduled for April 22 at the SkyDome against the Cleveland Indians. That at least boded well for his comeback. The last time Stieb had faced the Tribe he had no-hit them. But that, as it turned out, was then. This was now, and it wasn't very pretty.

He appeared in the familiar surroundings of the Blue Jays clubhouse on the afternoon before his scheduled start and was greeted with a bear hug from Joe Carter. When he spotted his old nemesis, Jack Morris, Stieb said: "Hey, great club. Every game's a chance for a victory." Then he shook hands all around. That night, while sitting in the dugout, his face was flashed on the JumboTron in the second inning and the crowd gave him a standing ovation.

A similar salutation greeted him the next evening, as he trotted in from the bullpen to start the next game. The relievers, anticipating the moment, had donned squirrely wigs in tribute to the colleague they called The Mossman, on account of the straggly mane that poked out from underneath his ball cap and curled over the nape of his neck. The goofy denizens of the 'pen salaamed, too, as Stieb took his familiar place on the hill. Confronted by these comradely hi-jinks, Stieb laughed. But the smile was soon wiped off his face.

The Indians, unmoved by the occasion, welcomed him back to the majors by tearing a strip off of everything he delivered to the plate. The fastball was leisurely, the curveball a puny imitation of its former self, and the slider sagged instead of snapped. He began with a strikeout, which had the crowd cheering in recognition of the Stieb of yore. Then, BANG, a home run to former teammate Glenallen Hill on an 0-and-2 pitch. That was followed by a four-pitch walk and two more strikeouts, one swinging and one called. When Stieb left after six innings, the Jays were down 4-0.

Still, he was just glad that it was over. Even in a losing cause, he had been triumphant. He had made it back, nobody could take that away from him. "It wasn't a total disaster," he told reporters. "There's plenty of work to do but I've got something to take into my next outing. The delivery's got to be more fluid. Got to get the ball down on a more consistent basis. Got to find a more consistent release point." What mattered more was that Stieb's problems on the night were the same problems faced by any other pitcher who'd made a few mistakes in a game. This was something he could deal with, it was within his range of experience. Best of all, there was no pain, at least nothing out of the usual for a 30-something arm.

On his next turn in the rotation, April 28 against California, it was harder to extract any positive notes from the affair. Stieb was rattled by the Angels as they trounced the Jays 9-5, led by former Blue Jay Junior Felix who drove California's 14-hit attack by cashing in three runs. Meanwhile, Stieb's control was so poor that he beaned second baseman Bobby Rose in the head with a pitch, following a home run by Lance Parrish. Everyone involved concluded it had been unintentional. Rose was taken to the hospital where he stayed overnight as a precaution.

After the game, Stieb had nothing to say to anybody. But it was obvious that he was furious with Gaston for pulling him at the end of the fourth inning, trailing 4-1. The two could be seen having a brief discussion in the dugout about what Stieb clearly considered a premature exit. There were more words, some of them heated, behind closed doors in the manager's office later. The shouting could be overheard down the corridor. "We were just talking," Gaston understated to the media later. "But, hey, I don't dictate how long he pitches. Guys dictate whether they stay in the game by the way they pitch."

Baseball, for all its sentimental trappings, is a hard-hearted endeavor. It was becoming clear that Stieb would not get any special treatment, or any greater latitude than what his own performance dictated on the mound. (This was not entirely true with everybody on the Jays staff. Jack Morris was routinely allowed to stay out there longer than seemed appropriate, especially since Toronto boasted one of the deepest bullpens in the game. But his record for longevity, and his knack for inspiring the team to come back from lop-sided scores, meant that he was accorded this respect.)

Finally, on May 3 at Milwaukee's County Stadium, Stieb got his first victory of 1992 — his first in almost a full year, 51 weeks to be precise. He managed it with a complete game three-hitter too, walking four and plonking Franklin Stubbs in the process. Otherwise, it was a tidy 98-pitch performance and observers hoped that this signaled the end of Stieb's trials and tribulations. "I'm pleased. I'm glad to finally win again but I'm far from satisfied," said Stieb, always the perfectionist. "I walked far too many guys and four innings without a hit wasn't at all indicative of how I was throwing. Every inning was kind of hit or miss. I didn't know where the ball was going. I did make some good pitches when I got in a few jams, but I also got some great defense. The Brewers were hitting bullets all over the place."

But it wasn't the end or the beginning of anything. It was just one fairly decent outing abetted by, as Stieb pointed out, some good luck. In Anaheim next time out, Stieb served up a dinger to Rene Gonzales — yet another former Blue Jay — in the seventh inning, surrendered another run, and was out of there. Jays lost 4-1. "I was okay for six innings," he said. "Then it all blew up in my face. One horrible pitch, a hanging curveball. He (Gonzales) couldn't pop it up or swing through it. Oh no, he had to take it deep."

This, while said partly in jest, was also typical Stieb. He had never been able to understand why things didn't go his way or how any given situation could unravel so quickly. To some extent, he was obsessive about the pure chance element of baseball. He took any eventuality personally, as if he were being mocked by fate. "I have a lot of pride. I have a hard time accepting when bad things happen because I'm never expecting bad things to happen. When it does, it's embarrassing, to a degree."

This is what led to those conversations Stieb regularly had with himself on the mound, which were so often accompanied by gestures and pantomime. It was the fingerprint of his style as a pitcher. "Sometimes, I can be cruising along, having a great

game. I start thinking to myself, oh God, just look at that stuff.
And then maybe I try to turn it up one more notch. I'm not trying
to embarrass the guy at the plate or anything. But I figure, if I'm
throwing this good, why not try to make it just a little bit better.

"So now I start rushing the pitches and suddenly I'm in
trouble. But still I say to myself, okay, I've got runners on base but
I've got my teammates standing out there behind me. What's
wrong with a line drive that's caught right here, right now? Why
can't I have that? Hell, I see games all the time where that
happens, why can't it happen to me when I'm in a jam? But, you
know, it seems so often that the worst thing that can happen, does
happen. To me anyway. I mean, I look at the batter and I think,
this guy is not that good, what are the odds of something bad
happening right here? Then, bam, it's out of the park or it's in the
gap or it just gets by somebody's glove.

"Sometimes, I think you're almost better off to start a game
struggling. Then you concentrate on settling down, establishing
control. You're not out there overly confident, trying to raise
your game to this other level because you think you're so damn
hot. It seems, with me anyway, that I can never make that one bad
pitch and *get away with it*."

This is, in part, a reference to what Stieb considers a lack of
defensive support from his teammates. Over the years, he had
earned a reputation for showing up his own players, sometimes
quite publicly, when they have not performed to his expectations. To some extent, his displeasure was based on hard evidence: by subconscious design or rotten luck, the Jays did appear
to make more mistakes when his turn in the rotation came
around, they did seem to fumble ridiculously (remember those
back-to-back no-hitters gone bust) or simply play conservative
baseball. They didn't make the spectacular plays when they were
required. And, throughout his career in Toronto, he was victimized by a maddening lack of run support. His reality was the
exact opposite of Jack Morris.

"I had a bad rap from the beginning," Stieb admits. "That I
was selfish and that I only cared about myself, that I wasn't a team
player. Yes, I used to get on my teammates, yes I would glare at
the opposition. But I started out in this game as an outfielder and
I know how that position should be played. When I played the
outfield, I had nobody to blame but myself. Then I became a
pitcher. Now, as soon as I let go of the ball, whatever happens is

completely out of my hands. Who's gonna care later whether it was a clean hit or there was an error on the play if that run comes around to score? The next day, that L is going to appear next to the pitcher's name in the newspapers. That makes me a loser and I hate to lose.

"So, in those earlier years, I saw things that I could not accept and I showed it. I vented it. I saw guys booting balls all over the place. I'm sorry, but we're playing at a level now where stats matter, that's what determines how we're going to get paid. I didn't like what I saw. But that was also a long time ago. The team has changed a lot since then and so have I. I don't think it's fair to continue to criticize me for the way I behaved when I was younger."

But the pitcher he was as a younger man continued to be very much on Stieb's conscience. He couldn't reconcile himself to the reality of the here and now. "I used to throw these fastballs in on a guy, whoooeee! I was throwing on the black without even thinking about it. I knew this pitch was gonna be down there. Or the slider away on a three and two. I was so confident. I lost it for a while, back in '86, '87, so I changed my mechanics. I started to throw more curves and changing the speed on my fastball."

By June, this is how Stieb was describing his latter-day arsenal: "My slider's been brutal and I don't have an out pitch."

His confidence, his sense of self, was in tatters. While an athlete's ego can be both looming and brittle at the same time, Stieb in conversation could sound both arrogant and touchingly insecure within the same sentence. If that was confusing to the public, imagine how he felt. "Confidence comes and goes," he said one day. "I know I have a special talent on the mound. But baseball is a humbling game. You can be far from special on any given day."

It is revealing, perhaps, that throughout his career — and especially as his comeback attempt last season progressed from a sense of hope to a feeling of dread — Stieb has been his own harshest critic, even as he recoiled from the censure of others. He was so displeased with his performance following one game against Milwaukee that he turned to a reporter and suggested maybe he was just a seven-inning pitcher after all. His self-loathing was chilling. "I'm harder on myself than anyone can ever be on me. I can have a game like I did against Milwaukee where I won but I pitched like shit. I got away with it, that's all.

I'm not the kind of guy who can measure my worth based on what I did two years ago. I build upon what I'm doing now."

What he was doing now was imploding. In early June, he dropped to 3-5 on the season after a 7-1 loss to Baltimore wherein Stieb allowed five runs on seven hits in only five innings. But what was most telling about this particular effort was the way Stieb disintegrated on the mound after the plate umpire called a ball on what the pitcher was adamant was a strike, which would have rung up Cal Ripken. The Oriole shortstop, after laying off a ball and fouling off two pitches, rifled an RBI single through the right side. "That was weak, pathetic," Stieb fumed afterwards. "The pitch was right there. I had him punched out at a critical time in the game and (the umpire) blew it."

But so did Stieb. He was unable to forget it, to proceed with any degree of coolness. Ripken's hit touched off a four-spot in the inning and when the frame was finally over Stieb continued jabbering at the umpire all the way to the dugout. This, too, was vintage Stieb. The Jays lost the game not because of a blown strike-call, as he saw it, but because he could not regroup after an incident which is common to all pitchers. And his club had suffered because of it. Stieb denied any culpability. "I can get as mad as I want but when I pitch, I'm pitching. It doesn't affect me."

His next turn, Stieb gave up a grand slam to Boston's Wade Boggs in a 5-0 shutout of the Jays and dropped to 3-6. It began inauspiciously enough with a one-out walk to Tony Pena in the fifth. Scott Cooper doubled and Jody Reed walked to load the bases. Stieb got Luis Rivera on a fly ball for the second out. But Boggs, with only one hit in 13 previous at-bats, deposited a hanging breaking ball over the right field fence for his fifth homer of the season. This was the third grand slam Stieb had given up in his career, and they were all to Boston.

Gaston said later that he intended to keep sending Stieb out there, particularly since he was having problems getting decent efforts from another starter, Todd Stottlemyre. But against the Tigers in his next start, Stieb lasted just 1 2/3 innings and left with Detroit up 6-0. This just couldn't go on. One solution was to dispatch the pitcher to the bullpen where he might be able to resolve his difficulties while facing less pressure. "He would probably get more work out of the bullpen rather than working every five days," Gaston told reporters. "But I don't know if that would help."

In Arlington, late in June, Stieb was rescued by a sudden squall and the game was called with the score tied 1-1 after 1 1/2 innings. Against Texas again a week later, Stieb started digging a familiar hole when he allowed the Rangers to come back 5-4 after being down 5-0. After the Rangers loaded the bases with one out, Pat Hentgen came on to stonewall Texas and the Jays eventually won 11-4. But Gaston had seen enough. Stieb had pitched his way out of the rotation and into the pen.

The veteran moundsman was not happy as David Wells took over his starting role. "I haven't pitched that badly," he told a television reporter. "It just seems like everything is going against me...Sure, I've made some mistakes but I've usually kept us in the game. It's so easy to criticize me from afar but I'm the one down on the field. I know what's going on out there and it's not that bad."

Stieb was frustrated and miserable. He found little solace in the 'pen although he performed adequately out of the chute. In a game against Oakland he retired the six men he was asked to face in his second relief appearance. But he still didn't see the need for this entire exercise in what he considered an unacceptable demotion. "What is going to the bullpen supposed to do for me?" he wondered aloud. "Is it supposed to make me more relaxed because it certainly hasn't done that. Is it supposed to relieve the pressure I was under? If anything, it's added a lot more. Because the way I see it, I have to go out there now and not give up any runs. When you start a game, that's the objective, but no one actually expects you to get every single guy out. Now, I figure I'm out there for two innings at a time and I feel like I'm in a no-win situation. If I go two shutout innings, then it's no big deal. But if I give up some runs, everyone's going to say, Stieb's still struggling. There goes his chance to get back into the starting rotation."

He vehemently denied the suggestion, floated by some baseball connoisseurs, that he was a pitcher who had never had to learn how to pitch, simply because he had such overwhelming talent throughout his 20s and early 30s. "This has nothing to do with learning how to pitch," he snapped. "Learning how to pitch means knowing what to throw and when to throw it. It means knowing how to think on the mound. I know how to pitch. If not, what the heck have I been doing for the past 13 years? No, this has been about correcting some mechanical flaws. Maybe it's taken me longer to do that than I would have liked. But people don't realize how difficult it can be to deal with the windup and delivery when you've been struggling with it. Usually, I just go out there and I do it. Now I have to stop and remember what it is that I'm supposed to be doing. So I'm thinking about five different things in my delivery at the same time that I'm thinking about trying to get major league hitters out."

The reluctant reliever was about to catch a break. In this case, his sudden good fortune was contingent on somebody else's bad luck. Starter Juan Guzman had suddenly pulled up lame for the first time in his pro career. He had come out of a game against the Athletics because of recurring muscle tightness in the back of the right shoulder. Stieb took over the chores to finish that game, retiring 12 of 14 over the final four innings to pick up his first win in relief.

There had been talk, in those days, that Stieb might actually be released outright by the Jays. After all, as a 10-and-5 player (10 years of service, at least five of them with the same club consecutively), the rules stated that Stieb would need to be protected by the Jays in the expansion draft that was coming up in the fall. Perhaps it would be wiser to just buy out his contract now — for a million bucks.

But with Guzman ailing, the Jays needed Stieb again. He had been given a new lease on life. How ironic, too, that it should have come at Guzman's expense. After all, the young Dominican had been ushered into the majors the year before precisely to fill the job vacated by Stieb because of his own injury. Subsequently, the young phenomenon surpassed Stieb's record of nine consecutive victories by a starter, and set the new mark at 10. Now the roles were reversed.

As an emergency starter, Stieb came out against the Kansas City Royals and gave the Jays a solid six innings in his first effort. From a total of 92 pitches, the righthander offered 50 strikes and demonstrated some fairly effective control. He walked two and struck out a pair, and even picked off Gregg Jefferies at first. The game was 1-1 when he departed, and the Jays eventually lost 5-2. But Stieb was pleased. "I threw well. A good breaking ball, good location, not overpowering."

Yet, there were new signs that not all was well. With Guzman still on the DL, Stieb started feeling twinges of pain in his elbow. Pitcher and manager held their breath. Stieb also held out his arm

for a cortisone shot. On August 8, he went to the hill against the
Tigers in Detroit and lasted only three innings. His elbow was
throbbing, and he allowed the Tigers to seize a three-run lead in
the third on two walks, a single, and a bases-loaded double. The
next day he had another cortisone shot and was placed on the
disabled list.

In the weeks ahead, anxious to return to active duty, Stieb
would continue to test the elbow, throwing on the side and off the
mound. The results were not encouraging. "Very disappointing," he reported on August 22, after throwing off the mound in
Minneapolis. "I get two cortisone shots. I rest it completely for
seven days. Then I play catch and more catch. Then I throw —
and it's still there." The burning in his elbow had not abated.
Doctors concluded it was not quite tendinitis but an irritation
where the tendon touches the bone on the inside of the elbow.
More rest was recommended. Stieb was running out of time as
time was running out on the season. He did not want more rest.
"It's such a lame thing to do nothing," he complained. "Eleven
years and never on the DL and now I've lived on it. The thing
about the rest option is there's no season left when I get back. I'll
be resting up for next season."

That, as it turned out, was an accurate assessment. Stieb went
to see a specialist in Birmingham, Alabama, who told him the
problem was medial epicondylitis — a fancy name for what he
already knew, an inflammation of the tendon. He stood on the
sidelines and watched as Jack Morris became the first Jays pitcher
to win five games in a month since he had done it in 1988. He was
stoic as Morris then surpassed his 18 wins in a season record, then
extended that mark to 21. His career, his place in the team
biography, was being overtaken and there was nothing he could
do about it. It also looked doubtful that the Jays would reactivate
Stieb so he could be included on the post-season roster.

Stieb threw off the mound for the first time in 18 days on
September 24 and came away disheartened. When asked how it
had gone, he responded: "It didn't. It hurt. After 10 minutes
throwing it hurt, so that's it. It's just more rest now — a whole
winter of rest."

One had to wonder if this was, in fact, the beginning of the
end. Or maybe just the end period. Stieb himself had discussed
the eventuality of retirement or banishment from baseball earlier
in the season. Years before, when he had written his biography

with Toronto journalist Kevin Boland, Stieb could barely envisage a time when he would no longer be in his prime, when he would no longer be playing. He said then that he would not try to hang on, would not make a fool out of himself if it looked like he was turning into a pale imitation of the brassy pitcher he had been. Now he wasn't as willing to go gentle into that good night.

"I will miss it more than I thought. But I'm not anywhere close to that point right now. As long as I'm physically able to go out there and pitch, then that's what I intend to do. You always have to believe that you are going to be able to find your groove, that you are going to get better." He was fretful, though, about how he would be remembered. "I've had a mediocre career, won-lost-wise. And some people will say that I was not a big-game pitcher. But give me five or six or seven opportunities and I will be a big-game pitcher. I'm afraid that I will be remembered for what an animal I was on the mound. But I was a severe competitor and a perfectionist.

"I guess maybe I'm the best pitcher who never won 20 games."

Stieb's season of humility was not yet over. There would be one more indignity to be suffered.

On the afternoon that the Jays clinched the American League East demi-pennant, there was a whole lot of championship nonsense going on in the dressing room. Stieb didn't stick around for much of it. The rollicking celebration was led mostly by young kids, many of whom had contributed little to the Blue Jay success of 1992. Fine. Kids are supposed to have fun at moments like these. But somewhere along the line, things got out of hand. The celebrants attacked Stieb's vacated locker.

Perhaps it was unintentional. Perhaps it was just a bunch of thoughtless young men having some fun at a veteran's expense. Just an act of carelessness where youthful exuberance turns surly — mob mentality writ small in a champagne-drenched locker room. But what transpired was still a regrettable gesture of disrespect.

Stieb had been one of the first to dress after the game was over. He did linger for a while, watched as the young'uns poured beer over their heads like this was a novel gesture. Later, he went into a backroom with Kelly Gruber. After that, he headed upstairs where he spent about 40 minutes in the company of Pat Gillick, Paul Beeston and his own agent, Bob La Monte. And why not? These were the men who had known him the longest. They had passed the seasons together. Maybe they even had some business to discuss up there.

But the baby Jays didn't know or care about the details. They didn't realize Stieb was still in the building. As ringleader Derek Bell put it to his raucous foot soldiers: "He left early because he doesn't like to party. So I think we should drench his locker."

There was some discussion about this. Most of the veterans wanted no part of this prank. Someone at least had the foresight to remove Stieb's dry cleaning from his cubicle. Then the locker was spritzed, sprayed and soaked. But that wasn't enough. All of a sudden, twisted beer cans came flying in — a cannonade, a rat-a-tat of tin. This was no longer an immature prank. This was a pathetic spectacle with a subtext of malice.

The next morning, told about the incident, Stieb was more hurt than angry. He sat in front of his locker, picking through his possessions, trying to determine if anything had been damaged. "I've been here for 14 years," he began, a perplexed expression on his face. "It's not the way it used to be, everything's changed. People don't have the same respect for older players anymore. The main people involved in this stuff were young. It's...weak. We're talking about kids and, basically, immaturity. But I would never have done anything like this when I was young."

He was annoyed that, yet again, his actions had been misinterpreted. "I was here, I didn't leave. But I didn't particularly want to get sprayed with champagne either. So I took my shower, and then I went upstairs to congratulate Beeston and Gillick. Everyone around here seems to think that I dashed out to go to a concert or something. Maybe I didn't feel as emotional about (winning the division) as they did. But I'm 35 years old and I've been through this before. The way they feel now is the way I felt in 1985, when it was my first time. Hey, they can take it any way they like, that's their option. But this just leads me to believe that they don't care about me. If you liked a person, you wouldn't just jump to conclusions about them."

He was unsure, then, whether he would remain with the team as a non-playing cheerleader through the post-season. Ultimately he did stay. He stayed because he could not bring himself to leave. He stayed because he wanted to be a part of it. And, in his own fashion, he was.

But, in the end, baseball had not been kind to Dave Stieb.

# Glory Jays

## *Quite Simply, The Franchise* 5

Some athletes play ball for the money. Others, regardless of how much they earn, just play ball. They are the ones who do it with glee, as if there were no other place they'd rather be than on a field of green. They skip on the grass, get dirt all over their uniforms, and slide head-long into first base even though they've been told that there is no particular advantage in this mode of arrival. It just *feels* good.

That is why it feels so good to watch them. There is an endearing quality in their enthusiasm, a look-at-me jauntiness that is becoming, rather than egocentric because it is delivered with such delight. These players may have graduated to the major league parks, but they still have sandlot baseball in their soul.

Robbie Alomar is this kind of ball player. He not only lives for baseball, he actually lives in the park. To be more precise, when he goes to sleep at night, he does it in a hotel suite that is attached to the SkyDome. And when he goes off to work, all he has to do is step into a service elevator that will deliver him to the club-house in the bowels of the complex.

Roberto Velazquez Alomar came to the Toronto Blue Jays in tears. But life in Toronto has been a jubilee for the young man ever since. He is a smile personified and, quite simply, the franchise. All this from a 25-year-old who wiggles when he walks and giggles when he talks. Life must be grand when you're young and hot.

When Toronto traded for Alomar in December, 1990, he was an unknown quantity to most self-proclaimed baseball savants in the American League city. Few Blue Jay fans even realized that Cleveland catcher Sandy Alomar Jr. had a kid brother who could sort of play this game. Robbie Alomar was the undercard in the deal that sent Joe Carter north of the border from the San Diego Padres. Most fans were too busy mourning the sudden departure of Tony Fernandez and Fred McGriff to find much solace in the arrival of this kid with the vaguely familiar surname.

To be sure, Alomar wasn't thrilled either with this unexpected turn of events. He was a 22-year-old bachelor who owned his own house in San Diego and he admitted he cried when he was told that he had been traded. Perhaps he should not have been so stunned by his fate. Only a year earlier, the Padres had shipped his brother, Sandy Jr., to the Indians in exchange for Joe Carter. Then they fired his father, Sandy Alomar Sr., a one-time all-star second baseman who had been employed as third-base coach with the Padres. For whatever reason, the club was clearing its house of all Alomars.

Toronto fans may have been ignorant about Robbie Alomar's credentials but even a cursory perusal of the stats should have set them at ease: a switch-hitter with a slick glove who had just hit a career-high .287 with six homers and 60 RBIs in his third season as a Padre regular. Of course, there was that small matter of his league-high 17 errors at second base. And doesn't that seem like an incredulous figure in retrospect? Then again, there's a fine line between a breathtaking play and an error. If it works you're a genius, if it fails you're a bum. Robbie Alomar is no bum.

The first thing Alomar did in his post-Padre period was take the Blue Jays to arbitration. There's a fine how-do-you-do but, as his agent and the Toronto brass agreed, it was nothing personal. This is the way things are done in baseball these days. He had made $400,000 in 1990 but he cooly demanded $1.25 million. Toronto countered with an offer of $825,000. The arbitrator sided with Alomar's version of reality, thereby handing the Jays their first salary arbitration setback since 1983.

How could he have been denied? Alomar was the son of one all-star, brother to another, and in his first campaign as a Jay, was destined to be selected an all-star himself for the second year in a row — a fan ballot choice at second base, outpolling his nearest rival almost two to one. The annual contest of superstars was held in Toronto in 1991 and on hand to see their sons play side by side were both Alomar parents. "He was such a good little boy," recalled his mother, Maria, who had recently won an award of her own when she was named Mother Of The Year in the town of Salinas, where her youngest son had grown up dreaming of the big leagues. "The only trouble I had with him is that he was always running after his father. Always wanting to go to the ballpark. And if I wouldn't let him go, or when his father left to go to America, he would just cry and cry. He would go to his room by himself and later I would find him sleeping with his glove and his bat and his ball."

His dad told another story, of the time when he first started to believe the little rugrat might follow in his footsteps. It was during winter league ball and, of course, young Robbie had tagged along to the ballpark. "The kids were out there, playing catch and running. And this scout from the St. Louis Cardinals, he's looking at Robbie and he says: 'Save him for me, Sandy. I'm gonna sign him some day.' The kid was only six years old at the time."

To talk to Robbie Alomar is to understand that there was never any doubt in his young mind that he was going to make it to the majors. "My family never told me, you have to do this or you have to be that. There was never any pressure to play baseball. But that's all I ever wanted to do. To be just like my dad. And I loved the game. I loved it more than anything else."

One night, in his first season with Toronto, Alomar dredged up childhood memories of those sun-burnished days when all the world a ballfield and the big people mussing his hair had names like Catfish Hunter and Nolan Ryan — the same Nolan Ryan who was on the mound when Alomar got his first major league hit in 1988. (Alomar also happened to be the last out in a '91 game when Ryan threw a no-hitter against Toronto.) "I remember a day in Texas when my father was playing there. It was one of those father-son days at the ballpark. All of the kids were there playing with our fathers. Me and Sandy and my sister, too. Nothing special happened. It just felt special to me, all of us playing with my father."

His father had taught him well. From the beginning Alomar enlivened baseball in Toronto, whether diving into the hole to prevent a line drive from scooting to the outfield, or leaping and pirouetting in the air, or rapping out another one of his ho-hum doubles, or swatting home runs from either side of the plate in the same game. Hell, his first year at the SkyDome he even led the ranks in sacrifice bunts, the most unselfish of baseball maneuvers, and one that had only been rumored around Toronto in years gone by.

One day, as a reporter waited to speak with Alomar, someone whispered in her ear that he was in a tetchy mood for some inexplicable reason. "Me?" gasped Alomar, when this was repeated to him later. "Someone said I'm in a bad mood? Who was it? Not true, not true. I'm never in a bad mood."

This is, by and large, the truth. Alomar is rarely snappish. For that, he credits his parents. "If I know how to treat people well, it's because of my mother and my father. That's the way I was brought up. To be a good player but to be a good human being first. Where I come from, everybody knew the Alomars, because of my father. Everybody was always looking at us, so it was important for us to behave properly and to treat people with respect. If one of us did something wrong or said something wrong, the whole town would know about it by the end of the day.

"I was lucky. I learned baseball from one of the best, from my father. He taught me that the key to this sport was discipline. And never to be a selfish player. But my mother was the real inspiration in my life. She was a good mama. She gave us the confidence to go out and do whatever we wanted to do. It was a dream, even when we were little, to come to North America and play baseball. My mom said, go there, do what you need to do. If me and my brother are in the majors now, it's all because of her."

As a family, the Alomars tend to spread the credit around. Maria Alomar says it was her husband who provided the best example for the children, even if too often it was from afar. "They knew from the beginning what it meant to be an Alomar. Me, I tried to teach my children to respect other people, to love one another, to always have lots of friendships, and to work hard."

Sandy Sr. insisted his wife was too modest. "When they were little, it was my wife who was the one at home with them every day, teaching them. She's the one that would take them to their ballgames. All I tried to do was teach them that if they were nice to other people, then people would be nice to them. I see no reason for anyone ever to be rude."

It is true that with Sandy Sr. away for so much of the year, it was Maria Alomar who had to take on the role of baseball expert and instructor. That meant she had to teach herself the finer points of the game, which involved many long-distance phone calls to her husband. "I had to learn to understand when they were, say, batting too desperate or something like that."

To hear Robbie Alomar tell it, his youth was idyllic. "Me and Sandy, we were always close. But I don't think we were very competitive with each other. We both wanted each other to succeed. Even when we were little, I think it would have been hard to say who was the better athlete." When the boys became adolescents, their father retired from baseball and came home to the island. "They were starting to get a little too much for my wife. They started to think that they were men."

Sandy Sr. opened up a service station and for a time his sons worked there. "But me and Sandy built this board with holes in it and spent all our time trying to throw strikes," Robbie recalled. "Finally my father said, forget it, go home, you're not doing any work standing around here."

A shared passion for baseball aside, the brothers were quite different. They don't even look like siblings. Sandy is 6-foot-5 and dark, like his father. Robbie is a compact six-footer with paler skin and gentle features, like his mother. "Me, I just loved baseball, that's all I wanted to do, all day long. That's the one thing I focused on. But Sandy, he had other interests. He loved motorcycles and taking apart radios. I played a little basketball and I used to like to go down to the beach to water ski. But it seems as if doing anything else was taking time away from baseball." Sandy was the adventurous one, Robbie the shy one, "more close to the family" according to his mother, and the last one to learn to speak English.

He was only 17 when he left the island to play pro ball in Charleston, South Carolina. Not that it was a major adjustment since both his father and brother were with the club. The following year he was sent to Reno in the California League. "That was very hard for me, very rough. I was alone. I was cold all the time. I wasn't making any money and I was very homesick. All the time, I was calling my mother to ask her, how do you do this, how do you do that? I had to learn to live by myself. That is where I learned to live the life, you understand? The baseball life. When you're not making money, when you have to go out and buy sheets for the bed, when you have to teach yourself how to cook. My mother was so worried. She'd phone and say, 'Listen to the older people, pay attention to the manager.' I spoke only a little bit of English, not real well like I do now. I was different from everyone else. I came from someplace far away, from Puerto Rico. But I knew the secret. To work hard. You have to work real hard to make it in America. You're living and working in a place that is not your country. So you have to do a better job than your peers just to be considered equal with them. That's what it means for a Puerto Rican to come and work in the Americas."

By the time he turned major league in San Diego, Robbie Alomar was a veteran of the baseball life, even though he was the youngest player to start a game in the majors in 1988. Again, he had family for company. His father had delivered Robbie to the Padres on the understanding that he would come to the team as coach. (The Jays had, in fact, offered Robbie more money to sign with them.) Sandy Jr. became a Padre too, though he would shortly be traded to the Indians — exactly 365 days before Robbie was forwarded to Toronto.

Then came the news that he had been dealt to the Jays. Robbie was dumb-struck. "I kept thinking, where's Toronto? What's Toronto? I'd never even seen the city before. And I was so happy in San Diego." This even though the team, under new management, had treated his father shabbily by firing him too late in the year for Sandy Sr. to line up another job with a major league club. "They did not treat him like a man," says Robbie, the anger still in his voice.

But it didn't take long for Robbie Alomar to adjust to life in the new, big city. "I started thinking, wait a minute: I'm going to a winning team. I'm going to a place where they like to play baseball. I was a little scared of coming to a new country. I thought it would be like Montreal and everyone would speak French until my brother told me not to worry about that. And the other thing about the trade was, I had to ask myself: What are you doing in the middle of all these big guys? You have Carter and Fernandez and McGriff, and then over here you have Robbie Alomar. Who is even going to know Robbie Alomar? So I said to myself, I will go out there and I will play hard and I will teach them who Robbie Alomar is."

His agenda then was simple, straightforward: "I want to win a championship. I want to help create a good attitude for the team. I want to play hard all the time."

Those were vows he kept. In his inaugural season with Toronto, Alomar won his first Gold Glove as a second baseman.

The local chapter of the Baseball Writers Association of America voted him player of the year. In May of '91, he connected for five home runs, including a two home run game against Chicago in which he became the 55th player in major league history to swat dingers from both sides of the plate in the same contest. Against Baltimore, he tied a club record when he stole four bases in a game. His base thievery provided tremendous entertainment for the fans — he was successful in swiping third on 21 out of 22 attempts — while fueling the Blue Jays offense. He finished the season second only to Rickey Henderson in stolen bases with 53, and second in sacrifice bunts with 16. He was third in triples (11), seventh in at-bats (637), eighth in hits (188) and doubles (41). In the division championship series against the Minnesota Twins, he was one of the few Jays who didn't gag, hitting .474 in the five-game encounter.

No wonder then that the Jays elected to sign him to a new contract just before spring training opened last February — an $18.5 million package over four years, making him (briefly) the highest paid second baseman in baseball. "I'm real happy about it," said Alomar. "It's fun to play in Toronto and I want to be here for years and years." At the same time, he was enjoying an endorsement bonanza as his marketing agent secured several lucrative deals with companies eager to have their products associated with the handsome, affable Blue Jay stalwart. It was all a heady whirlwind of baseball blessings but Alomar remained realistic. "So I had a great year, all right," he told a reporter in Dunedin. "But baseball is baseball, you know. You have to expect good times and bad times. That's the key. You don't get high and you don't get low. My approach is to work as hard as I can at every last detail, all the time. I came here to training camp with that in mind, as if I was trying to make the opening day line-up. And then what will happen will happen. *Que sera, sera.* That's the way it has to be."

*Que sera sera?* How about a .500 batting average in spring training? Did that presage good things for the season ahead?

That season began with Alomar's first-inning double in the opener against Detroit and, shortly after, Toronto's first run scored as the Jays beat the Tigers 4-2. How fitting. In the second game of the series, his first homer of the campaign was a three-run shot that set Toronto on its way to a messy 10-9 decision. When the team returned to the SkyDome to get reacquainted with the hometown fans, the dramatics continued. His pressure-packed single over second base in the ninth inning delivered Devon White and a 4-3 victory over the Baltimore Orioles. "The important thing was the first game here in Toronto," he said afterwards. "The fans expected a win and we're really happy to give them the win."

With White hurting, manager Cito Gaston moved Alomar up one notch to the lead-off spot when the New York Yankees followed the Orioles who'd been swept into the SkyDome. Alomar responded with two hits, including a three-run homer as the Jays doubled up the Gotham crew 12-6. Two nights later he scored the game-winner in a 7-6 affair over the Yankees when centre fielder Roberto Kelly, trying to nail him at third, threw the ball into the Jays' dugout.

Moving into Fenway, Toronto split a hard fought four-game series with the Red Sox. In the final encounter, it was Alomar's third hit of the game, in the 13th inning, which drove in the winning run in the four-hour and twelve-minute marathon. That raised his average to .322 in the still fledgling season. Facing the Cleveland Indians back at the SkyDome next, Alomar's third four-bagger of the year provided all the runs necessary in a 2-1 victory for Jack Morris. He also swiped his sixth stolen base, this time off his brother. In fact, because Sandy Alomar Jr. had missed most of 1991 due to injuries, this was actually their first major league showdown. The siblings didn't speak to each other at all during the game. "We didn't say a word," insisted Roberto. "People see us talking, maybe they think he's giving me the sign." Responded Sandy: "He looks like anybody else out there. He's having fun but I'll get him back."

He had some fun next at the expense of the Kansas City Royals when he scored the game-winner by scoring all the way from first on a wild pitch by reliever Rusty Meacham, a throwing error and a fielding error. Next night, he fouled off five pitches from reliever Curt Young in the sixth inning before tapping a two-out, two-strike single to deliver the tying and go-ahead runs as the Jays polished off the Royals 6-4. His three-hit afternoon nudged his average to .403, if only until a ninth inning pop to first sent that stat backsliding to .397. His 19 ribbies also gave him a share of the lead in that department with Cecil Fielder. This, insisted Alomar — 17-for-28 in his last seven games — was a temporary anomaly. "I'm not the RBI guy."

Things were perhaps going too well. In that same game, few took much notice of a play wherein rookie shortstop Rico Rossy kneeled on Alomar's pinkie knuckle when the latter was attempting to steal second base. Rossy, a fellow Puerto Rican, had apparently dropped a similar block on the bag with both Alomar and White in spring training. There were subsequent whispers about dirty tactics by the recent Triple A call-up but Gaston wasn't having any of that. "Rossy was just playing his game. It's baseball. These things happen."

Alomar was a scratch for the next game, though his injury didn't stop him from signing about 900 autographs earlier in the day at a card show. "It was no problem," he said, showing how he had held the pen between thumb and forefinger. He was back in the lineup the next game and, in the interim, had been named American League player of the week. He had led the league with 15 hits, scored seven runs, driven in nine, sported a .643 on-base percentage, had a stretch of seven consecutive hits and had reached base nine consecutive times. "I guess it has to be my best month," he shrugged. "I never had these numbers before, the hits, the RBIs. But you never think you have a good month going. It's just trying to do the job. I don't think I tried to do too much."

An 11-game hitting streak came to an end in early May when the Jays visited Milwaukee. It was only a tiny blip in the stats. When the action shifted to Oakland, Alomar drilled a Ron Darling offering about 10 feet to the right of second base with two out, runners on second and third, and the score tied 3-3. The two RBIs lifted Alomar's total to a team-leading 21 as the Jays ended up 7-3 victors. Twenty-four hours later, he went 3-for-5 against the Athletics in a 5-1 win, yanking his average to a league-leading .396.

Alomar's consistency at the plate, while providing offensive impetus for his club, was less dramatic than the acrobatics he exhibited afield. This was where he shone most brilliantly, whether leaping for line drives or diving for a squibbler and throwing out a runner from the seat of his pants. Many chroniclers of the sport paid tribute to his "thinking-man" version of baseball but more often than not his defensive executions were instinctive, spontaneous with little time to ponder what he was about to do. He was reactive, finely attuned to the ebb and flow of the game, the demands of the moment. Whether in tandem with Manny Lee or

Alfredo Griffin at shortstop, he could turn the double play with a swiftness and a poise that had become commonplace.

On the basepaths it appeared sometimes that he was brash and reckless, the way he continually gambled on a pitcher's delivery to the plate or a catcher's throw to second, but there was a method to his madness: he was clever and he was fast. Moreover, he was supremely self-confident and studied the opposition closely. That put even more pressure on the other team, leading to hurried throws and haphazard relays.

Against the Athletics, he stole two bases on May 13 as the Jays edged Oakland 4-3. When Toronto then lost five in a row, Alomar was among those who refused to panic. "This is not the end of the world," he pointed out after the Jays dropped a 7-1 decision to the Minnesota Twins. "We have to go out there and try to play better baseball. Do your best and not think a lot about the past."

This wasn't just pacifier talk. The Jay bats came alive — if only for a brief resuscitation — in Chicago when Toronto smashed four home runs to defeat the White Sox 6-2. One of those four-baggers belonged to Alomar, a towering 433-foot shot, his first homer since April 21. He was an opportunistic hitter, not a basher, but he almost whacked the skin off that pill from Jack McDowell, as he was the first to point out later. "I killed that ball," he croaked. "I crushed it. I can't hit a ball any better than that."

The Sox had a return engagement in Toronto the following week and the hometown fans were feeling restless. One sign hung in the uppermost tier of the SkyDome summed up the public's discontent with the club's late May stumble: "OK Blue Jays, let's wake up." They did, and swept Chicago in three games. The initial encounter ended up 3-0 and it was Alomar who opened the scoring in the eighth, with his fifth dinger of the season, a bolt to left-centre. "The first swing, I was thinking home run," said Alomar, who paused at the plate for a moment to admire the trajectory of the ball. He insisted he wasn't trying to show up the pitcher, he was simply impressed with what he had just done. "It felt great to hit a ball that hard." The next day he enjoyed a three-hit afternoon, driving in the tying run on a two-out single in the eighth as the Jays scratched out a 2-1 victory in 11 innings. He was now 19 for 42 with runners in scoring position. At the end of May, he was named the Jays' top player of the month, for the second time in the young season and the fifth time in seven months if you went back to '91. He had led the team with 32 hits and 15 runs in May and had a .314 average.

Not everybody around the league was impressed. In Minnesota, where the Jays won 7-5, Alomar had (unusual for him) declined to attempt the potential inning-ending double-play with human blimp Kent Hrbek barreling into second base. Meanwhile, the game-tying run crossed the plate. A Minneapolis sports columnist opined in print the next day that Alomar "looked a little chicken" and should have made the play. This was nasty criticism indeed but Alomar waved it off. "I didn't have a good grip on the ball," he explained. "You've got to have the ball before you throw it. I never left the bag. I'm not scared of anybody coming in. Writers? They can call me anything they want."

In New York, the team shook off its ennui and swept the Yankees in a three-game series but the general merriment was marred when Alomar suffered a ligament sprain in his right knee. "Just a little sprain," Gaston assured reporters but it was not so inconsequential as that. Alomar would miss five games and was replaced by the useful Jeff Kent. His return to the line-up coincided with another Toronto frisson of futility and the team actually slipped out of first place in the American League East — for about a minute and a half. But they climbed back atop the division with a 6-1 verdict over the Royals in Kansas City. Alomar contributed a two-run single with the bases loaded in the ninth. When the team hopped down to Texas, he hit an RBI triple and scored on a wild pitch to cap a three-run rally in the fifth as the Jays fought back 3-2.

In early July, Alomar learned that he was a runaway fan-selection to start the All-Star game at second base, the second year in a row he had been so recognized. His brother made it too and, with the game in San Diego where Robbie still owned a house, it would be a kind of homecoming for the entire clan. Ironically, all the players involved in the deal that brought Alomar to Toronto — himself, Joe Carter, Tony Fernandez and Fred McGriff — were part of the All-Star festivities. In the meantime, he continued to serve admirably for the club that was paying his salary. Against the Athletics on July 9, Alomar led off with a double in the ninth and was running on the play with Candy Maldonado at the plate. His aggressiveness ensured the run — his third in Toronto's 4-3 victory — would score as he barely beat a strong throw to home by left fielder Eric Fox.

Heading into San Diego for the All-Star spectacle, Alomar sported a .323 average. He was the undoubted catalyst in the Blue Jay line-up at the midway point of 1992, having hiked his average by 40 points from the previous year. And now he was scheduled to bat leadoff among the stars of the American League. "Lead-off?" he wondered. "I guess I just go out there and swing."

The year before, when the All-Star show had been staged at SkyDome, Alomar had played the entire game but was a dreadful 0-for-5 at the plate. In fact, the second-inning single he slashed in San Diego was just his first all-star hit, though it was the third time in his career that he had made the team. He then sped home on Joe Carter's single and became the first man ever to steal two bases in the same inning of an all-star game.

That done it was back to the real business of real baseball as Alomar rejoined his club in Seattle. The Jays took three out of four in the Kingdome but the series also provided a most embarrassing incident for Toronto's second baseman when he was forced to leave the third game after injuring his head in a bizarre accident. According to Alomar, he had gone to the bathroom while the game was in progress, and smashed his cranium on a wire rack when he reached down for a newspaper. "I hit it hard, it was really bleeding," he told reporters, somewhat shamefaced. The injury required a single stitch to close and Alomar tried to get back in the game, wobbling back to the bench, late for his turn at the plate. A weak groundout to third ensued. He played the next inning on defense but then, still dizzy, he called it quits for the day.

It was not an entirely ridiculous afternoon for Alomar or the Jays, who won 3-0. In the first inning, he had laid down a perfect bunt behind Devon White's lead-off single to right. When Carter dropped a blooper behind second base, scoring White, Alomar sped toward third. Centre fielder Ken Griffey Jr. pumped a low, hard throw to third baseman Shane Turner but the ball and Alomar arrived at the same time. Turner thought he had made the catch and looked with disbelief into his empty glove. Alomar, realizing that the ball had rolled into foul territory, jumped to his feet and hustled home with the Jays' second run. Shortly afterwards, he responded to the ill-timed call of nature.

The next day, Alomar didn't want to talk about his potty blooper anymore. Nor did anyone else on the team. But somebody had hung a hand-drawn sign over the washroom door that read: Hard Hat Area.

The Jays moved on to Anaheim and then Oakland. And, with Devon White getting a brief rest, Alomar moved into the leadoff spot. He singled, walked twice and stole his fourth base in three games but he was also twice stranded at third as the Jays went 1 for 7 with runners in scoring position and 9-1 on the scoreboard.

That was the ugly conclusion to a dissatisfying 5-6 roadtrip. Back in the friendlier confines of the SkyDome, they took two of three against Kansas City and then swept a troika from the visiting Yankees. On the road again in Boston, the team dropped two straight to the Red Sox but salvaged a 5-4 win in the final encounter, though not before Alomar — along with Gaston and starter Todd Stottlemyre — got tossed for various disagreements with the umpires. Alomar was heaved in the fourth for arguing a third strike call with plate ump Terry Craft. Then Gaston got in on the act by offering a few observations of his own with similar consequences. As one Boston writer snootily reported: "Teams in first place should be more composed."

Throughout August, the Jays were up and the Jays were down, but they were never out of first place. They allowed the Orioles and the Brewers to huff and puff their way back into the pennant race but, to their credit, the Jays never faltered irrevocably. When Baltimore traveled to the SkyDome in the second week, Toronto seemed ripe for the picking yet the visitors could only manage a split. In the fourth game, which the Jays won 4-2, Alomar messed up two bunt attempts with Devon White at first. Then he rung one up the left-centre gap enabling the fleet-footed White to score the game winner.

Toronto took two from the Tribe and then gave two to both the Brewers in Milwaukee and the Twins in Minnesota. At Comiskey, Alomar swiped three bases, giving him 37 for the season as Toronto blanked the White Sox 9-0. The Jays then split another series with the Brewers, including a surreal 22-2 loss, before prevailing in two out of three confrontations with the White Sox.

The month continued and ended in yo-yo fashion for Toronto but as September dawned the club appeared to right itself.

Alomar was one of the few Jays who didn't share in the erratic conduct of the club — his single in Kansas City, where the Jays shut out the Royals 5-0 on September 8, stretched his hitting streak to a season-high 14 games. That streak would continue for just two more games before Alomar was stonewalled in Texas. The team, however, took all three games from the hapless Rangers.

The most intriguing story to come out of that weekend deep in the heart of Texas had less to do with what was happening in the field than what was apparently going on in the dugout. At the centre of this loopy story was Alomar, who had complained to a Toronto reporter that someone with the team — he never named the culprit — had been giving him the evil eye. Or, to be more precise, the evil moue. According to these newspaper accounts, this unidentified member of the Jays had "scowled" at Alomar when he returned to the dugout after laying down a bunt with none out. Devon White reached third safely on the play and then scored on Joe Carter's one-out sac fly.

Alomar had been upset by the glowering reception he was given on the bench but, when the incident was made public, he clammed up. "I don't want to talk about it," he said, brushing off a reporter who approached him at his locker the next day. Provocatively, for the press anyway, he was a last-minute scratch from the next night's game against the Indians, which Toronto lost 2-1. According to the Jays, Alomar was suffering from sinus congestion but he did make an appearance as a pinch-hitter in the ninth, drawing a walk.

Manager Gaston said he was certainly not the one who had scowled at his second baseman. "I have no problem with the way Robbie plays," Gaston told the Star's Jim Byers. Added batting coach Larry Hisle: "My only problem with Robbie is that he doesn't have four brothers on the team just like him."

Sportswriters, suddenly assuming the role of investigative reporters, appeared to narrow the field of suspects to a non-playing member of the club. Perhaps bench coach Gene Tenace? "It beats the hell out of me," he told Byers. "You can't criticize Robbie." And general manager Pat Gillick was dismissive of the entire mini-tempest. "If Robbie has a problem, he should speak to the guy."

The curious controversy had a short life-span. The Jays were up to their eyeballs in a demi-pennant race that provided diversion enough. The next evening, Alomar lofted a sacrifice fly to centre to score a run as the Jays nudged the Indians 5-4. He also swiped his 42nd base of the season. Against the Rangers on September 19, Alomar drove in Toronto's lone run in a gutsy 1-0 victory. It was his 69th RBI of the season, equaling his career-high total from the previous year. No wonder hearts started thumping anxiously  the next week when Alomar — who had been playing MVP baseball for months — cartwheeled over a sliding Joe Carter when both attempted to reach a flare in right field. For a few moments, Alomar lay there motionless. Then he bounced to his feet and trotted back to his position and everyone watching went back to breathing normally.

Alomar was resilient. So was the team. The players did not tremble and collapse under the grind of September baseball. They actually seemed looser now then they had through the doldrums of August. Time was running out on the onrushing Brewers and the Orioles had already sagged out of contention. There was a convergence of elements which seemed to augur well for the Jays, including Jack Morris' 20th victory on September 27, 12-2 over the Yankees in Gotham. Alomar chipped in with a couple of singles, a walk and scored three. He was now one of only five players in the American League who had scored 100 runs in 1992.

When the Tigers ventured into the SkyDome for the last series of the season, the division was still undecided. The Brewers, nipping at Toronto's heels, were doing battle with the Athletics in Oakland and hanging tough. But the Jays, while following the west coast action closely, understood that they were the masters of their own fate. If they could take care of business in their own backyard, whatever Milwaukee accomplished from here on in would be irrelevant. It was their ballgame to win or lose.

They won.

On October 2, the Jays clinched no worse than a tie as they battled it out 8-7 with the Tigers, made possible in part by Alomar's two-run first-inning homer into the Detroit bullpen. He also doubled and came around to score in the second frame. The next afternoon, with 50,412 fans poised for a celebration, Toronto did not disappoint. The Jays flicked off the Tigers 3-1, then rushed onto the field for the tribal pile-up thing.

In the clubhouse, corks popped and champagne bubbled. Grown men poured ice water down each other's pants. They danced, they sang, they frolicked. But in his own little corner, Robbie Alomar was unusually subdued. A year earlier, when he'd scored the winning run that made the Jays division champions, he had wept with joy. Now he was dry-eyed, almost stolid. A reporter wanted to know, why so dispassionate?

Alomar stripped off his jersey, tossed it into a bin, scratched his belly. "Last time, I'd never been in one of these things before. It was my first time. Now, I want to know what it's like to get to the World Series. That's what I'm looking forward to."

Then he got dressed, walked down the corridor to the elevator, and retired to his room above the ballpark.

# Gl⚾ry Jays

## *The Curtain Call Kid*        6

Baseball has never been a pristine pleasure. Even from the days of its infancy, as it rocked in the cradle, so was it rocked with scandal. But those were innocent times for our universe, and we did not realize the depth of our ignorance. We were treated like children as were the sometimes-errant ballplayers who occasionally crossed their owners and threatened to bring their game into disrepute. They were dealt with sternly, dictatorially, behind closed doors. Nor was there any recourse for punishment that may have been out of proportion to the perceived offense. The sanctity of the game was all that mattered even though the satraps of the sport often displayed behavior far more odious than anything their indentured servants could manage. Baseball was heavy-handed and the owners, their whims duly expressed through the office of the commissioner, omnipotent.

The deception held firm for generations weaned on the notion that baseball held special, mystical properties that elevated it beyond the status of mere sport. It was closer to the heart of Americana than football or basketball or hockey because it was homegrown and corny. And who cared if it was a derivative of English rounders transported from north to south by Union soldiers during the Civil War? Folklore had it as American a creation as jazz.

It has continued to be a symbol of something that perhaps no longer exists — goodness, virtue, the small-town values of neighborliness. Baseball was our friend and the men who were privileged to play it our companions. They may have been phenomenally gifted, but they were really not so different from you or me. They chewed tobacco and they scratched their genitals, they labored on the farms and in the steel mills during the winter months. And, when they lost, they cried.

It is not very much like that anymore. Barry Bonds gets almost $44 million, while owners cry poor and ticket prices are jacked. Egos run rampant, and players run for the money. They carry briefcases to the clubhouse but not their own luggage to their rooms. They sign autographs but mostly for cash. Loyalty is quaint cant.

In this increasingly unpleasant environment, Pat Borders is a throwback. He is a modest man in a world fueled by vanity and wretched excess. He is, well, decent. That is no small feat in baseball in the '90s.

In the World Series last autumn, Borders astonished himself and everyone who tuned in by hitting so well that he was named Most Valuable Player. Such laurels were completely unantici- pated and Borders was near speechless in his abashment. Here was a converted third baseman, recast as a catcher only a few years earlier in a desperate attempt to make the major leagues, who had been routinely castigated for his deficiencies behind the plate. In October, with the world watching, he had metamor- phosed into a self-deprecating star. And, within hours of propel- ling Toronto to its first championship, he was at the centre of trade rumors.

It has always been thus for the fair-haired country boy with the tobacco juice-stained uniform and the near-impenetrable hillbilly accent, a pokey inflection that belied the fact he was a schoolteacher's son who possessed honest, homespun insights into himself and the game he played.

Coming out of Lake Wales High School in South Florida, Borders had high hopes and low prospects when he signed on with the Blue Jay organization in 1982. He spent six years bouncing around the minors, from its nether regions to the apex of second tier ball: the Pioneer League, the South Atlantic League, the Carolina League, the Florida State League, the International League. In 1986, stuck in "A" ball and disillusioned with his chances of breaking into the majors as a third baseman who couldn't catch or throw very well, Borders concluded that some- thing drastic had to be done. Fearful that he was about to be released outright, Borders approached Bob Mattick, former Toronto manager and supervisor of instruction, and suggested that perhaps he would have better luck as a backstop. The organization, with two aging catchers handling the chores in Toronto, agreed to the experiment.

"I started to think that maybe I would never be able to make it any further than that," says Borders. "I was in "A" ball for five, six years. I didn't have enough power to play first or second. So I was the one who suggested that I try catching instead. That was the only option I had left. Otherwise, I felt like I might not get another chance to play. I'm grateful that they gave me that chance."

The most difficult part, he said, was neither catching nor throwing but learning how to block the ball at the plate. "I was always trying to catch the ball instead of blocking it." But he still maintained that learning a new position from scratch was an easier assignment than trying to improve himself as a third baseman. "It was do or die if I wanted to make the team. I think, in a way, that made it easier for me. I didn't have any bad habits like you can develop if you start catching as a kid. Now I think it's the most fun you can have. You're more into the game, involved in every single thing that's going on. It's given me new energy and a new life."

He studied and he persevered and, ultimately, he got his opportunity. Filling the spikes of Ernie Whitt and Buck Martinez, however, was a thankless assignment. His mistakes, which were still frequent and often blatant, subjected him to constant ridicule. To his credit, he was thick-skinned — or maybe thick-headed — enough to brazen it out. He was not easily unsettled by his critics though he often appeared rattled behind the plate. Nor was he a tremendous offensive threat when he discarded his chest protector. Borders began 1991 with an 0-for-21 streak of futility, before connecting for his first hit on April 24. In some quarters, his courage was also questioned. There were those who maintained that both he and platoon mate Greg Myers were prissy about blocking the plate. They had each been banged up quite substantially in the past. In one game against Chicago, Borders had been knocked out cold by Robin Ventura. During that collision he had almost choked on the wad of tobacco that he always kept tucked in his cheek. "I've been hit harder than that, actually," he said. "But that was a good, clean shot. I'm sure I'll be hit a lot again. You always set up in position to block the plate, but you're never sure where the ball's going to be coming. You end up reaching for it, one way or the other."

His defensive shortcomings were most evident during the American League Championship Series with the Minnesota Twins in '91. Of course, he was encumbered by having to catch knuckleballer Tom Candiotti twice in the five-game set. Candiotti's lack of confidence in Borders was obvious too, which is why he resisted throwing the knuckler that was his bread and butter pitch. The ex-Indian, rescued by the Jays in mid-season, continued to toss his curveball instead and the Twins, licking their chops, kept crushing it. "I told Tom to just go ahead and throw it, not to be afraid. If I missed it, I missed it. That was my problem. But, you know, some of those pitches you just can't catch. Nobody can. Yeah, it bothered me."

The most glaring evidence of Borders' inadequacy, the image that haunted him and fans over the long winter, was the phantom tag the catcher put on Shane Mack, who was charging home from third in game 5. The Jays had just fought back to take the lead as they battled to extend the series to a sixth game. The score was 5-2 Toronto with runners at the corners as Dan Gladden grounded to third. With a three-run lead, the play should have been to first but Kelly Gruber figured he had enough time to erase Mack so he fired home instead. The relay was not on the money but Borders compounded the error with a pathetic slap of his hand on the tag. Unfortunately, the ball was still in his mitt, which was on the other hand. How embarrassing. "My feet were straddling the baseline. I knew I had the plate covered. The runner had to go around me. Gruber threw it kind of underhanded and the ball crossed in front of me. I tried to get the ball over to the other hand but I knew there wasn't enough time. It's hard to put it in words, but it's like the brain is saying one thing and the body is doing something else."

By the time he got to Dunedin last February, Borders was just grateful that Candiotti had relocated to Los Angeles. "Nothing personal but I was very happy when I heard that he'd moved on. I definitely was not looking forward to catching him again," he said. "Tom told me I caught him as well as anybody had but I don't know. He gave me nightmares. Besides just trying to catch the thing, it is practically impossible to throw anybody out at second and, with a guy on third, that's all he ever wanted to throw."

Two different versions of events. Either way, it was all behind him as the team reassembled, with some key revisions, in the sleepy hamlet of Dunedin. One morning, with the rain pounding the ceiling of the dugout, Borders sat down to talk with a reporter. His uniform was a dirt-caked mess and his hair was matted. That was the familiar part. But this was a different looking Borders who had trudged off the soggy field, dragging behind him the tools of the trade: bats, mitt, chest protector, shin guard, facemask, helmet. He was pumped up, literally, with corded shoulder muscles and beefed up biceps. Borders had spent the winter respite working with weights, a return to a regimen he had abandoned the previous year when some genius had suggested that laying off the iron could contribute to a quicker bat. He didn't get his first hit till April 24 and finished off the month batting a horrendous .071. "In the off-season (before the '91 campaign) I pretty well laid off the weights. I did a lot lighter weight and I think that hurt me. Maybe it was just mental but the bat felt heavier. At the All-Star break, I started lifting more weight but I never really got my timing. Hitting, for me, is a combination of strength and timing."

It was an altogether bizarro year for Borders in 1991. He didn't hit his first home run until July 30 and then had four down the pennant drive stretch, including two crucial game-winners. "I didn't cope with it very well at all. It was so frustrating. I was taking tips from anybody who would offer them. After the All-Star break I began working with the weights again and I think the extra strength helped my confidence."

Strength, or stamina to be exact, is a prerequisite for a catcher. The brethren spend most of their time in a squat, dragging their buns in the dirt. Runners try to steal off them, pitchers shake off their calls. Fastballs bend back their knuckles and homeward-bound marauders slam into their chests. It is a wearying profession. It's a different perspective from down there, too, when you're the only guy on your team facing in the opposite direction. And there was no rest for the weary at spring training either.

"I hate to say we're the hardest-working guys at camp," he drawled, after scattering bits of his catching accouterments in a haphazard trail of fatigue. "But we have to practice catching popups, blocking balls, strengthening our legs, remembering the various signs. Then the last thing we have to worry about is our hitting."

As if the quirks of the job weren't tough enough, Borders had to cope with swirling rumors about his imminent departure for distant parks. The season began — and ended — with his name most prominent in trade talks. For a while it seemed a done deal that he would be sent off to San Diego in return for problem child, and fellow catcher, Benito Santiago. "What's the deal supposed to be now?" he asked one afternoon, as the rumors reached a crescendo. "I don't guess you ever feel secure unless you have one of those contracts." Meaning the kind where a player who has 10 years in the majors, five consecutive with the same club, has veto rights on any trade.

One day, manager Cito Gaston penciled Borders into the designated hitter's spot and that ignited speculation that the Jays were trying to showcase his offensive talents. He responded by executing a home run and a double but Borders remained confused about the situation. Not that there was anything he could do about it. "I guess it's just the stuff they pull in spring training," he shrugged. "In the past, I've played third base and the outfield and you'd never see me do that during the season. I've just got to be positive and motivate myself by thinking that some other team wants me. I can't be mad about it. The Blue Jays have been really good to me."

He may not have been as unperturbed as he was trying to let on. In the clubhouse one day, as Borders continued to maintain that he was unbothered by the trade gossip, the clubhouse attendant stopped in front of his locker and said: "Have your stuff packed right after the game." Borders' mouth opened in a wide "O" of exclamation. All the attendant meant was that the team was leaving for Miami directly after the game and no delays would be tolerated.

Borders was more distracted by his efforts to quit the tobacco chewing habit, which would have come as a relief to Gaston who was tired of being inundated with mail from people complaining about Borders' propensity for masticating and spitting on TV. He knew, intellectually, that the vice was bad for his health but he was not entirely convinced by the prophets of doom. "My grandmother chewed until she was 97. I'm not even 30 and I have to quit?" he complained to *Toronto Star* reporter Tom Slater. But he had a little girl at home, daughter Lindsay Rae, and he was worried about not being around to watch her grow up. "I just figured, why should I be taking the chance — you know, cancer and all that. Why, some year down the road, should she be left by herself just because I wanted to chew?" Besides, that hunk of

chaw bulging out his cheek was not exactly pleasing aestheti-
cally. "I know it didn't look too good. I've got a couple of baseball
cards that are pretty ugly."

To satisfy the urge to cud, Borders figured he would experiment with other concoctions, perhaps mixing dried maple leaves
with a little molasses for texture. The ground tea leaves he'd
mashed with honey a few weeks earlier had proven to be a sad
substitute. Not only was the yield bitter but it had irritated his
gums. "Got a pretty good caffeine rush though."

Stripped of his wad, Borders was behind the plate when the
Jays opened their season in Detroit on April 6. In the fourth
inning, he was standing in the batter's box, minding his own
business while trying to take care of business, when a generously
endowed lady rushed onto the field and attacked him from the
rear. The cantilevered Lulu, as she was professionally known
across the border in Windsor where she performed as an exotic
dancer, pounced with a two-strike count. Borders, having no
idea what had just befallen him, swung around in self-defence,
his bat poised like a club. The damsel was lucky she didn't get
herself swatted upside the head. Perhaps she just found the 28-
year-old Borders irresistible. After all, Bill James, in his best-
selling *Baseball Book 1992* had proclaimed him the most handsome player on the Toronto squad.

After Lulu was taken away, perchance to assault another day,
Borders fouled off three balls, then smashed a solo home run to
right off Bill Gullickson, thereby putting him nearly four months
ahead of his dinger pace from the year before. "Yeah, I found it
real hard to regain the hard focus I'd had," deadpanned Borders
when reporters caught up with him in the dressing room, with
the Jays 4-2 victors. "I know it's only one but, believe me, it's a big
one," he added. "It was sure in the back of my mind that I didn't
want to go through all that again. Maybe I'll ask Lulu to come
back tomorrow."

Alas, there was no encore from Lulu but Borders did not
suffer from her absence. The next game, he crushed another four-
bagger as the Jays outdistanced the Tigers 10-9. And just what
was this sudden power all about? Back in Toronto for the home
opener against Baltimore, Borders unleashed more fireworks
though saving his dramatics for the bottom of the ninth. The Jays
were down 3-2 when he took a fastball from reliever Gregg Olson
and pummeled it into the second deck in left centre to tie the

game with one out, before 50,424 suddenly animated fans — the largest regular season gathering up till that time. Devon White later slapped a double and Robbie Alomar followed with a little flare to win the game 4-3. That lifted the spectators out of their seats and into a brand new season.

In the clubhouse, Borders was saluted by his teammates who immediately tagged him the "Curtain Call Kid" because he had been cajoled into stepping out of the dugout to wave to the crowd after delivering his home run shot. "Aw, half the dugout shoved me, they kept on pushing me," he insisted. "I didn't know if any of the fans had seen anything like that here. I didn't want to be the first." He speculated that his new-found pop may have had something to do with the new bats he was borrowing from Joe Carter. They were a half-ounce heavier but with a slimmer handle. Or maybe it was just that aforementioned weight-lifting program. Then again, perhaps it was only a question of confidence. "Look, my head might be the weakest part of my body," he quipped to one columnist. "Last year, I know I had no confidence at all."

It was not a pace he would maintain. Who could? But it soon became clear that Borders had the catching job almost entirely to himself in '92. He would, in fact, end up catching 136 games in the regular season, more than any other backstop in the American League. The mighty bat may have become somewhat subdued after that noisy first week but Borders continued to connect for timely hits. He was also taking instructions well from kindly hitting instructor Larry Hisle who had been encouraging him to hit the opposite way. On April 15, against the New York Yankees, it was Borders' wrong-way single in the second that got the slow-of-foot John Olerud all the way around to home, and his leadoff single in the seventh that eventually produced a 2-0 victory for Toronto. Typically, Borders was more anxious to commend the effort of Toronto starter Jimmy Key. "As far as location goes, it's one of the best I remember. The fastball was almost pinpoint and he seemed to be able to drop the curve in there for a strike any tme he wanted. He was over the middle of the plate maybe twice the whole game."

A week later, against Cleveland, Borders slapped two doubles and a single in a losing cause as the Indians tilted the Jays 7-2. It was a game Borders had begun on the bench with Myers getting only his second start of the year. Halfway through the contest, the latter had to exit the proceedings after a jangling shoulder-to-shoulder collision at home plate with his counterpart, Sandy Alomar Jr. So much for a wee rest.

In early May, at Oakland, Borders connected for the 300th hit of his career (he had a single and a triple on the night as the Jays prevailed 5-1) but it wasn't until the following week, back in the SkyDome and facing those same A's, that he managed to rediscover his long-bomb stroke, which had been missing for more than a month. He drilled Dave Stewart's first pitch of the seventh inning into the foul-screen in left, a scant few inches from being called back and just clearing the fence by about a foot. That made the score 3-0 Toronto, which is how it remained. Even Stewart was impressed. "He smacked it. That was the hardest hit ball I've seen in a long time. Cec (Fielder) don't hit 'em that hard. I'm surprised it didn't bounce all the way back to home plate."

Shortly thereafter, the Jays went into a five-game tailspin, dropping three to Seattle and two to Minnesota before righting themselves with an 8-7 squeaker over the Twins. That match was punctuated with a bench-clearing free-for-all, an official protest about an alleged corked bat from Gaston and five home runs. Borders didn't get any of them but he was the one standing at the plate with the bases loaded after Derek Bell was intentionally walked in the bottom of the 10th. That brought manager Tom Kelly out to the mound for a pow-wow with his troops. The ensuing strategy saw right fielder Randy Bush position himself in the infield, just a little to the right of second base. And that permitted Borders to drop what would have been a routine flyball directly into the hole in centre field to bring home Kelly Gruber with the winner. "That was nice," observed Borders, about the convenient vacancy in centre. "But all you can think about is getting the ball in the air deep enough for a sacrifice fly; get it over all those infielders."

Facing the Twins again in early June, Borders came off the bench in the 13th to rack up a pinch double and then score the insurance run on a Manuel Lee single as Toronto ended up 7-5 victors. A few nights later it was Borders who prevented the Orioles from executing a similar comeback attempt in Baltimore. Tom Henke was on in the ninth nursing a 4-3 lead. After giving up a lead-off single, Henke got Billy Ripken, who was trying to bunt, to pop-up. Then Borders threw out pinch-runner Mark McLemore who was attempting to abscond with second. But

Henke was more grateful for the pop-up that had curled behind the plate. "That's exactly what you're trying to do when a guy is bunting. Throw a fastball up in the strike zone. Pat did a fabulous job finding it and catching it."

Nobody was laughing at Borders the backstop anymore. For a while there, he even led in fan balloting for the All-Star game though that all came to naught. A solo blast in Boston on June 11 helped lift the Jays to a 4-0 win over Roger Clemens and the Red Sox. That also marked only his second RBI in 25 games. What really got his goat was the next month, in Seattle, when his two hits against the Mariners (Toronto won 3-0) were described in a local newspaper as being so soft "they wouldn't make an impression in wet concrete." Just in case he hadn't noticed the article, his teammates constructed a bat with the newspaper sports section and hug it from the dugout ceiling. He then went out and rapped two more bloop singles, producing two runs as the Jays motored over the Mariners 8-4. Observers also took note that Borders was back on the 'baccy again.

In Anaheim later that month, Borders' two-run homer in the sixth squared things at five apiece, and Toronto went on to win by a 9-5 score giving Jack Morris his eighth straight win. Forty-eight hours later, Borders crank-started a 12-hit Toronto attack that made a 9-3 winner out of Dave Stieb, who came on in relief after Juan Guzman departed complaining of tightness in his right shoulder. Borders' contribution was a two-run double, a solo homer and a sac fly for four RBIs. He was now 10 for 28 (.357) with eight ribbies since the All-Star break. Further number-crunching showed he was also a perfect 3 for 3 off the bench — accounting for almost half of the Toronto pinch-hitting success ratio. Defensively, however, the Jays ranked eighth in thwarting opposing base thievery. Borders had a 30 percent success rate in throwing out rabbits.

In closing out the month, Borders had one of the best games of his professional career as the Jays clobbered the New York Yankees 13-2. He went 3 for 4 including a two-run homer and a three-run double for five RBIs, which equaled his career best. "I'm not concerned with hitting, I'm here to catch," he told reporters. "But the five RBIs helps build my confidence." It was a familiar refrain and one might have thought his confidence no longer needed bolstering. He had 10 home runs by now, all of them against righthanded pitching. Ah yes, there was a pattern developing. What did it all mean, the investigative scribes wanted to know. "I have no idea," Borders responded. "I don't make the pitch. I just hit it."

A new experience loomed on the horizon. In a game against the Red Sox at Fenway on August 3, Billy Hatcher stole home. That was the last thing the catcher was expecting. He had never before faced an attempted steal of his quarters. With Tom Brunansky facing Juan Guzman, Borders noticed movement out of the corner of his eye. Confused by this unexpected development, Borders stepped in front of the plate to intercept the pitch. Dumb. Had Brunansky been swinging, Borders might have been clobbered — and then called for interference. "I've been thinking about that," he said after some deliberation. "I don't know why I did it like that. It's like my head was on a tee."

On August 20, his 100th start of the season, Borders went 3-for-4 and rang up his 12th homer in a horrible losing effort — the Brewers capsized the Jays 16-3 and muscled their way back within 4 1/2 lengths of Toronto. A more pleasant outcome awaited the team in Minneapolis where, behind the pitching of Jack Morris, the Jays took the rubber in a three-game series 4-2. Borders was instrumental in the proceedings with a double into the left corner to kick-start the third and an RBI single in the fourth.

Border's equilibrium was given a jolt at the end of August when the Jays traded for David Cone. The national league strike-out leader possessed a sly backdoor slider but his high kick on every pitch made for a notoriously slow delivery to the plate. That was nirvana for base stealers who already posed a problem for Borders. He said there was no need for an intimate tete-a-tete with the newest Jay, that they would work things out as the season went along. "No big deal," he said.

But it was a big deal, as Cone's debut showed all too emphatically. The Brewers welcomed him to the American League by stealing eight bases on 10 attempts. Cone also gifted them with seven walks as the Jays surrendered meekly 7-2. (Still, a vast improvement over the previous night when they had been walloped 22-2 in a mind-boggling contest that saw the Brewers lash out 31 hits) "Geez, I'm just tickled for them," sneered Borders, referring to all those Milwaukee stealers. As if all this larceny still wasn't enough, the Brewers went out the next night and executed a successful double steal. As Milwaukee left town, Borders was last seen checking his wallet.

When the Jays opened a homestand against the Twins on September 4, Borders made his 111th start and 114th appearance of the season, making him the busiest catcher in the major leagues. It also moved him into second place on the Jays' career list of catchers with 442 games, one ahead of Buck Martinez but still a long way behind Ernie Whitt's total of 1,218 games as a Blue Jay lifetime. (Myers had been traded away to the California Angels earlier in the season, leaving Ed Sprague and the insect-eating Mike Maksudian to provide infrequent backup.) "I'm not tired, not at all," insisted Borders who had to now deal almost single-handedly with all those nasty forkballs from Morris and Henke, Cone's slider and Duane Ward's curve. "Cito seems to know when I need a day off. I've never had to ask for a day off but then I don't think I ever would." Certainly no fatigue was in evidence the next night when he connected for a bases-loaded smash up the middle, scoring two runs, as the Jays defeated the Twins 7-3.

Borders and Cone were also starting to click as demonstrated in a taut 1-0 victory over the Kansas City Royals on September 9. "I just felt relaxed tonight," said Cone who went 8 1/3 innings. "It was the first time I was able to use my back-door slider with Pat. He got the feel for it and we were able to use it."

It was Borders behind the plate when Morris notched his 19th win of the season, a new Toronto record, as the Jays prevailed 4-2 in Arlington. Shedding his armor, the catcher contributed with a double in the third. Within the week he also struck for a two-run single as the Jays shamed Texas 13-0 back at home, giving him a career-best 50 RBIs. That modest accomplishment was overshadowed by Dave Winfield's 25th homer of the year, which also give him 1,700 career rib-eyes. Borders didn't mind. Borders rarely minds anything.

The Cone-Borders synchronicity was apparent again on September 25 in New York when the battery functioned smartly on the way to a 3-1 Toronto decision. Cone, who said it was weird to drive up to the Bronx from Manhattan without making the turn towards Shea Stadium, conceded only four hits in seven innings. Meanwhile, his catcher supplied all the offence that was necessary with a two-run single in the second, as well as a double and run-scored in the seventh.

Finally, on the last game of the month, Borders took a break from his labors in order to rest the big toe of his right foot where an opponent had earlier fouled off a pitch. Back in the line-up on October 2, he smashed a Bill Gullickson offering for his 13th, and final, home run of the regular season as the Jays nosed out the Tigers 8-7. The next day, he cranked a nice double as the Jays finished 3-1 and guaranteed themselves a fourth visit to the American League championships.

While his teammates celebrated with champagne, Borders sucked on a can of beer. This seemed only fitting for a guy who had always considered himself a baseball grunt.

How was he to know that baseball grandeur awaited?

# Glory Jays

## *Winny— Forever Young* 7

Fifty thousand, four hundred and twelve people are serenading the birthday boy.

And that's what he is: a boy. Forever young, even on the day that he turned 41 years of age.

Dave Winfield is a baseball boy for life and, around the Toronto Blue Jays in 1992, he was also The Man. That is why all the fans at the SkyDome were on their feet and cheering on the second-to-last day of the season, the day when the club would clinch its fourth American League East championship.

It was a spontaneous display of affection from a city to a player because they had both believed in each other, loved each other, were beholden to each other. Winfield had come to Toronto looking for the World Series ring that had eluded him in a major league career that spanned almost two decades. The city had spread wide its arms in welcome because here was a man who could take them to the World Series that had eluded them all the days of their baseball life. It was, to use Winfield's own expression, a *symbiotic* relationship. And perhaps it was also a last chance, the last dance, for both partners. But they had made beautiful music together. In the clubhouse, the off-key salutation continued, kids and veterans squirting champagne in Winfield's face, singing "Happy Birthday To You." It was, he said, one of the sweetest moments he had ever known. "Beautiful...beautiful...beautiful. Today, I feel *young*."

It is appropriate, in this case, to begin the story at the end, or close enough to it. With Winfield wiping tears and beers from his eyes, one arm wrapped around his brother's shoulder, the other pumping any hand that was extended in congratulation. He is a big, strapping fellow and he dominated the room as he had dominated the season. It was the force of his will and the force of his bat that had on so many occasions picked the team up by the scruff of its neck and propelled it towards this day, this celebration, not to mention celebrations that were yet to come. In a city that is oftentimes shy and awkward about showing its feelings, Winfield induced roars and yelps and giddy shrieks. Go forth and make a joyful noise, he had urged in the shaggy days of summer when the club and its followers were struck dumb with ennui. He encouraged them to cheer with abandon and they, uncharacteristically, had responded. So did the team. "We need you," he had said.

Dave Winfield needed the Blue Jays in 1992, too. His grand, but in some ways ungratified career, seemed to be winding down with a whimper and a sob trapped in the throat. He was not ready to go gently into retirement after the California Angels released him from his contract rather than offer salary arbitration at the end of the '91 season. Of course, he did not view it as a release, per se. The way he saw it, the Angels had freed him to pursue his own fate in baseball, unencumbered by compensation requirements.

Just before Christmas, in 1991, Winfield signed with the Jays for $2 million, a straight-up one-year deal. Having just secured Jack Morris for megabucks, the addition of Winfield was unexpected, and perhaps an even bigger treat for the fans. It had seemed, over the years, that Winfield had been constantly Toronto-bound. It was no secret that general manager Pat Gillick had tried mightily to land the 19-year veteran but with no luck. The nearest miss had come in 1988 when it was widely understood that Winfield had vetoed a trade that would have brought him to the Jays from the New York Yankees and sent Jesse Barfield in the opposite direction. (As a veteran with 10 years experience, five with the same team, he had that privilege.) Except that's not quite the way it happened. Winfield said he might very easily have turned Blue Jay four years earlier than he did, if anybody had just asked. "I have never figured that out completely. I think they were discussing it one day. Pat Gillick was waiting and George Steinbrenner didn't show up. See, they had to ask me if I wanted to go in a trade. And the owner was never prepared to do that. Had he asked me to go, had we negotiated it or discussed it, we might have had a deal a few years ago. But nobody asked me."

All his life, Dave Winfield had tried to take the high road. But in finding his way to Toronto, he had gone the circuitous route instead. Not only by way of the California Angels either. He admits that he lingered too long at the Bronx Zoo as well. "I stayed longer in New York than I should have," he said one day at spring training last year, in that mellifluous Marvin Gaye voice. "Longer than I really wanted to. I guess I got stubborn. I didn't want to see HIM win."

The him, of course, is that renowned vulgarian, George Steinbrenner III, Winfield's adversary through most of what should have been his wonder years in baseball. There was glory enough for Winfield in his pinstripe period — a full decade — but not enough to suit the temporarily defrocked if not defanged principal owner of the Yankees; the most hated man in baseball, who found his own repository for venom in the unfortunate Dave Winfield.

Steinbrenner couldn't beat Winfield. He couldn't trade him either. So he decided to debase the man instead, heaping years of abuse and scorn on the player he once cruelly dismissed as Mr. May. It was a stalemate until Winfield finally agreed to pack his bags for California in 1990. He just couldn't take it any more and, quite frankly, the unsympathetic baseball public in The Big Apple couldn't take much more of him either. Everybody ended up bloodied in that mess.

It is telling that almost every extended conversation with Winfield winds back to George Steinbrenner's doorstep. There was, it should be admitted, no true victor in their dirty little war. Steinbrenner was booted out of baseball for his dealings with a two-bit gambler, a man he had paid $40,000 to dig up dirt on Winfield. But that banishment didn't last long and the resurrected, if not necessarily repentant, Steinbrenner is back in the saddle this year. Winfield survived the arduous battle but his reputation was ravaged in the process. "He tried to beat me, to demean me," the veteran said. "There were so many misconceptions, so much disinformation put out there about me. I'm glad it's finally been cleared up. But, man, it hurt. I suffered. My (charitable) foundation suffered. My friends and family suffered. You have to be strong to go through something like that. If it doesn't kill you, then you can learn from it. I've just gone on with my life and my career. They tried to take those things away from me but they failed. So now I've put it behind me because I can't dwell on it anymore. No complaints, no excuses. Just do it."

During the minuet of player transactions in the early winter of 1991, the Jays had expressed interest in Winfield again. But there was no serious offer on the table and the club told reporters that it had shut down business for the Christmas holidays. That's when Winfield's agent, Jeff Klein, contacted the Blue Jay brass. "The door opened and I walked through," Winfield said later.

He had been a frequent visitor to Toronto and not just as an opposing player. Local fans, normally unappreciative of talent not sporting a Blue Jay crest on its breast, were unusually fond of Winfield. In part, this attachment went back to a bizarre incident in 1983 at old Exhibition Stadium when the then-Yankee had inadvertently slain a seagull during a game. The big flap started in the fifth inning when Winfield and his teammates were warming up in the outfield. The slugger threw the ball he'd been tossing back towards the dugout, but it struck one of the more sluggish rats with wings that had settled on the grass. Death was instantaneous. A ballboy came forward to wrap the fallen avian in a white towel.

That should have been the end of that. But after the Yankees beat the Jays 3-1 — Winfield contributed a single and a double — a police officer who took his duties far too seriously put the collar on Winfield, dragged him to the cop-shop, and had him charged with cruelty to animals. The charge was dropped the following day since there was no proof that Winfield had intentionally committed murder most fowl, but by then the crime was well on its way to tabloid sensation legend. Remarking on whether the assault had been intentional, the late Yankee manager Billy Martin snorted: "They wouldn't say that if they'd seen the throws Winfield's been making. That's the first-time he's hit the cut-off man all year."

The seagull did not give its life in vain. The following year, Winfield commissioned a painting of a bird and had it auctioned off for charity in Toronto, to the tune of $32,000. It was the beginning of an affectionate relationship and Winfield would return to the city over and over again to participate in sports dinners and charitable events.

When he showed up in Dunedin in February of '92, Winfield was an immediate hit with his teammates and the hundreds of Canadian snowbirds who annually migrate to spring training for a Blue Jay preview. Never had the team had a bigger turnout for its first workout. The fans had waited a long time to see him in a Toronto uniform. He had waited a long time to don it. "It's been a pretty good welcome so far and I think it will be the same when I get to Toronto," said Winfield, who also made it clear that he had brought his glove to camp as well as his bat. The prospect of full-time designated hitter status was distasteful to him. "My frame of mind is, you go hard until you can't do it anymore and I have never acknowledged that I felt unable to do certain parts of the game."

With the Angels in 1991, Winfield spent about a quarter of his 150 games playing out of the DH spot, hitting .262 with 28 homers and 86 RBIs on the season. But whenever the subject came up, Winfield would babble about the joys of playing the outfield. The decision would rest with manager Cito Gaston, who just happened to have been Winfield's roommate in the latter's first season in the majors, with the San Diego Padres. (Gaston had lost his outfield starting job to the newcomer.) But Winfield was making his sentiments known and Gaston was receptive to the message.

That was the only (marginally) contentious area as Winfield embarked on his reincarnation as a Blue Jay. Most of all, he was delighted to be there and the franchise was delighted to have him. Year after year, the Jays had fallen victim to their own, imprecise inadequacies. They had this reputation for lacking grit or guts or toughness, or maybe just leadership, a vacuum that had not entirely been filled with the acquisition the previous winter of Joe Carter. They were perennial underachievers who could find all sorts of ways to beat themselves. Maybe Winfield would change that. He was hungry for it, having made it just once previously to the top of the pyramid, and not having acquitted himself well. He wanted a return engagement, he wanted it so much he could taste it. And he wasn't getting any younger.

"I had a few choices, but it came down to who I thought had the best chances of winning," he said one day. "I don't want to look down the road two or three years to win. That's for real young guys." Winfield was not young but he was in shape. The passing of the often turbulent years showed a little bit around the eyes but not much anywhere else. "Physically, I have always taken care of myself because I like to feel good in life, I like to look good. Believe me, this is a job. It's not just fun and games. There's a lot of science and technique, strength and endurance involved. One day I may say I don't want to do this anymore but I haven't even remotely considered that yet."

There was more to his renaissance than just Dave Winfield, ballplayer. There was also Dave Winfield, philanthropist. That was why one of the earliest discussions he had in Dunedin with reporters was about his long-standing Dave Winfield Foundation, a charitable organization he founded early in his career to raise funds for impoverished children, and which he now brought to Toronto. All year long, he would be in the forefront of charitable drives and good-deed causes. Yes, it is easy to be cynical about these things — for athletes, charitable contributions are dramatic gestures more often motivated by tax write-offs. But that does not entirely comprise such efforts. "If the media covered each player who has done things for the public, on his own, people would learn that there are a lot of good people in this game who try to make a difference," Winfield observed. "People just don't know individuals. They don't know me, know the way I was raised, which was to do things for other people. You didn't wait to be asked. You did them."

What he didn't have was the familiar Number 31, which he had worn for all those years in New York. Duane Ward already owned those integers and he was unwilling to part with them, so Winfield had to settle for Number 32, which he had also worn in California. "Wardo just said 31 had been pretty lucky for him, so that was that. You just can't influence these young guys anymore."

Gaston slotted Winfield into the cleanup spot in the batting order which proved advantageous for Joe Carter who, as number three hitter, was now assured of seeing better pitches. Just a little more symbiosis at work there and the formula proved effective through spring training and into the season. It had looked for awhile, though, as if Winfield would not be in the lineup when the season opened. He had been hampered by a troublesome hamstring that had kept him out of the final 10 exhibition games. But opening days are special, even if is your 20th year in the major leagues. When Toronto unveiled the 1992 version of the Blue Jays in Detroit on April 6, Dave Winfield was the DH. He tossed three singles into the mix, including an RBI that scored Toronto's first run of the game and the season, as the visitors prevailed 4-2.

In 1992, it seemed like Winfield set some kind of new record every time he touched the ball — which was not just a function of longevity as a player but a direct result of his own prowess. His third hit on the first day was also the 2,700th of a major league career that had begun in 1973, when he was drafted by the Padres from the University of Minnesota. He had hit 20 homers and driven in 75 runs as a freshman and he had continued to post similarly impressive numbers down through the seasons, except for 1989, which he had to sit out entirely because of back surgery.

"Three-for-four, I'm real happy with that," Winfield said after game one of 162. "I've played so well against Toronto all my career (.313, 84 RBIs, in fact), I'm just glad I started out doing something for 'em. Toronto fans? Sure, they can be happy with this team, but that's not their goal. I know they want to see what it's like to have their team win it all." He could understand the feeling. "Winning the whole thing, that's big motivation for me and, coming here, well, this team's close. I got a gut feeling." The moral: Never underestimate Winfield's gut.

Two days later, still in Detroit, he cranked his first home run of the season, the initial one of 26 as it turned out. That made him 6-for-13 in the opening series. "Three wins was the best but I'm happy I got off on the right foot too. The hamstring's been a worry but when the bell rings, you've got to get it going."

He got it going well enough when he made his official debut as a Jay at the SkyDome on April 10 with a long double against Baltimore that had the fans jumping up and down in their seats. Baseball players are itinerant tradesmen by definition but there was an immediate sense that Dave Winfield had found a home. A safe place. It felt as natural as if he had been there all along.

When the Yankees came to town on the 14th, Winfield performed like a man who had something to prove, even though his Yankee incarnation was long past: a home run, two run-scoring singles, four RBIs on the night. Take that, Georgy-Boys. The four-bagger was the 408th, major league life-time, and bumped him to 22nd on the all-time list. The quartet of ribbies gave him a grand total of 1,611 and 16th spot on the tote-board. This kind of number-crunching and statistical calculation would send reporters rifling through the reference books all season long.

The following week, his hamstring coming along nicely, Winfield got his first assignment in the outfield. Gaston had listened to Winfield's appeals and had agreed that his middle-aged slugger should get routine opportunities in right field. The next night, he proved that there was still some thrust in the throwing arm when he smoked one from right smack into catcher Greg Myers' mitt with Cleveland's Sandy Alomar charging for the plate. A few evenings later, he executed the same quick delivery to home, which stopped Kansas City Royal Bob Melvin dead in his tracks. Winfield may have been two-score and a few months, but he wasn't a defensive pushover in the field. With Joe Carter suffering a slight groin pull, he made six consecutive starts in right. Returning to DH duties, he uncorked two home runs on April 28 against another former squad, the Angels, but the Jays succumbed 9-5 at home. Later in the series, Winfield was nailed at second when he tried legging a single into a double — something he would attempt frequently in '92, sometimes foolishly. The Jays still won that contest 1-0.

In Milwaukee, the Jays dropped three in a row before saving at least a minimum of face with a 4-1 decision to escape the sweep. Winfield contributed with his fifth dinger which extended his hitting streak to 11 games, five short of matching his career best from 1988. That was nothing compared to the whammy he had saved for the Seattle leg of Toronto's road trip. Two out in the ninth inning, bases loaded, Jays down 7-4. Winfield comes to the plate, slaps his hand against his batting helmet as is his habit, digs his toes into the dirt. And launches his 10th career grand slam. That made the score 8-7 Jays and, with the Mariners thoroughly stunned, it stayed that way.

Winfield said afterwards that he had started to contemplate the possibility of a grand salami as he sat on the bench in the ninth, waiting his turn. He thought about it some more when he got to the on-deck circle. And he thought about it a lot as he circled the bases before a shocked, silent audience. "You have to be man enough, or have the heart, to want to be up there in those situations."

Rookie Pat Hentgen had come on in relief and was suddenly the winning pitcher of record. He had watched Winfield's at-bat intently from the dugout. "Between pitches, when he stepped back, I could see the intensity in his eyes. He wasn't going to give in."

Give in? That's not in Winfield's lexicon. He was now batting .375 in the seven games in which he had played the outfield and

.353 for the 22 in which he had appeared as DH, with a .358 mark overall. He was also in the middle of a career-high 17-game hitting streak. Alas, it would go no further than Anaheim when Winfield crapped out 0-for-5 against the Angels on May 10, though the Jays won 4-1.

Seven times in his career, Winfield had chalked up 100-plus RBIs, a statistical category that is the real mark of a player's effectiveness. But he was not one to look backwards at conquests long past. He was aiming to do it again, as a Blue Jay, because the eighth time is as gratifying as the first time, if not more valued still. Besides, it was all ammunition for the final tally — the numbers that he hoped would put him in the Hall of Fame some day. As Gaston once observed: "He's playing in a Hall of Fame league."

He was pulling up the team with him. There was a tremendous home run shot to dead centre at the SkyDome in mid-May as the Jays edged the Mariners again, 7-6. Two nights later, legs pumping, he stole his first base of the season, against the Minnesota Twins. Still flush from that blaze of speed, Winfield went into Chicago and connected for his eighth round-tripper, which gave him 414 life-time, tying him with Darrell Evans at Number 21 on the big board, a dozen behind Billy Williams and an even 300 back of Babe Ruth. Meanwhile, though the oldest member of the squad, he was also the only Blue Jay who had played every game thus far in the '92 campaign. Which may be why Gaston imposed a rest and sat him out against the Brewers on May 27.

Back in the line-up, Winfield was in the DH-mode for what was his 2,600th career game. His infield single in the first inning of a 3-2 heart-thumper over the Chicago White Sox gave him his 2,750th career hit, good for 35th place on the all-time list, just ahead of Luke Appling.

The previous year, in California, Winfield had slumped sharply in July and August, no doubt tiring. It's no fun piling up decent numbers while your team trails along in the nether regions of the division. But there seemed no hint that this recent history would repeat itself. In Minneapolis, he contributed three hits, including a double and an RBI single as the Jays dumped the Twins 7-5. In fact, he had two three-hit nights in succession. Moving to Camden Yards in Baltimore, the Jays squeaked by the Orioles largely because Winfield managed to swoop slide past catcher Chris Hoiles' tag in the second. He was hittin', he was throwin', he was slidin', hell he was even stealin'. He was The Man.

When the Jays blanked the Red Sox in Boston 4-0 on June 11, behind Jack Morris' stellar complete game, Winfield chipped in with a homer that moved him into a 17th place tie with Baseball Hall of Famer Ernie Banks, with 1,636 RBIs. It also snagged him a piece of 21st place on the extra-base hits toteboard with 972, which he now shared (fleetingly) with Al Kaline. (Ruth, Appling, Banks, Kaline...heady company Winfield was keeping these days.)

It was a happy time for Winfield, though marginally tarnished when word came down that George Steinbrenner was about to be un-banished from baseball. In fact, Commissioner (but not for long) Fay Vincent soon announced that Whiny Steiny could return to active control of the New York Yankees March 1, 1993. Winfield was unimpressed. "I don't have to be happy or comfortable about it," he told *The Star's* Allan Ryan. "The only thing I can say is that I feel it's been played down just why he was suspended from the game." He continued to maintain that Steinbrenner's involvement with two-bit wiseguy Howard Spira was only the tip of the iceberg. "It's what he did as an owner to Dave Winfield that got him suspended. Basically, he tried to ruin my life."

More heartening news was the decision rendered by a judge in Texas to set aside an order for Winfield's arrest. That development was part of an ongoing court battle with a Houston woman who claimed to be his former common-law wife. The decision nullified an order, issued June 11, which said Winfield had failed to appear in court to answer a complaint alleging he owed $10,000 in child support to the woman. He had acknowledged paternity of the little girl.

Perhaps cheered by this verdict, Winfield went into Arlington Stadium and collected five RBIs, as well as one of Toronto's homers, as the Jays routed the Rangers 16-7. He got another one to lead off the second inning the next night but it didn't count because the game was called on account of a sudden thunderstorm. The one a few nights later did count, however, as Toronto flattened the Indians 6-1 in Cleveland, for three road wins in a row. On his return to Toronto, Winfield stopped by a recreation centre on his way to the SkyDome, where he recounted to a bunch of ogling youngsters how he and his mother would sit together on the couch and "add words to each other's vocabulary." His favorite books, he said, were a dictionary and a thesaurus.

These days, his bat was doing the talking for him, and supplying all the adjectives necessary. With the Angels back in town, Winfield connected for his 14th homer and 46th RBI of the season, as the Jays took an 8-6 decision in front of their hometown fans. He was now the proud owner of a .309 batting average, fifth best in the league. These were all-star numbers here, he reckoned. In fact, Winfield finished fourth among outfielders in the fan balloting, behind leader Jose Canseco, who wasn't even playing due to an injury. The game was scheduled for Jack Murphy Stadium in San Diego, where he had played for eight years, and he was looking forward to a triumphant return to the National League park.

It was not to be. American League manager Tom Kelly passed on Winfield, opting for his teammate Joe Carter instead. The rejected Winfield was annoyed by his exclusion though he could hardly dump on Carter. This was a tricky situation. "I won't get into it," he snapped to reporters in Toronto, unusually testy. "I earned a spot and it didn't happen."

Did he take it personally? When regular season play resumed after the all-star break, Winfield was responsible for the Jays' first two runs in a 7-2 victory over the Mariners at Seattle. He drove in Carter with a triple and then hustled home to score after Randy Johnson unloaded a wild pitch. Against the same team, Winfield homered again, alongside teammate Candy Maldonado, both of them two-run shots as the Jays doubled up the Mariners 8-4. Maldonado didn't get the spotlight often with the Jays and on this occasion, when he could have preened over his own performance, he preferred to pay tribute to Winfield. "When you retire (meaning himself), you can tell your grandson that you played with a player like Dave Winfield, a Hall of Famer."

Tom Kelly may have overlooked Winfield's heroics. His teammates did not.

August would prove to be a crucible for the Toronto Blue Jays. They tumbled and stumbled, slid and skid. They left the door ajar for the Baltimore Orioles and the Milwaukee Brewers, then they almost invited the division stalkers right through it. Come on in, come on in, no one home but the Blow Jays. Had it not been for Jack Morris and Dave Winfield — one a perennial champion, the other a perennial wannabe — the season may have been lost then and there.

Tangling with the Yankees on August 2, he singled, doubled, and tripled as the Jays overcame a shaky start by Jimmy Key to nose past the Yankees 7-6. He homered in a futile effort against the Red Sox at Fenway, then launched a two-run double the next night to help Toronto nudge past Boston 5-4, salvaging one win in the three game series. "We can play better than this," Winfield insisted. "But it's not the end of the world. I think we showed some character by coming back to salvage something. We just don't want to be salvaging all the time." When he wasn't providing leadership with his bat, he was trying to settle down the youngsters who had become fidgety and flighty under the pressure of a pennant battle. Fighting off the flu, he connected for two hits, including a homer, and three rib-eyes when the Jays doubled up the Orioles 8-4 in a critical confrontation at the SkyDome. But it was on the road that he was demonstrating his true value: Winfield was the team's top run-producer away from the SkyDome, with 39 RBIs and 10 homers.

In Cleveland, on August 16, Morris and Winfield joined forces in the bottom half of a double-header, which enabled them to get out of town still hanging on to a three-game lead over Baltimore. With Morris limiting the Indians to two runs on five hits over seven innings, Winfield did more than his bit by driving in five runs with a home run (his 20th) a three-run double and a single in the nightcap, ensuring a 6-2 Toronto victory. Typically, he was unforgiving with himself for a base-running error that may have cost him a triple and the elusive cycle. The mistake he said he made was stopping at second base after hitting a bases-loaded line drive over centre fielder Kenny Lofton's head. "I should have gone for the triple there but I wasn't sure if Robbie (Alomar) was going to score and I didn't want to make a mistake and over-run him. I should have realized he was going to score there and kept going. I would have made it." No matter, he was still the oldest man in the majors to get a cycle, a feat he had accomplished in June the year before, with the Angels.

In Milwaukee, in mid-August, he connected for five RBIs in two games. The games were blow-outs, in opposite directions, on consecutive nights. But Winfield played them the exact same

way — as if the score were tied 1-1 in the ninth. He never slacked
off. He didn't know how to slack off. It seemed at times as if he
was running for his life. No pause, no respite, no peace. And yet
he was delighting in the rigors of the chase. Those who chronicle
these things had expected him to run out of gas round about now
but he just revved up the engine and kept motoring. By August
20, he had 20 RBIs in 18 games that month, had hit in 13 of his past
14 games (.351), and was putting his junior Jays to shame. He
insisted he wasn't playing for individual goals, but every time he
came in contact with the ball, it seemed, another record was
equaled or surpassed. "I don't want anyone to think I will
continue in baseball just to reach certain individual goals. If I stay
healthy I will reach 3,000 hits but I don't sit with a calculator in
my hand, thinking of things I might do," he told *The Star's* Milt
Dunnell. "A long time ago, in San Diego, I learned a lesson about
that. I made predictions of what the team would do. It didn't. I got
the blame. On the other hand, you make a prediction for yourself
and if you do well, they say you're an individual, rather than a
team player."

At Comiskey, on August 26, Winfield smoked his 21st round-
tripper and his 1,000th career extra-base hit (no stat is too
picayune to pass unremarked), while driving in three runs to
lead the Jays in a 9-0 pasting of the White Sox. Back in the
SkyDome to kick-off a 10-game homestand, his three-run homer
helped the Jays dust off the Brewers 5-4 in yet another critical
confrontation. But he was still worried that his ballclub was
losing its stomach for the battle that had been enjoined with the
Brewers and the Orioles. So, at the end of the month, he called a
whither-goest-we meeting of the team personnel. The message
was simple: we have nothing to fear but ourselves, because we're
better than the rest. Let's play that way. Hup-hup-hup.

On the final day of the month, Winfield unleashed a 386-foot
blast with two on that helped the Jays sweep past the White Sox
9-2. It was his 23rd homer of the year and gave the big guy 32 RBIs
for August — a club record for a month, erasing the mark set by
George Bell in May of 1987. He had batted .303 with seven home
runs and he was the Blue Jay player of the month. "I didn't know
there was a record involved," Winfield declaimed afterwards.
"A good ballplayer had that record and I'm proud to surpass it."
It was a month in which he had carried the load. "This team was

getting complacent, sitting back and just watching. If the pitchers fell behind, it was 'Here we go again.' Well, there's 20 per cent of the season left and no one's going to let this team not put out and fall by the wayside." Not if Winfield had anything to say about it.

And he had a lot to say about it. His timing and his words were impeccable.

The conduit for his message was *Toronto Star* columnist Jim Proudfoot and the epistle from Winfield was this: He wanted to hear a lot more noise from the SkyDome throng throughout each of the remaining 15 home dates. He insisted this kind of support was necessary if the team had any designs on a division championship. "I'll tell you this. When you sit on the bench, the players have about the same drive and enthusiasm as the fans. It's almost like they don't want to make more noise than the spectators. This is a symbiotic relationship, if I can use that expression. The fans need us and we need them. We feed off each other. And with the right lead, the right prodding by the Toronto organization, we'd get a lot more out of our fans. The way it is here, the teams we're attempting to beat have an advantage over us at home and are playing on neutral ground in Toronto."

There was more. "There'll be crucial times in these next few weeks when we need this sort of thing. I believe there are things the Toronto baseball public wants very badly. Maybe they even expect certain accomplishments. They need to realize there are things they can do to help this team bring about what they're hoping for. I guarantee that what I'm talking about will make a difference."

Professional athletes are handsomely paid to perform, and if they can't find self-motivation in a pennant race then they're a disgrace to the uniform. But Winfield's plea did make a difference in how baseball felt at the SkyDome from then on. A few churlish souls were offended by his guilt-inducing lecture but most responded lustily. One of the most familiar sights in the waning days of the campaign, and through post-season play, was someone in the park holding aloft a sign that said: Winfield Wants Noise. And whatever Winfield wants, Winfield gets.

The Jays, similarly inspired, went out and whipped the Twins 16-5. Winfield contributed a single and was cheered even after he was thrown out trying for second. Hustle is forgivable even when it's ill-advised. But the crescendo of support seemed to startle the man who had ordered it. "I saw one (fan) working so hard, he was sweating," Winfield marveled later. "If their lungs are tired and they've got a smile on their face, then they did their job."

Meanwhile, he kept his side of the bargain. Against Cleveland, his two-run homer helped the Jays come back from an early 3-0 deficit for a 5-4 win. Homers or no, he had become the key element in getting his teammates across the plate. With runners on third, and less than two out, he now sported a .484 average; with two out, it was .375, for a combined .429. On September 18, when the Jays decimated the Texas Rangers 13-0 at home, there was a tweaky sign in the stands that read: "Hey Winfield, grow up! You're playing like you're 24!" He liked that. He liked it enough to stroke his 25th homer of the year — 22 as the designated hitter — to match a club record established by Cliff Johnson in 1983. It also gave him 1,700 RBIs for his career, two short of equaling Reggie Jackson for 15th all-time. The accolades, and the milestones, just kept coming. His exploits were elevating him towards legendary status. Concurrently, reporters jostled for a piece of the story, the saga. Winfield rarely said no to an interviewer, even when he was at his most distracted. This, he knew, was part of the job, his specific job, on the club.

One day in particular comes to mind. Winfield had just finished taking BP but the path to the dugout was like an obstacle course. Over here was a scrivener from New York who wanted a word, over there a local television crew that needed to film a promotional spot. Someone wanted a ball, someone else an autograph. A child in a wheelchair waited to have his photograph taken with The Man. Sign this, hold that, give us a smile, a word, a touch. *Talk to me.*

The object of all the commotion lowered his buttocks onto the bench, folded one long leg over the other and raised a hamhock paw, fingers splayed. The gesture said: Just a moment. The Man said: "I'll be there." That was an expression that Winfield used often. "I'll be there." But it had also become an ethos.

Win With Winfield was the name of a charitable campaign that the athlete-cum-philanthropist had brought to town along with his considerable talents. It was, as well, an apt summation of the promise — the covenant — that Winfield had made with the ballclub and the town. His accumulative stats over nearly 20 seasons of baseball may have had bound-for-the-Hall written all over them, but his immediate objective was the World Series. He was famished for an October classic and, damn, one of those rings. He'd only been to the charmed circle once before, as a Yankee in 1981, and all he had to show for it was an .045 average. Mr. May, as the Other Man, had sneered. Said Winfield: "I know, more than anyone else, that you don't get this opportunity often."

This was a bitter lesson to have learned and one that Toronto teams seemed unable to absorb, even though they had been routinely involved in pennant races and playoff appearances. It had seemed, so many times, as if everyone had put their faith in next year, blithely assuming that there would always be a next year and another playoff encounter. But, as the end of baseball '92 approached, everybody realized that baseball was changing and the Jays organization would be compelled to change with it. Many familiar faces would be gone in 1993, lost to free agency and the expansion draft. Winfield might even be gone, though few took that notion seriously.

So the moment was now, for The Man and the team. And the job Winfield had accepted, perhaps tacitly, demanded not only offensive production but to inspire, to cajole, to lead — by whatever means necessary. In the past, others such as George Bell and Ernie Whitt had tried and failed. Now it was Winfield's turn, though he was loath to discuss this aspect of his tenure as a Jay. "No one has asked me to do anything in particular," he maintained. "They didn't ask and they didn't write it into my contract either. First thing, most important thing, is to come here and play well. If you hit .210 or .220, you can't say much. Beyond that, well, you could do a book on the intangibles. It's presumptuous for me to talk about my role on this team. I do what I have to do. I do what I feel I have to do to reach a defined and envisioned goal. Everybody looks at these things differently and reaches for them differently." Winfield, the man who is never at a loss for words, even 50-cent words, was suddenly all bashful and tongue-tied. "How do you talk about yourself? I don't think it's my place."

So listen to Gaston talking about Winfield instead: "Dave Winfield has a goal. He's playing in a little bit higher league; he's playing in a Hall of Fame league. The players respect him and Dave certainly deserves that respect. He's a leader in a lot of ways, but mostly he's a leader because of what he does on the field. If you can only do it off the field then you're just another clubhouse lawyer." Judging from the sour expression on his face, it was evident what Gaston thought about clubhouse lawyers.

"Baseball's a funny game," sighed Winfield, pulling on his lower lip. "Sometimes you can be appointed or anointed. Sometimes people go out and proclaim it. And sometimes things can just happen with age and certain things become acknowledged. I've been around a long time, seen a lot of people come and go. I keep trying to do the right thing because I know that I'm just one part of the whole, one slice of the pie. As long as I can prepare myself in every way to contribute — because you don't want to be the weak link — then I'm doing my job. It's preparation meeting opportunity."

Winfield talked like this a lot, in inspirational phrases that sounded as if they should be posted on a clubhouse wall. Some may have heard, in these pronouncements, an echo of something slippery, something slick. He evoked, at times, the guy on late-night TV who claims we can all make a million bucks if we follow his business direction and just send your cheque to this address. There was something disturbingly evangelical in Winfield's platitudes. But short-hand messages that drive home the point, that stir the adrenaline and percolate the testosterone, are what is required in sports. Baseball may be one of the more cerebral athletic diversions but it is still played by sweaty jocks, most of whom are not poets or philosophers. Subtlety is lost on them.

"You've got to have everyone wanting it at the same time," Winfield continued as he got up to stretch the muscles in his legs. "But as well as talent and determination, you have to have luck, desire, teamwork and a tremendous drive to reach your goal. You can't look for just a few people to carry a team. When the responsibility and the accomplishment is distributed, it makes it easier to play because it's not such a heavy load for one individual."

But he had picked up much of the load, especially through the month of August. "A lot of people can give their all on the field but they're not actually prepared. There's a lot that goes into preparation: the physical part of it, the mental part of it, the review and education part of it, the sports medicine technique, whatever."

And the tension-relieving extras too. It was Winfield who resurrected the hoary kangaroo court to deal with lapses of judgment on the field. "We don't want people not to communicate or not to laugh or not to have fun. That's what this should be. It's all part of making it a memorable, positive year."

To that end, he had also encouraged his teammates to assemble ego-boosting videotapes of themselves, their best plays. "I include only hits and well-hit balls in mine," he explained. "When you're hitting the ball well, you're technically or fundamentally doing things correct. I remember one time in New York — and this is probably why we were always at odds — the principal owner was very negative; he wanted every player to make a tape of all the errors they had made. Before the season started, he wanted us to review all those errors and bad plays. I said to the coaches: 'No way. I'm not going into that room to watch that video. Put on The Three Stooges or something. I don't want any negative reinforcement.' "

That, in a nutshell, was the key to Winfield's personal philosophy. "You can't afford to let negative thoughts creep in. Each day I come to the stadium, I'm smiling because I know it can be good. I go to home plate, I have to think I'm better than the pitcher each time. Each part of the game, anything you do. You can't leave any room for 'I should have, I would have, I could have.' There are some ballplayers who are always crying and moaning. I don't appreciate them; I don't want them around me. I don't want it to rub off on me. Send me negative mail, I might look at it for a moment, then, BOOM, it's gone."

That was why he refused to dwell on what could have been, and what should have been, for the Jays in the past. "I've only been here for a year so I can't talk about what happened here before that. How much negative emotional baggage does this team have? I'm not a psychiatrist, I don't know that. But I don't try to analyze it from a negative standpoint. What we're trying to do is to instill, to inculcate these guys, with positive reinforcement."

Baseball was a joy to Winfield. Again. But it had not always been thus. In his autobiography, *Winfield: A Player's Life*, he had written that "baseball is rarely fun -- though I suppose those of us pulling down million-dollar salaries shouldn't expect it to be." But those were sentiments fostered by his pinstripe era.

"It was only in the last couple of years I realized that baseball didn't have to be the way it was in New York. Don't get me wrong. I loved playing in New York. But if I had finished my career there, I wouldn't have known how different this life could be. Part of it came from playing on Yankee teams with unfulfilled expectations. But beyond that, personally, I worked for an organization that tried to hurt me every day that I came to work. They tried to take my money, ruin my reputation, hurt my endorsements. At least, late in my career, I've gotten the experience that it isn't like that everywhere."

Watching Winfield through the last gasps of the season was like watching pages of the baseball annals turning. His history, the game's history; they had merged and become one. On September 24, in Camden Yards, he became the first 40-year-old to ring up 100 RBIs. He did it with gusto too, knocking in two with a monstrous first-inning homer and then two more with a second inning double. Equally important, from a collective point of view, the Jays dumped the Orioles 8-2 and it was bye-bye Baltimore in the pennant sweepstakes. "I really can't understand why no 40-year-old has done it before," Winfield mused later. "Maybe everyone else retired and was playing with their grandchildren. It is an achievement. The oldest guy, that's nice. It's something I thought I could do but it wouldn't have been as probable on a team that wasn't in it. I wouldn't have had the energy, the enthusiasm I'd have needed. It's kind of like we were all working on this together."

In the last game of the regular season that meant anything, the day they beat the Detroit Tigers 3-1 to lay claim to their fourth division championship, Winfield was a mere footnote to the proceedings. His groundout allowed Manny Lee to score the third run in the fifth inning. But it was his 41st birthday and the rejoicing that resounded through the SkyDome was at least in part directed at the Man who had emboldened The Team.

In the clubhouse, Winfield was overcome by the tenderness he had felt from the crowd. "Beautiful. We win it on my birthday, too. Beautiful. Wow, a whole city acknowledges my birthday. That's more acknowledgment than I've had for any other birthday in my life. It's great. I love sharing it with Toronto. I love sharing it with Canada."

It was not just the birthday or the championship. For one shining season, Dave Winfield had shared all of himself with everyone who had watched and hoped and dreamed.

He had been asked, a few weeks earlier, what he would cherish the most about his first year as a Toronto Blue Jay. And his last year as a Toronto Blue Jay, as it would turn out. "The best part? Well, you know, if we can reach the goal that I have in mind, then every day has been the best part."

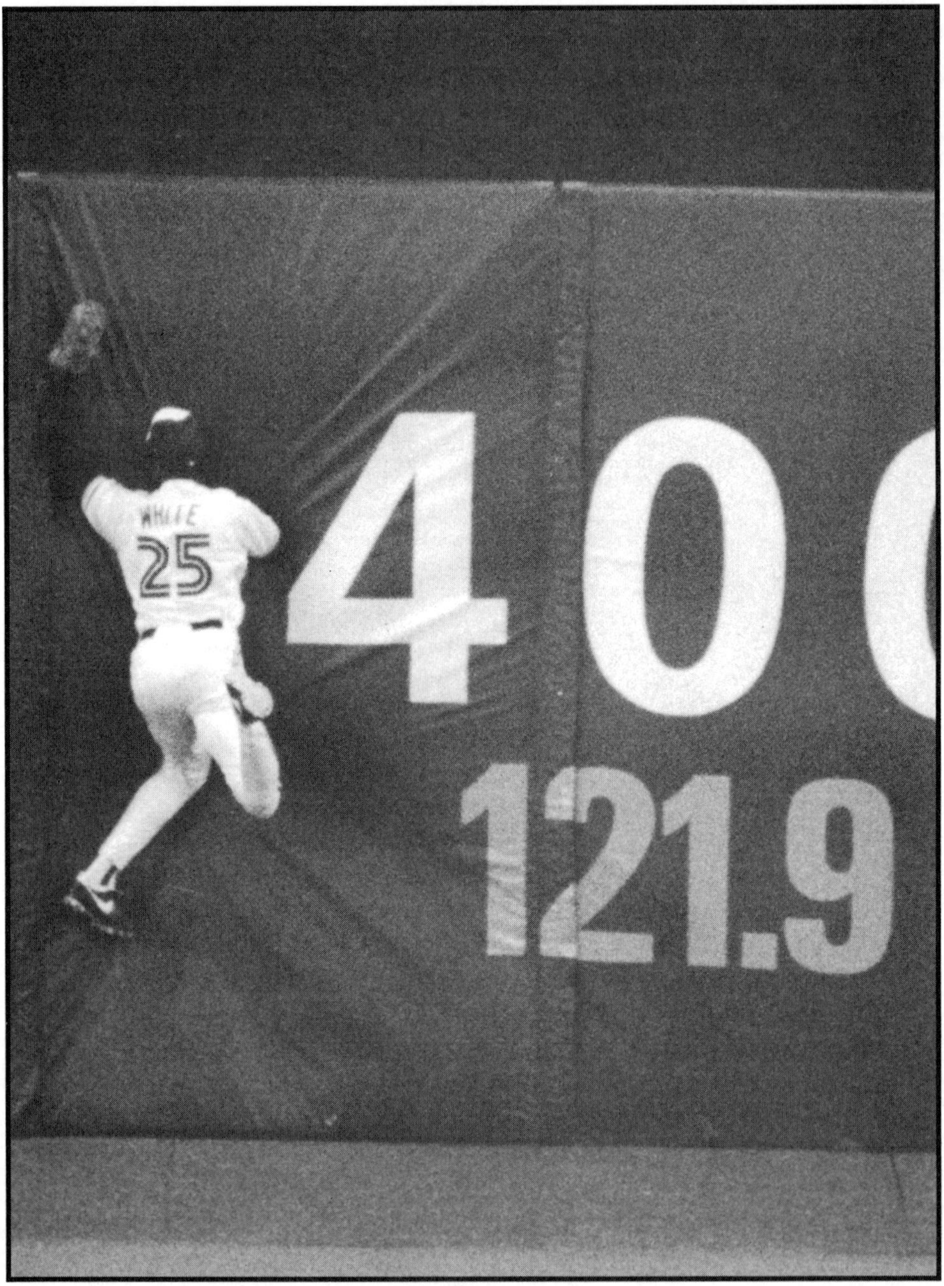


Jeff Goode—*Toronto Star*

# Glory Jays

## *If He Can't Make the Catch, It's Not Do-able*     8

There is a grace even in his stillness. In the hands, one bare and one gloved, that hover just above the knee caps. In the torso, bent slightly at the waist, undulating ever so gently from side to side. In the chin that juts forward and the lips that move but make no sound.

Devon White, the man who doesn't much like conversation, is talking to himself.

He is also moving in tandem, almost imperceptibly, with the man on the mound. With the coil of the wind-up and the grunt of the release and the torque of the follow-through. But while the crowd is still in its first syllable of exclamation as cowhide cracks against ash, the nimble centre fielder has already sprung off the balls of his feet. He is tailing back, eyes glued to the arc of the ball's trajectory. Floating...floating...floating...

Somewhere in the recesses of his mind, White makes a quick calculation and a split-second decision. By now his reflexes are more instinctive than intellectual. It is not a process he will be able to explain. *But he turns his back on the ball.*  Lopes in his long-strided gazelle gait to a point at the centre field wall, a spot where his impulses have propelled him. Turns, leaps, and traps the fleeing orb in the rim of his glove. For a moment he is suspended in space, spread-eagled against the padded fence. Then gravity takes over and he is alighting again on the warning track at the SkyDome, his cap askew but the ball cradled against his chest.

The crowd roars and roars and roars. Finally, White has to acknowledge the applause. He doffs his lid. "Well geez, I had to do something," he remarks with a self-conscious grin after-wards. "They were giving me a standing ovation." For a fleeting second, a jumble of emotions flits across White's whippet face.

There is pride and shyness and then something that might almost be a wince of pain — an admission that the fans' tribute was sweet and precious and coveted.

Defence is so often a quiet art. For every heart-stopping catch that White makes on the fly at the wall, there are a dozen that fall without fanfare into his outstretched glove. No drama, no theatrics, just the confidence that is shared by all White's teammates on the Toronto Blue Jays — and the SkyDome patrons — that *this* man will get to *that* ball. Former Jay Mookie Wilson, who patrolled the meadow on occasion during White's first season in Toronto, once put it this way: "He makes everyone's job easier. If I'm playing left field, I know I just have to cover this little amount of ground. Devo will get the rest. You know, a lot of good centre fielders can catch anything they get to, but the trick is getting to them. Devon can get to just about everything." A superb catch may elicit oohs and aahs but there is never a sense of incredulity. "We expect him to make those catches," Mookie added. "We forget sometimes that he's only human."

The consensus is, if White can't make the catch, then it's simply not do-able. In 1991, his freshman year as a Jay, he had a fielding percentage of .998 — almost perfection. In 156 games that year, White committed only one error on the way to earning his third gold glove. "I'm not sure about the one I missed," he reminisced one day. "I think it was that time I bobbled a ball." *That time I bobbled a ball.* That isolated case when he didn't do the expected, which somehow should make it more memorable.

Thirty-year-old White is an amiable fellow but a reluctant interview. He is almost fanatically private about his feelings and elusive about his past. It is why he has been able to retain a certain equanimity in a career that had its share of setbacks before he got the break of his professional life and was traded to Toronto from the California Angels on December 2, 1990. "I'm the mystery man," he said one day, pleased with the metaphor. "And that's the way I like it. Basically, I don't need the public to know too much about me. I come out, I play hard, I want to win and be successful. That's all anyone can ask. That's all anyone needs to know."

Needs to know, maybe. Wants to know? Not a chance. Ballplayers, like other entertainers, are a public commodity. The fans are proprietary about their athletes. But White's attitude, while largely defensive posturing, also had a lot to do with old-fashioned bashfulness. He is, in essence, a shy guy. "I don't say too much to people I don't know." And not that much to people he does know. To some extent, that attitude has changed in the past two years. He has come to trust the fans in Toronto as they have embraced him. The ramparts of self-preservation have been steadily breached. He has grown comfortable in his own skin as he has matured on the field and off. But while he is good-natured enough at the ballpark, as ready to huzzah-huzzah before and after the game as anyone else, there remains a solitariness to White. On the road, he will go out for an occasional meal with teammates but more often he'll keep to his hotel room, amusing himself with movies, music and "my toys" — hand-held diversions such as Game-Boy. His focus away from the park is his family: wife Colleen, son Thaddeus and daughter Davellyn Rae. He has been able to separate the baseball life from the personal life, something a lot of ballplayers find very difficult to do. But the family spends much of the season at the White residence in Mesa, Arizona, meaning that he is often alone for long stretches of time.

The public recognition in Toronto has startled White, who came to the Jays in the trade that sent Junior Felix and Luis Sojo to the Angels. "I'm not a superstar," he insisted near the end of his first campaign as a Jay. "I don't want to be noticed. That's why it's been tougher for me in Canada than it was in California. There, I wasn't considered one of the big guys so not many people noticed me on the street. They'd have to see my name on my jersey to know who I was. Here, I can't believe it. Everyone seems to know who I am."

Celebrity is not so much an imposition as an adjustment. "I'm not nervous or ashamed about anything in my life. It's just that I get uncomfortable when people stare at me. It's like they want to know something." He stops, looks at his interlocutor with genuine curiosity. "What it is? What do they want?" Then he ducks his head into his shoulders. "I'm pretty much a loner, that's all." A natural centre fielder, in other words. The sentinel who stands way off, 325 feet-or-so from the plate. The loneliest man in the ballpark.

There were other reasons for White's natural reserve when he first came to Toronto. Back then, there was still the residue of his last year as an Angel, a fallen Angel. His first full season in

California, in 1987, White had led the American League in put-outs with 424, while racking up 16 outfield assists, tying him for third in the AL. But in 159 games started — more than anyone else on the club — he had also delivered unexpected offensive numbers for a guy who had shone defensively throughout his minor league career. He was the first Angel rookie to record more than 20 home runs and 20 stolen bases in one year (24 and 32 respectively). In one game against the New York Yankees, White had even homered from both sides of the plate. His clutch of rookie records with the franchise included most at-bats (639), runs (103), total bases (283) and extra-base hits (62). Round off those numbers with 87 RBIs and a .263 batting average and you've got a decent candidate to build a club around. But that stellar debut may have been the worst thing that could have happened to the young man.

White regressed in each of the next three years (putting aside for the moment a 1989 game against Boston where he stole for the cycle), bottoming out at .217 in 1990 with 11 homers and just 44 RBIs. Not only had he fallen from grace with the organization but he had toppled all the way back to the club's Triple A franchise in Edmonton where he was dispatched for an ego-crushing three weeks at midsummer. It was a humiliation and sent a strong message that the Angels had given up on their incorrigible "head-case." The demotion only served to scramble what was left of White's confidence. "I played there for four years and then they decide to demote me?" he recalled long after the fact, the wound still not healed. "Man, that was new. I mean, first they send me down to Edmonton because I'm not hitting. Then they bring me back up and I'm hitting in the third spot. That doesn't say too much for management."

There was undoubtedly bad blood between White and then-manager Doug Rader. The two were barely on speaking terms as their last campaign together concluded. Much of the feuding evolved from Rader's insistence that White bat lead-off, which he had no taste for. But the Angels were also convinced that White was a screw-up who could never be straightened out. After the trade to Toronto, Rader said of White: "He's the kind of player who has a tendency to grate on your soul." Those were harsh, cruel words. White's rebuttal: "Hey, it's coming from Doug Rader so I gotta say, check the source. When you trade someone, you're always afraid that they're going to turn into the type of player you wanted them to be in the first place."

That's exactly what happened in Toronto, right down to White's assignment as lead-off hitter. "The thing is, in Anaheim they tried to mess with my head. As you can see, they didn't get in there. How do you keep them out? You think of where you can be that's even worse than where you are. You don't let them wear you down. Me, I'm a tough street kid. I grew up in New York. Ain't no one can mess with me."

He took virulent exception, however, to the suggestion that he had been a depressing element on the Angels squad. "My attitude doesn't change, no matter what kind of year I'm having. Go ahead, ask my teammates. They'll tell you I'm not a difficult guy to get along with. But playing in Toronto is different. Playing in Toronto is fun. It's a first-class operation. When I came here, Cito (Gaston) said, we're gonna have you hit leadoff. And it was never mentioned again. No problem. I don't care where I hit as long as I know what it is they want me to do. That's the way I like it. I go out there every day now and I'm laughing."

Although he is a man of few words, White can get quite animated when he discusses the fine art of fielding. He sounds cocky at times, almost arrogant, but this is practically a prerequisite for self-confidence among athletes. And he's only being honest. "I position myself well, as far as knowing the hitters. You know all that stuff you hear about some centre fielders being so good? Well, they're really not as good as they should be. You can't just have the ability, you have to have the instincts. That's all I'm doing. I'm anticipating where the hitters are going the majority of the time."

It may be instinctive but it doesn't necessarily come naturally. It takes serious study and hard work. It means doing the drills and shagging the ball, night after night, during batting practice. *Envisioning* where it will go.

His first year with the Jays, *Baseball America* picked White as the fastest runner in the American League. He was also given the nod as second-best defensive outfielder behind Ken Griffey Jr. of the Seattle Mariners. That latter designation as a runner-up did not sit well with White. "I think what Ken Griffey Jr. has on me is that he's made a couple of great plays that everyone remembers. Hats-off plays. With plays like that, they show them over and over again on TV. People can't help but remember them. So I guess I'm a little bit jealous," he admitted in late '91. "Because a lot of people don't get to see the great plays I make. Also, I make it look too easy. It's like, well, that's no big deal. But go out and ask the baseball managers who they'd rather have on their team, a Devon White or a Ken Griffey Jr. The people who know baseball know who the better outfielder is."

Devo knows.

But who is Devon White anyway?

He was a kid from the sun-drenched island of Jamaica who grew up with no fantasies of baseball or a life in the big leagues. Baseball was neither seen nor heard on the streets of Kingston, where he was reared with his four siblings. On the island, the children were weaned on the pleasures of British colonialism.

His father, Thaddeus White, was himself a fairly renowned athlete on the island in his younger days. For 10 years he was in the army, as an instructor with the Jamaica Battalion in Montego Bay, where he excelled in cricket and soccer. Those were the sports that Devon played as a child as well, long before he'd ever heard of baseball. "I played soccer and some cricket when I was a child. But I don't think I was very good at either one. What I remember most is that I was one clumsy kid."

White, the younger, has made off-hand remarks in the past about the endemic poverty of native Jamaicans. He says now, however, that he was too young to understand the situation. He remembers only how grateful the locals were for the tourist dollars. "I don't think anyone ever resented them. We lived off tourism." The Whites were better off than most. Devon's dad was a butcher who ran his own business. "He was pretty successful in his own line of work. He owned his own cows. Me, I don't know anything about cows."

When he was six, White's parents emigrated to New York City, leaving him and his siblings behind with his grandmother until they got settled. Three years later, the reconstituted clan was living on the upper west side, in an area known as Washington Heights, just across the river from Yankee Stadium. "We moved to Manhattan because my parents were looking for a better life for the family." His father continued as a butcher for a while before returning to school to qualify as a nursing attendant.

There were cultural bridges to cross. White says he took the changes in stride, in spite of a thick patois accent that earned him the ridicule of his new classmates. "We were more excited to be in the United States than worried about how we were going to be accepted or that we were different. It wasn't until we got to school that we even realized that maybe we were not exactly the same as everyone else. They rode me about the accent for a while. When that happens, you learn to talk like everyone else pretty fast. But I think I was accepted. See, I was such a quiet person anyway, there was no reason for anybody to even notice me. Or not to like me. So I didn't have to change my personality. I just stayed the way I always was."

Toronto has a large Jamaican community, much of it only recently transplanted. This has caused some problems and resentment, not unlike the American experience of big-city racial disquiet. But White has become something of a hero to young Jamaicans, bereft of their own role models. "I haven't seen a lot of the Jamaican kids," he maintains. "But some of the older ones, the men, they have approached me. They say, 'We're proud of you, Devon.' It's funny. They're only proud of me because of where I come from. I understand it, of course. They look at me as a countryman and I'm glad that they have a countryman that they can be proud of. But it's also a little bit sad because that's the only part they can see. We shouldn't care so much about where a person comes from. It should just be who you are. But I guess they have to look at it that way."

He claimed, in his early days as a Jay, to know little about the racial difficulties that some Jamaican Canadians had encountered in Toronto. "But I hope that I can be a role model, if that's what Jamaican kids need. I sure hope Toronto doesn't become like the U.S. with all the racial problems they have there."

He was asked, one time, about his personal experience with racism in America. White measured his response carefully. "I was brought up in the States. I knew when to say things and when not to. I knew when to keep my mouth shut." It was a cryptic answer but, after a pause, he continued. "They say there isn't any prejudice in baseball anymore but that's not true." (This conversation took place long before the revelation of Marge Schott's remarks about blacks.) "There is still prejudice against Latinos and blacks. Even though there have been some pretty good teams that were almost all black or Latino, like the Pittsburgh Pirates when they won the World Series. If there's no prejudice, then why can't a guy like Bill Madlock get a coaching job anywhere in

baseball? How come he's knocking around, trying to get someone to hire him as a hitting instructor? So you can't really tell me
there's no prejudice in baseball."

It had been, for White, a long speech. He cleared his throat.
"The Blue Jays, though, this particular organization, I've never
seen any prejudice here. You know, prejudice is just something
that you have to accept and then go on with your life. You can't
be a rebel all the time. You can't try to change everything in the
world. You can only take care of yourself and your family."

He had discovered baseball in New York with his family and
the love of the game had been a shared experience, nurtured in
that small apartment on the west side. "It was pretty much my
father who taught me what was the right call, the right thing to
do in a situation. We both learned the game together, sitting
there, watching it on TV."

Thaddeus White remembers those days quite clearly. "At
first, Devon played a lot of basketball. But back then we were
living right by Yankee Stadium and both of us started going to a
lot of ball games. I became a fan right away because it was so
much like cricket." Both Whites became avid students of the
game, often sitting together on the couch in front of the TV, trying
to decipher the intricacies of this American pastime. "We had five
children and Devon was the baby," White Sr. reminisces. "When
we started watching baseball, we were Yankee fans. For a while
there we switched to the Mets but then we went back to the
Yankees. I used to love watching that Dave Winfield and now
he's playing with my boy! There was that other guy, too, the
manager, the one who was always coming out and kicking dirt
at the umpire. What was his name? Billy Martin, that's it."

Thaddeus says he encouraged Devon to pursue his baseball
dreams, even though the youngster was shy and smaller than
most of his friends. "I knew what it was like to love a sport the
way Devon loved baseball. And I had faith in him. His mother
and I, we would pray every day that Devon would make it to the
major leagues."

He was an obedient son, the father adds. Never caused any
problems, never gave his folks reason to worry. "He had a couple
of friends I didn't like too much." Pool sharks, apparently. "I said
to him, 'Son, you stay away from those boys.' And he did. He
never talked a lot either, he wasn't that kind of person. But he was
always laughing."

In his little section of Manhattan, Devon White also was introduced to stickball, the asphalt version of baseball. He took to it quickly and enthusiastically. But it wasn't until he got to high school that he had any official involvement with baseball proper. "I came late to baseball and I started playing later. You might say I'm a late bloomer. I only played a season and a half of Little League my whole life." His real love, back then, was basketball. (He is still crazy for the Phoenix Suns.) But the notion of a major league career never crossed his mind. "It's just not anything I ever dreamed of. It all seemed so impossible, something that could never happen. Until it actually did happen."

In those days of adolescence, White was aiming for a career as a mechanic, or perhaps even a fireman. "Little boy stuff. Although I guess you could say that professional baseball is little boy stuff too." Accordingly, he transferred to a school that was some distance from where he lived — Park West High, which is smack in the middle of Hell's Kitchen. But it was a well-regarded vocational school, particularly noted for its mechanics and cooking courses. It was at Park West that White attracted the attention of baseball coach Gilbert Rose, the man who would become his mentor and life-long friend.

"I came across him when he was a freshman in high school," recalled Rose, who went on to become an assistant principal of health and physical education in Brooklyn. "Back then, he used to be called DEHV-on (as in Devonshire), not DEE-von which everyone calls him now. He was only about 14 or 15 years old at the time and he was still rather small. But he tried out for baseball and he made the varsity team, which was very unusual for a freshman. But you just knew, you could see it, that this one was special, that he could make it. He had such natural ability. He could run, jump, catch. It was all instinctive to him."

White, the consummate centre fielder, played shortstop and second base in those salad days. "But I think his first and primary love was basketball," Rose confirmed. "He had a nice jump shot, I remember." The Blue Jay is still fondly recalled among the alumni at Park West and whenever the Jays visit New York "it's like a family reunion" says Rose. "Devon was a good student, never got into trouble. A lot of teachers liked him. He was one of those kids who was always hanging around the gym. He was a gentleman."

It wasn't until the California Angels plucked him right out of high school in the sixth round of the 1981 draft that White began to hope that perhaps he could make a career out of baseball, especially after his third year in the minor leagues when *Baseball America* voted him best baserunner and best outfielder. "Whenever anyone talked about prospects, my name was right on top. That's when it finally hit me — maybe I can do this."

He did it in Anaheim but then it all went sour. Arriving in Toronto he knew he would have to prove it all over again. At least he was starting clean. No grudges, no conflicts.

He had proven that in Anaheim, before it all went sour. Now he was going to prove it to the Jays.

White went 3-for-5 in his second game with Toronto, including two doubles, though his first home run did not come until May 31, versus his former club. At the All-Star break, he led the club in multiple hit games and had a four-hit encounter in a losing effort against the Boston Red Sox on August 9. His second four-hitter came against the Cleveland Indians less than a month later. Twelve of his 17 home runs in 1991 were executed when he was leading off an inning and six of those were to lead off a game. Who said he didn't like batting first in the order? He was second on the team in stolen bases, too, with 33.

In the American League he was tied for fourth in runs (110) and triples (10), seventh in stolen bases, fifth in at-bats (642), eighth in multiple hit games (56), ninth in hits (181), and total bases (292), and tied for ninth in doubles (40). He ended 1991 with a respectable .282 average and a third Gold Glove. For his efforts, the Blue Jays rewarded him with a $10 million contract last February, guaranteed over three years with a club option on 1995 worth another $3 million.

When he reported to Dunedin for spring training in '92, White had his 75-year-old father in tow. The elder White had never been to the spring camps. In fact, he had seen Devon play in only one major league game, at Yankee Stadium when his son had still been a California Angel. "I told him to hit a home run for me," the father recalled. "And he did. That boy has always listened to his father."

On this sunny morning, under a molten Florida sun, Thaddeus White was sitting in the dugout with his legs crossed and his arms folded over his chest. Out on the field, his son stood with legs splayed and his arms whirring overhead. It was a pleasing picture, with endearing symmetry. Then the elder White rubbed his knees, got up to stretch and walk a bit along the chain-link fence. He didn't move too well anymore but there was still a faint echo of the son's athletic grace in the father's stride. It was in their faces, though — one youthful and the other wrinkled — where the family ties were most evident. They both had the same shy smile.

Devon White's mother, Gloria, had died suddenly the previous month at the family home in Kingston, where the senior Whites had returned to live after their children had grown. Gloria White was only 67 when she passed away in her husband's arms. The couple had been married for 36 years, during which time they had never spent more than a couple of weeks apart, usually when she went to visit Devon in America. Thaddeus White, so recently widowed, was lonely and his son knew it. That's why he more or less ordered his dad to visit him in Florida. "He's such a good boy. He took care of everything, all the funeral arrangements. There were so many people, so many beautiful flowers. He said to me: 'Pops, you're coming up to be with me.' He forced me and I'm so glad he did. We're staying together, just the two of us. He's been taking me to the show and to dinner. He introduced me to the players and the manager. Everybody's been so nice."

Thaddeus White may have encouraged his son in his career choice but by the time White turned professional, his parents had already returned to Jamaica. Mother and father watched their son's career blossom from a distance, on television. But Devon White was still something of a celebrity in the neighborhood and his father admitted that he reveled in that spotlight too. "Oh, people will come up and talk to me on the street about Devon. They'll say, 'We saw your son on TV last night. Hit a home run and stole two bases. Don't you think that calls for a drink, Thaddeus?' "

No doubt Thaddeus White had plenty of visitors dropping by in search of alcoholic hospitality last season, too. Devo's stats were not quite as lofty as the ones he had recorded as a Blue Jay frosh — his early season average would drop in alarming fashion before rebounding to a quasi-respectable .248 on the year — but the power numbers stayed healthy. There would be renewed debate about his qualifications as a lead-off hitter but no complaints about his acrobatics afield.

As spring training wound down White was troubled by a strained hamstring that would continue to cause discomfort as the season progressed. He was 0-for-5 in the season opener at Detroit. In fact, he went 1-for-13 in the series but did manage to steal his first base of 1992 in the third encounter as the Jays swept the homeside at Tiger Stadium. Opening at the SkyDome, White slashed a two-out double to left and was delivered home by Robbie Alomar as the Jays secured a bottom of the ninth 4-3 victory over Baltimore. The next night, White's performance (3-for-5, 2 RBIs) suggested that his early-season difficulties may have been an anomaly. "I didn't start the season like everyone expected," he conceded "You know, lead-off base hit. It didn't happen that way in Detroit. I think it was a little too cold for me. But now everything's rolling and my individual stats will come along if I don't put pressure on myself, as long as I go out there and have some fun. And that's what we're all doing."

A brief battle with the flu aside, it looked as if White was finding his stride and his groove. Against the Cleveland Indians on April 23, he rapped a two-run homer, his first of the campaign, as the Jays annihilated the Indians 13-8. When the Tribe moved on to make room at the SkyDome for the Kansas City Royals, White was among those who had harsh words for rookie Rico Rossy, who had blocked the bag on a sliding play by Robbie Alomar — a move reminiscent of a similarly aggressive defensive maneouvre by Rossy in a spring training encounter. This time around, Alomar suffered a sprained knuckle on his right pinkie. As far as White was concerned, Rossy had traversed the fine line between playing hard and playing dirty. "He knows and, now that we know...let's just say that, next time, we'll be coming into second very hard," he warned. Responded Rossy: "I remember Devon in Florida, too. He spiked me coming back in (feet first), but that's the price I got to pay. I'm trying to make the club. It's kind of hard to time it sometimes but if I've got a chance to block the bag, I block it."

In early May, White enjoyed one of his finest turns in the still young season as the Jays pounded the Mariners in Seattle 12-4. He contributed three hits including a lead-off single that bumped his puny average to .231. "The fact of him getting a hit first time up does a lot for his confidence," observed Gaston. "We need him to have a good year. If we get him and Robbie on base, we're going to score a lot of runs."

Hosting the Mariners on May 14, White connected for a two-run blast in the seventh inning as the Jays scraped out a 5-4 decision. The tater was something of a called shot as White had promised a home run as a gift for his daughter's first birthday. "I don't call too many, but sometimes I feel good about trying to hit them for my kids. I wanted to hit a home run for her today." The last time he had called one for his kids was in 1987, when he was still an Angel, and that had been to celebrate the birth of his son. His second paternal present also broke up an 0-for-9 slump at the plate. "It hasn't been too good a season for me so far. I'd like to say it's over but we'll have to see. It's only one hit. I'll need a few more before I know I'm out of it."

The team had spent much of that first month on the road so White couldn't even blame the lousy air inside the SkyDome for his troubles; tests conducted by the *Toronto Star* had shown that carbon dioxide levels during games were above the comfort zone as determined by the province of Ontario and air-quality experts. No doubt this concentration of unpleasant elements, which could cause headaches, itchy eyes and lethargy, had been compounded by the addition of fireworks displays before the start of the game and after every Blue Jay four-bagger. The concentrations were particularly elevated just beyond the centre field level where White patrolled the green.

In the open-air of Comiskey, White assisted the Jays to a 6-2 victory over the White Sox on May 22 with a two-run dinger in the third, his fourth of the season — it traveled some 420 feet into the cheap seats in right-centre. Just over a week later, in the Metrodome at Minneapolis, White accomplished a rare feat when he connected for two home runs, one from either side of the plate. What's more, he nailed the first one as the lead-off hitter in the game while the second one, in the 10th, was an inside-the-park job. It had looked like a blooper, just missed by the fully-extended left fielder Shane Mack. Then the ball took a huge hop past the on-rushing Kirby Puckett. "When I saw Kirby jump, I was thinking a sure double," said White. "That's all I figured, though. I guess I just pretty much flicked it into the right place." It was his first-ever inside-the-park four-bagger. The other homer on the night, accomplished in a more normal fashion, was his first leading off a game in 1992. Meanwhile, the inside-the-parker was the 17th ever hit by a Blue Jay.

Those theatrics took some of the pressure off White but by mid-May he was still hitting only .234 with 55 strikeouts, hardly the kind of numbers one would expect from a lead-off hitter. On June 18, he assembled four hits, equaling a career high, but the effort was wasted as the Tigers dumped the Jays 14-10. The season was unfolding as a frustrating exercise in inconsistency at the plate for White, with one step forward and two steps back. Then the Angels came to town and, perhaps inspired to prove his former club had been wrong in trading him away 18 months earlier, White was instrumental in Toronto's series sweep. Next up were the Mariners and White's run-scoring single in the bottom of the ninth helped the Jays rally for a 4-3 final, their sixth straight victory and the 51st win of the season. The oddity in that encounter presented itself in the sixth inning when White lined a ball to right that Jay Buhner couldn't find. White, naturally, raced home but when first-base umpire Tim Welke ambled out there to solve the mystery of the missing ball, he found it wedged between the Detroit banner and the wall. White was ordered back to second with a ground-rule double.

The beginning of July also saw White enjoying an eight-game hitting streak (it would go no further) but another streak was about to come to an end. In a July 12th date with the Oakland Athletics, an 8-0 fiasco for the Bluebirds, White's uninterrupted trail of 13 consecutive stolen bases was derailed as he was caught leaning in the first inning. By mid-July White's batting average was hovering around the .252 level but he was balancing that out nicely with 39 RBIs. A plateau of futility of sorts was reached in Anaheim on July 20 when he struck out three times.

The current batting slump had started just before the All-Star break when White went hitless (0-for-15) in four successive games against Oakland pitching. Following the break, he had been blanked in three of the first seven games during Toronto's west coast trip and, as of July 23, had only four hits, all singles, in his last 48 at bats. He'd scored only one run during that stretch and hadn't driven in any. His average nose-dived from .252 to .231 and his on-base percentage for the season was just .290. Still, Gaston refused to move him further down in the order. That night, what looked like a sure home run for White was pulled back at the last moment by a leaping Willie Wilson. Gaston, faced with this untenable situation, opted to give White a rest against

Oakland, substituting Derek Bell at centre. The shake-up didn't help the team, as the Jays fell hard, 9-1.

His legs rested — at least that was the hope — White was back in the line-up *tout-suite*. Returning to the friendlier confines of the SkyDome, White smoked a vicious line-drive that right fielder Gary Thurman misplayed into a three-base error. White scored soon after and later knocked home the Jays' fourth run with a sacrifice fly as the Jays dismissed the Royals 6-4. Against the Red Sox in Boston on August 3, Devon's 11th home run of the season was all the offense the Jays could muster as they submitted meekly, 7-1. The Jays were mired in a disheartening August swoon but at least White looked to be righting himself. His on-base percentage may have been nothing to jump up and down about but, once on base, he was among the most notorious thieves in the league; in fact, he was fourth in the majors, good on 27 of 31 attempts as of August 8th.

In Cleveland on August 14, Gaston again rested his centre fielder — whose average had skidded to .233, though that accu-satory figure was augmented with 13 homers and 47 RBIs — and called on Derek Bell once more. The problem, said Gaston, was that White was still ailing from a sore quad muscle in his left thigh. White responded to these concerns by coming out in the next game and cranking his 14th homer. It was the fourth time in 1992 and the 10th time in his career that White had opened a game in that manner. The Jays nevertheless lost the upper-half of that doubleheader to the Tribe 4-2. White's four-bagger in the futile venture, on the second pitch offered by Dennis Cook, left him less than charitable towards the Cleveland starter. White accused Cook of nagging umpire Greg Kosc for favorable calls. "He doesn't have enough time in this league to be begging for pitches like he does," White sniffed afterwards. "We'll remember." So too would he remember losing a C-note on the night — the penalty he was assessed for disagreeing with the ump on a called strike, then flinging his bat and batting glove in disgust. Less than a week later, in a stinker against the Brewers in Milwaukee, White was ejected by plate umpire Terry Craft for another argument — this time over White's insistence that he had slid home safely on a Dave Winfield dribbler. He still hadn't learned that you don't win tiffs with the men in blue.

White, and the Jays, survived August. Both would prosper in September. For the centre fielder, there was another four-hit affair on the 4th as the Jays overpowered the Minnesota Twins 16-5. He missed a start on September 6 because of a strained thigh muscle but was back taking care of business in centre when the team traveled to Kansas City. White's key contribution to Blue Jay folklore there was his discovery of a two-inch-long, bright green locust in the grass which he brought back to the clubhouse. Rookie catcher Mike Maksudian, accepting an $800 challenge, promptly ate it.

Still marveling over his teammate's peculiar gourmet tastes, White opened the next series against the Rangers by crushing a Scott Chiamparino fastball into the right field grandstand. That made it five lead-off homers on the season, 11 for his career. Toronto toughed out that contest, 7-5. The following evening he smacked a three-run double in a 4-2 affair that made Jack Morris Toronto's first 19-game winner in a season. Back in T.O., White collected a double, scored two runs, took a walk and swiped his 33rd base of the year as the Jays nipped the Indians 5-4. With those numbers, he had lifted his average to .339 for the month (19 hits in 56 at-bats), which concurrently yanked his season average to .242. He also had 15 homers and 54 ribbies on the year.

White, more than anybody else, appreciated that this was what the team needed from him as Toronto, Baltimore and Milwaukee hurtled towards the finish line in the pennant race. He admitted to one reporter that he had spent much of the earlier months swinging at bad pitches, curveballs in particular, that he should have eschewed. "You have to go back to the basics sometimes and look for the pitches that are best for you. And I'm pretty much a fastball hitter."

In a big game against the Rangers at the SkyDome on September 18 — the Rangers were humiliated 13-0 — White drove in four runs and scored three times, notching his 16th long-ball of the campaign. The next afternoon was a far different entry but with the same ultimate verdict, a 1-0 squeaker for the Jays. That encounter was notable for some heads-up, daring base running by White, assisted by confusion on the Texas side. The shenanigans started innocently enough with Alfredo Griffin blooping a one-out double down the line in right. That brought up White, who slapped a single through the right side. Griffin trotted to third and stopped, following orders from coach Rich Hacker. But White, watching as Jose Canseco's throw arrived in the infield, just kept motoring past first to second. First baseman Rafael

Palmeiro cut off Canseco's crooked relay and it looked as if White was hopelessly hung up between first and second. That's when Griffin came to the rescue, faking towards home, thereby compelling Palmeiro to fire to the plate. But Griffin put on the brakes and scrambled back to third. Meanwhile, White was standing unmolested on second. Next man up, Robbie Alomar, tapped a slow ground ball toward second and now Griffin did make it home for the only run of the game. White was asked afterwards if he had just been lucky on the curious play. He disagreed adamantly. "Running the bases like I did, aggressive, with one out, caused that play. We're taught to keep going on that play and force them to cut the ball. If they get me out, so what? The run scores."

The books were balanced the next night, though, when White dropped an easy fly ball that allowed the Rangers to mount a three-run uprising and avoid the sweep, winning 7-5. "That shows I'm human," said White, who was nevertheless annoyed with himself. "There's no excuse for it."

His 17th, and final, home run of the regular campaign came during a key game in Baltimore on September 22. It followed a two hour, 42-minute rain delay at Camden Yards. And it followed almost immediately, at that, on just the fourth pitch from starter Rick Sutcliffe. It was a resounding thwack, bouncing off the top of the out-of-town scoreboard in right. When the contest was finally done, almost an hour and a half past midnight, the Jays had prevailed 4-3 and the Orioles' division-hopes were all but dead.

Now Toronto had to hold off the persistent Brewers as Milwaukee overtook the Orioles in the standings. Towards that end, the Jays knocked off the Red Sox at the SkyDome 5-2 to stay just ahead of the Brewers with time running out. The catalyst in this encounter was again Mr. White, who had a single, double and triple while driving in one run and scoring twice. When he came to the plate in the eighth, needing a homer for the cycle, the crowd cheered him lustily. The fans continued to cheer even after he grounded out.

That salutation was nothing compared to what transpired the following evening. Back in April, the Beantowners had been expected to give the Jays a run for the division but nothing had come of that prediction as the Sox floundered early in the year and then stumbled from bad to worse. Now, in the waning days of the season, with Frank Viola facing off against former New York Met teammate David Cone, there was little at stake except pride.

The determined Viola frustrated the Jays through eight and looked good for his first-ever no-hitter as White dug in at the plate to open the ninth frame. And laced a single over second base. Boston won the game 1-0, behind Viola's one-hitter, but the Jays had just narrowly averted being no-hit for the fourth time in team history. White's connection had saved them that ignominy.

Two days later, Toronto clinched the division. White had two hits as the Jays polished off the Detroit Tigers 3-1. The following afternoon Gaston rested most of the regulars, including his centre fielder. But White did make an appearance. Between innings, he and Joe Carter and Candy Maldonado came motoring out through an opening in the fence in the left field wall. From inside a bright green Jeep, the trio waved to the fans. That Jeep just happened to belong to Derek Bell, his most prized possession, and the rookie's face fell as word spread that the Jays were about to auction off his beloved toy. Well, of course, it was a gag.

White was not behind the wheel on that occasion. And he was a passenger as well just over a week later when the Mercedes-Benz 500 SEL he was thinking of buying went out of control and crashed into a hydro pole, snapping it in half. White and his wife Colleen, both of whom had been riding in the back seat during the test-drive, miraculously escaped injury.

Puts the game of baseball in perspective, a thing like that.

# Glory Jays

## Trying to
## Regain Favor
9

Heroism is often a transient state of being. There are heroes of the moment, heroes of a season and heroes of an era. Only very rarely, and it usually requires that you also be very dead, can a mere mortal be a hero for all eternity. Even then, with revisionist historians sifting through the bones of one's legacy, the skeletons are apt to come clattering out of the closet.

We love our heroes. But many is the time that we build them up only to tear them down. This is called empowerment of the people. Our admiration is on loan and can be recalled at any time. We extend to individuals all the perqs of idolatry, elevate them to dizzying heights, mount them on plinths of devotion. But woe betide the man or woman who is untrue to our expectations, who lets us down. Or maybe just starts to believe his own press clippings.

The public can be remorseless in its disdain of those who have betrayed our trust.

For athletes who fall down to earth, the shock of it can be overwhelming. It can happen in the blink of an eye or the slip of a tongue; it can occur slowly, in excruciating increments over the course of a season from hell. A handful, those with insight and a willingness for self-examination, can perhaps make sense of it all. But most, raised from their first childish flashes of brilliance in the comforting knowledge that they are better than all the rest, are ill-equipped to deal with failure — even in a sport like baseball, which is more about striking out than hitting home runs. Some, unfit to handle the whims of public sentiment, will become inconsolable. Others grow hard and niggardly with their feelings, distancing themselves from the disapprobation of the crowd. They will hurt you as you have hurt them. And some just keep stumbling and bumbling along, trying to regain your favor.

Kelly Gruber would probably fall into that last category. He was not a bad man and not a bad ballplayer but he hadn't turned out to be what the Blue Jay devotees had anticipated. He gave them one season of magic in 1990 and then he fell apart, certainly physically, perhaps emotionally. Fans, and even some of his teammates (behind his back), began calling him Mrs. Gruber and Scrap Iron last year when a litany of physical complaints took him out of the line-up for a total of 42 games, 49 the year before. Some of those injuries seemed like small hurts, nothing to go lame over, especially in the heat of a pennant battle that rarely waned from April through September. There were whispers that he was malingering, that he didn't have the guts or the grit to play hardball. He was ridiculed in the media and on radio phone-in shows. His own manager, a man noted for his forbearance, lost patience with him. One summer night in Boston, Gruber arrived at Fenway Park an hour before game time with a package of magnetic resonance imaging (MRI) negatives tucked under his arm. Griping about a sore neck, he had been sent for tests by the Jays' orthopedic specialist and here now was the evidence that he had been seeking though it was hardly irrefutable. When reporters tried to question Cito Gaston about this latest development, the skipper snapped: "I don't even want to talk about the guy." And that was the part that was quotable.

But there were other worrisome developments in the soap opera that Gruber's career had become. In Toronto, rumors were flying about the problems he was supposed to be having off the field and in his head. Some of the tittle-tattle was downright vicious though no less eagerly imparted or avidly absorbed. Reporters were sent off on wild goose chases to track down the source, any source, to nail down even a fraction of a fact on which to hang the swirling speculation. There was a tip-off that his wife Lynn had arrived at a local hospital emergency ward covered with bruises but no evidence to back that up. Another informant insisted a drunken Gruber had been tossed out of a downtown watering hole but that intelligence was not supported by proof. Still, the jungle drums continued to beat out a tattoo of gossip and malice.

Was it getting to Gruber? One evening, during batting practice at the SkyDome, the third baseman interrupted an interview he was conducting in the dugout with a reporter on another matter to fly off on a bizarre tangent. "Have you heard the rumors about me?" he demanded, his pupils dilating. "Have you heard that I beat my wife? Have you heard that I'm a homosexual? Have you heard that I left a bar the other night with a blonde on each arm?"

The reporter, stunned, stopped taking notes. Inadvertently or by design, Gruber was legitimizing the rumors by addressing them. He was putting them on the record. But did he understand that the conversation had been, indeed, on the record? It may have been the wrong decision but the reporter did not write the story. Gruber looked and sounded like a man coming unhinged. It was a sad and pathetic revelation.

How had this happened? Toronto had gathered this Golden Boy to its breast not all that long ago. He had done all the right things, at his job and in his life. He had even married a lovely local girl, a one-time cheerleader for the football Toronto Argonauts, and his two young children were both born in the city. He was also the only Blue Jay who lived in the greater Toronto area during the off-season — at least he had the previous winter, instead of migrating south to his home in Austin, Texas though he wasn't sure he wanted to repeat the experience. "I'm a Pisces. I love the sun, I love the water. Those winter months are a good time to be in Austin because I can take out my jet skis and get out on the lake. That's not something you can do in Toronto in January. The other thing is, by staying in the town where you work, you never really feel like you've had a rest. You need to knock off a bit, get some time away."

He had made a valiant attempt at learning how to play hockey, the sport that truly identifies Canadians, which draws together all the quarrelsome regions of the country. He had skated late at night on a frozen pond, which is a rite of passage for those north of the 49th parallel. "My ankles weren't happy about it at all," he joked. His face had been everywhere, whether promoting the Jays, endorsing a product, or assisting in charitable events. He had launched his own good-deeds organization, Kelly's Kids, which each year undertook to send ill or disadvantaged youngsters to ballgames at the SkyDome. And he was voted the most popular athlete in a newspaper survey.

On the day of his birth, in 1962, his name was Kelly King. He became Kelly Gruber when his mother remarried, some time after his natural father — a football running back who once

played for the Saskatchewan Roughriders of the Canadian Football League — abandoned his beauty queen wife, with their son
still in diapers.

In Toronto, he had become King Kelly. And now, suddenly,
he was a bum?

To understand this transformation, one would have to back-
pedal a couple of seasons. In 1990, his third full year as a Toronto
starter (he had been snatched from the Cleveland Indians in the
1983 draft after being left off the 40-man winter roster) Gruber
had propelled himself into the near-superstar category. He racked
up 31 homers and drove in 118 runs while garnering a .274
average. Now here was a ballplayer to build a franchise around.
It helped, too, that Gruber was handsome and personable. The
fans liked what they saw and heard. The offensive numbers only
reinforced their good judgment. Not to be overlooked, either,
were his solid defensive attributes at the hot corner.

The following February, Gruber signed a three-year contract
with the Jays for $11 million, making him the highest-paid third
baseman in history. This was in keeping with the club's well-
earned reputation for fair-handed treatment of its baseball chat-
tels; fine efforts were rewarded with equitable payment. As the
season got underway, everyone settled back prepared to be
marveled again by Gruber's gifted athleticism. But just barely out
of the block, Gruber became bothered by an irritation of the
tendon sheath of his right finger. Then, in a rundown on a play
against the Texas Rangers, he suffered a sprained ligament and
chip fracture at the base of his right thumb. He went on the
disabled list but even after returning to the line-up he continued
to have rotten luck with his throwing hand, a rather important
extremity for a third baseman. During batting practice one day,
he was hit in the very same spot with a hard linedrive. The
baseball gods seemed to be toying with him.

For much of the season, his hand would resemble mashed
eggplant and it felt even worse than it looked. The whole year,
during which he missed about 10 weeks accumulative, was an
ordeal. Both his hitting and his fielding suffered. His output
dropped to 20 home runs, his RBIs to 65 (48 of them after the All-
Star break) and his average to .252. In the post-season, the Blue
Jays' frustrations and ineffectiveness against the Minnesota Twins
were most acutely symbolized by Gruber's awkward thrashing

at the plate. He was always a first pitch swinger but now his futility was taking on comical proportions. In the first game of that five-chapter fiasco he committed two errors in the field. There was no sanctuary during that revolting series.

The season was barely over before Gruber's name was bandied about in trade talks, but competent third basemen are as rare as happy marriages in the Royal Family. "Why should we be thinking of trading anybody right now?" wondered Toronto general manager Pat Gillick. "We don't have to do much, and we're happy with Gruber. We think he's the best fielding third baseman in the league if not in baseball." Meanwhile, the magazine *Inside Sports* ranked Gruber number four in the game at his position, behind Wade Boggs, Matt Williams and Howard Johnson, who was only keeping the bag warm.

When spring training rolled around, Gruber was healthy, healed and looking forward to a return to form. The Golden Boy understood that some of the sheen had rubbed off his halo the year before and he wanted to atone. A lump of calcified tissue had taken permanent residence at the base of his thumb, a reminder of his physical misfortunes from the previous season, and a fresh blister had popped up to boot. But these were inconsequential abnormalities.

"That was no fun at all," he reminisced, dredging up the miserable memories of '91. "It seemed like I sat out an eternity. When I came back, I would find myself doing the things that I most especially didn't want to do — looking at the scoreboard, looking at the stats. You try to stay within yourself and play through the pain. More than anybody else, I wanted the kind of season that I had dreamed about. But it seems like time just ran out on me."

Gruber admitted he was hurt, too, by the dirt that had been dished in some quarters of the dressing room, the buzzing that he had refused to bite the bullet when the team needed him. He didn't know it then, but this was an echo of the same murmurings that would be heard as 1992 gathered steam. "People didn't realize how much it was affecting me because that's not something I wanted to talk about. You don't want the opposing teams knowing about the extent of your injuries because they're going to use that against you. I recognized that there was a certain expectation of me because I guess I'm one of the roots on the ball club. I mean, I know how I felt when I watched Joe Carter go up the wall (in the playoffs) and hurt his ankle. I wanted him to be able to come back right away, too, because we needed him.

"It doesn't matter who said what. You've just got to put that stuff behind you."

But he more than his teammates was haunted by his performance of the year before. "What people could see on my face probably told the whole story. Man, I had enormous problems at the plate. My defence was all right, but because the bone in my hand was still tender I was having serious troubles getting the bat around on the ball. I couldn't get the bat head through the strike zone. I was way behind the pitches. I don't think I've ever had as many broken bats."

Against Minnesota in the playoffs, "what you saw was a grown man trying hard not to cry at the plate."

It did not help matters that Gruber's season of discontent had coincided with the publication of his autobiography, *Kelly: At Home On Third*, written with Toronto journalist Kevin Boland. It revealed a man with more than his share of self-doubts and adolescent angst as it charted his surprisingly rocky road to success, a road that had become even more pitted with potholes since the book had hit the store shelves. "That's one reason I wrote it, to show people that I've gone through trials and tribulations, too. So often the public will put you on a pedestal. They think that you're different. But I've had my lows, and I was hoping that people could equate to that, to see that there is an alternative to taking a gun and putting a bullet in your mouth. It hasn't all been peaches and roses."

He talked, then, like a man who had wrestled his demons to the ground. He could not foresee that there would be few peaches and roses in the season that lay ahead.

Of course, Gruber also started the campaign by putting his big foot in his big mouth. The Grapefruit League had not even ended and he predicted to a reporter that the Jays would win the east by a good 15 games. Not a wise remark, even if he believed it (as many others did). All year long, that forecast would be thrown back at Gruber, sometimes hitting him upside the head. Opponents heard about the cocky remark and smacked their lips. His boast had become a direct challenge. Said Roger Clemens, a fellow Texan: "I know Kelly. He's a good kid, but he's getting carried away there."

Another day, munching on a big hunk of boiled yucca — he claims the foul stuff is full of healthy properties — Gruber mused aloud on his chances of reaching the century mark for runs driven in. "I think Joe (Carter), Winnie (Dave Winfield) and myself have the best shot of pulling away with over a hundred RBIs. But that's because we're going to bat third, fourth and fifth." This would become another unfulfilled prophecy.

The exhibition season concluded with an omen. Their last meaningless encounter was in Montreal, against the Expos. Kelly Gruber sat out with a sore throat.

But the only-season-that-counted began well enough. At Tiger Stadium on April 9, Gruber — batting third instead of his traditional fifth because Joe Carter was suffering from back spasms — swatted his first home run of the year in Game #3 of the Blue Jay schedule, and knocked the go-ahead sacrifice fly in a 3-1 Toronto victory. The round-tripper was Gruber's 700th major league hit. Two days later, against Baltimore, he was good for a triple and a double. Not a bad little clip for this fledgling campaign.

The next day, a rookie by the name of Jeff Kent was sent in to replace Gruber in the fifth inning against the Orioles. Gruber had to leave the game when he felt "something pop" in the left side of his neck while whiffing at the plate. Nobody was overly concerned. "We think it's no more than a kink in his neck," said Gaston. Trainer Tommy Craig revealed that Gruber had been experiencing some stiffness for the previous week in the right side of his neck. He figured the problem on the day was nothing more than a muscle spasm, between the shoulder and the neck: the shrugging muscles.

The 24-year-old Kent, meanwhile, had rung a double up the left-centre gap in his first major league at-bat. Gaston was impressed, as were the 48,309 patrons at the SkyDome, who watched the Jays dismiss Baltimore 3-1. Who could have envisioned how prominently this Kent kid was going to figure in the Blue Jay fortunes for '92, though he would end the year with the New York Mets.

Next night out, against the Yankees, Gruber was again absent-with-leave. The medical term for his condition was something called a wry (stiff) neck, and he was listed as day-to-day. Still, nobody was overly anxious about his predicament. "Don't know what started it," Gruber said, though he knew the problem had begun after the home-opener and had been aggravated by his last at-bat. "Maybe it was all the work, maybe the turf, but it kept getting stiffer and stiffer. That swing sort of pushed it over the edge. I couldn't lift my head up the rest of the at-bat."

Gruber didn't start again until April 17 at Fenway Park, a 1-0 loss to the aforementioned Clemens. The prodigal third baseman contributed a line drive single to left in the losing cause. Back in Toronto the following week, Gruber was a key factor in the Jays' 13-8 pasting of the Cleveland Indians, with two homers and a double. The brace of home runs marked the seventh two-homer game of Gruber's career and accounted for his 400th and 401st RBIs. But in the clubhouse he was unusually cranky. The neck, he told anybody who would listen, was still bothering him. "I'm actually surprised I had the kind of game I had. I felt really bad this morning, got some treatment, but had it stiffen up again during batting practice. Had to have more heat on it just before the game. I was a little irritable out there tonight. The players knew it. It's a struggle. It's taxing. It's hard enough to play this game when you're healthy."

Good health was a condition that would become increasingly alien to Gruber as the season progressed, but he was still looking at the bright side in April: "I guess you could say that injuries are one of the things that have made me a better hitter. Starting out, my strong point used to be the inside fastball. I pulled everything, never hit to right. When I've been hurt, I've had to adjust, slow things down, learn to go to the wrong field."

He sat out again three days later. And so it went: in and out, in and out. The fans were becoming accustomed to young Kent at third. They were in his corner while he continued to cover at Gruber's. Kent had grabbed the public's affection even though he racked up errors as consistently as the man he so frequently replaced. The latter came back one night, fouled a pitch off the inside of his shin, and promptly disappeared again, limping. Now he was hurting all over the place. He reappeared to crush a three-run homer against Goose Gossage as the Jays dumped the Oakland A's 5-1 on the coast and savored the moment. The shot traveled nearly 500 feet to the back row of the bleachers, but he claimed he hadn't been following its progress. "I don't make it a habit to watch them. I don't like it when (opposing players) watch theirs." That mighty wallop notwithstanding, Gruber was still batting a measly .226 as the Jays returned to their SkyDome bunker at the end of the roadtrip.

The boo-birds had again taken up their chorus but were momentarily silenced on May 14 as Gruber celebrated the birth of his daughter Cassie by cracking a two-run shot. He said afterwards that he hoped his wife, still in hospital, had been watching. "I tried to look right at the TV camera when I came back to the dugout and I mouthed the words, 'That's for you Cassie.'"

He may have been ailing, but Gruber was still playing an aggressive heads-up kind of ballgame — as in heads-up and head-first into first base, which is not a recommended procedure. Milt Dunnell, in his *Toronto Star* column, suggested that what Gruber needed during these discomfiting times with the fans was a touch of arrogance. Dunnel wrote: "He should tell somebody: 'Hey, I'm one of the best damn third basemen in the game today.' And he would be telling it like it is."

What remained of the public's charity towards Gruber was rapidly dwindling. Nor were fans the least bit appeased a few days later when Gruber cracked his sixth homerun of the season in a game against the Twins that featured a bench-clearing rhubarb. He repeated the feat two days later against Chicago at Comiskey Park. Of course, the day after that he committed three errors, equaling a team record for ineptitude by a third baseman.

When the Jays winged back to Toronto to take on the Milwaukee Brewers they were still grouchy. Again the players poured off the bench after Joe Carter rushed the mound, convinced that Jamie Navarro had been throwing at his noggin. In the melee that ensued, Gruber stood out as one of the most animated participants, but he suffered another boo-boo to his hand in the process. It looked like a sprained thumb and Gruber was out of the game, though the Jays insisted he had not hurt himself during the scuffling. Tests later showed that it was actually a bone bruise at the base of the right thumb. Status day-to-day.

This was probably not the wisest time for Gruber to do what he did next: admonish SkyDome fans for riding the players. The third baseman was miffed at the nasty treatment that had been accorded reliever Tom Henke in a recent contest. The message somehow got warped in the delivery. "We're all in this together," he had observed, "the players and the fans. If we're going to succeed, the fans are going to have to help. I just want the fans to understand something. Nobody likes to fail, nobody likes to have rotten days. Some of our players have had tremendous starts;

others slow. But the team is off to a pretty good start and it can only get better, if the fans stay on our side. We seem to have a few fans who come to the park with nothing to do but get on somebody, calling out stuff. They should realize when you go through bad times, nobody feels worse than you do. When (the fans) are at the office, nobody comes to call you a bum and boo you."

A couple of months down the road, Dave Winfield would try the exact same gimmick, and everyone would call him a genius as he got the desired effect. But Winfield is more articulate and couched his plea in appealing language. He was also having a hell of a season, unlike Gruber. Gruber's plaint sounded like sour grapes, as if he were taking the fans to task for their reaction to his own poor performance. They were not amused and let him know it, firing off letters to newspapers and delivering even more verbal venom at the park. As one of those newspaper letters declared: "If we are all in this together, then why doesn't he share the wealth with the fans?"

In July, the Jays called up third baseman Tom Quinlan from Triple A Syracuse and placed Gruber on the 15-day disabled list retroactive to June 28. He had wrenched his knee on a fielding play at Cleveland. The injury was diagnosed as a strain of the posterior capsule. He later underwent an MRI which revealed no serious damage but Gruber told club officials that the pain was persisting and he was unable to play.

On his own, he went and got a second opinion from a specialist in Los Angeles whose findings were pretty much the same as the first, with maybe a touch of tendinitis thrown in to compound the pain, and perhaps aggravated by a bit of a strained hamstring where it attaches to the back of the left knee. Gruber had been out of the line-up, at that point, for 19 straight games, 25 of 26. At the same time, he seemed heartened that the pain was not as severe as it had been up till the All-Star break. "We've gone and changed anti-inflammatories and the knee seems to be responding. The pain is very bearable. There are some lateral movements that bother me and running backwards irritates it but it's not like I've got a punctured lung or anything. The thing is, when I do come back, I just want to be absolutely sure there's no chance of me going backwards again. The pain's not too great to play but I'm concerned about being able to play right through it. I don't want them to take me off the DL, then, bang, have to put me right back on it."

Then a mischievous story broke in a Toronto paper. Marty York, a *Globe and Mail* columnist, quoted sources who maintained that Gruber had been seen playing tennis and water skiing at an Ontario resort during the All-Star break, when he was on the disabled list. General manager Gillick said he was unconcerned about the allegations. "I don't know what he did," he told the *Toronto Star's* Allan Ryan. "I don't know what he should or shouldn't be doing. Something like swimming, I'd imagine that's probably even good for his injury. The thing is, if a guy says he's hurt, and is physically and mentally not ready to play, there is not a whole lot you can do. You can't send a guy out there who says he's not ready."

At first, Gruber refused to defend himself but, as the account travelled to his teammates' ears, he tried to undo the damage. He admitted that he was in a ski-boat during the three-day break, which he had spent with his family at a resort in cottage country, "but that was as close as I got to skiing." He had splashed in a wading pool with his son Kody. "That's far from swimming. And I never stepped on a tennis court," he told Allan Ryan.

"Look, just because I'm hurt doesn't mean that life has to cease. I'm still doing all my work. I'm still taking batting practice. Just now, I ran my first sprints since the injury. Whatever I do, I try to stay within the boundaries. But the thing is, those are my three days off and, if I want to jump off the Empire State Building, by golly, that's what I'll do."

Whatever the case, on July 23 Gruber was back in the saddle at third base after 21 games out of the line-up. He contributed a single, a walk, a sac bunt and a sac fly in five trips to the plate during the 9-3 win over Oakland but he wasn't making any declarations that the knee was sound again. "There's no guarantees...there's no guarantees in life. All I can do is my best. That's all I can promise."

Within a week, he had struck for his first home run since returning to active duty. "It felt good to be back and doing something half-decent," he sighed with relief, after executing the 369-footer against the Kansas City Royals. It came in his first home park appearance since his extended hiatus and was also his first extra-base hit since June 2. "I was nervous," he allowed.

Ironically, the tater, which complemented some impressive defensive work, carried straight over the top of a sign in left field that read: "Gruber for rent, keep Kent."

He told reporters that it had been an awful year and that he was aware of the fans' disenchantment with his play, his frequent absences. "I know that no matter what I do, destiny will happen. Things are going to come crashing down sometimes but it's not going to kill me. It's not do or die."

What else could go wrong? Well, in a game at Yankee Stadium, Gruber threw a fit after striking out. He also threw a whole bunch of equipment, some of which struck shortstop Manuel Lee. This was adding insult to injury, and not even his own.

His return to the line-up was short-lived. After playing in seven games, he was back on the gimp because of continued soreness in his left knee and hamstring. And the neck, bothering him since Day One, had never really improved. In Boston, he went missing and showed up at the ballpark just an hour before game-time with his clutch of MRI negatives. That's when Cito Gaston hit the wall on his Gruber-endurance. With the third baseman continuing to resist a return to his position, the Jays went into Detroit and dropped three out of four.

Gaston was not the only one growing weary of Gruber's maladies, whether real or exaggerated. When the team wound its way back to Toronto after their miserable 2-5 road trip, a summit meeting was called in the skipper's office. On hand were Gaston, Gillick, assistant general manager Gordon Ash, and club president Paul Beeston.

Gruber would say later that he had already been mulling over his predicament, ruminating on his future. He had concluded that he had three options, which he says he presented to his quartet of inquisitors. "I was really hurting, I'd tried my durnedest to get in those games in Detroit. Every time I said, yeah, put me in coach, seems like 20 minutes later someone had planted a dagger in my back. Couldn't breathe, couldn't cough, it was killing me."

The options he presented to the Blue Jays that day were these: He could go back on the disabled list, he could return to every day status and do his job, or he could perform spot duty, riding the bench until called upon. The decision to resume full duties was made then, behind that closed door. "I told them I was willing to go back full-time," said Gruber.

This, in spite of the fact that his suffering had been more acute than many realized, or chose to believe. When swinging, his arm would sometimes go numb and when sprinting to the base, he often felt a stab of pain so piercing that it was "like sticking your finger in a light socket." On occasion, the pain would cause him to black out for a few seconds.

Beeston listened patiently to this recital of woe. Then he told Gruber he wanted him out there. The team needed him out there. "I think you're wrong," Beeston told his third baseman. "I think you can go out there. Let's do it buddy."

Gruber says he was heartened by the faith Beeston showed in him. "With all that was going on, I was confused," he would later tell his biographer, Kevin Boland. "I needed direction from the guys that invested in me. I'm glad Beeston helped me go the way we did. It built a lot of character in me. It made me grow a bit. It made me a better ballplayer."

If he had disappointed the team and the fans, he had most of all dissatisfied himself. "It's one thing playing with less than you want to have. It's another thing accepting you don't have it, and keeping your head up when you fail. Maybe I couldn't do all I'd come to expect of myself but I did what I could and had some success. That's what makes this game so great. It's not just offence. It's not just defence. There are so many sides to it. You can't let one affect the other."

He told other reporters afterwards that what he'd feared most was that he was suffering from a disk problem in his neck and was overcome with relief that this did not seem to be the case. "It eases my mind," he said, after that sobering conference in Gaston's office. "I just wanted to be able to rule out surgery, or any of those bad things."

On August 10, against the Orioles, Gruber was at his post. He executed a couple of nice defensive plays but left six runners aboard on an 0-for-4 night. The Jays were content to have his glove back in the game. His return also made it possible for the club to swing a deal with the Yankees. Gruber's constant replacement at third, Jeff Kent, was dispatched to New York along with outfield prospect Ryan Thompson in exchange for strikeout ace David Cone. And would the Jays have managed to win the division without Mr. Cone down the stretch?

Gruber's first RBI of the month came on August 30, in a 5-3 decision over the Brewers. The season moved inexorably forward, with the third baseman trying to shut out the jeers of the crowd. Then, on September 1, he was given a moment of grace. He had struck out in the sixth inning and, when he came to the plate one frame later with the bases loaded, the belligerent crowd heaped abuse upon his head. Gruber smashed a grand-slam homerun. The 50,409 schizophrenic patrons at the SkyDome leapt to their feet, all uncharitable thoughts of Gruber forgotten. The standing ovation continued as Gruber trotted around the bases and to the dugout. That may have been the apogee of his season. The regular season, anyway.

The fans, now that they were momentarily in love with Gruber again, wanted to have their affections acknowledged. They continued to clap and cheer, expecting to draw Gruber out of the dugout with some kind of salutation. After a few moments, he did step out onto the top step but only briefly, barely doffing his cap. Some of his teammates had suggested he not show the fans even this tiny courtesy, but Gruber did not wish to be vindictive, he wasn't playing hard to get. "I know they want me to do good," he said of the fans. It's just that they didn't know, hadn't been told, about the nature or extent of his injuries. He wanted it kept that way, he said. "I don't want to get into what my game consists of and what I can't do."

The fan support would ebb and flow as the season rushed headlong towards its conclusion. Those who cheered fondly one night would boo lustily the next. But that's baseball. Gruber finally understood that.

He would have one more evening of brightness in the regular campaign. It came in Arlington, in front of his fellow Texans, when his big stick led the way in a 15-hit Jay attack over the Rangers. In the 7-5 affair, Gruber drove in three runs with a 3-for-5 effort, including his 11th homer, his last of '92, excluding post-season. "Some days are good, some days are bad. This was one of the good ones."

If someone was keeping a ledger, then Gruber paid for his Texas triumph just a handful of days later in a game against the Tribe. He was covering third when former teammate Mark Whiten came sliding in hard. Blinded on the play, Gruber had his legs knocked out from under him, landing squarely on his tailbone. But Whiten's sliding effort brought his legs grinding into Gruber's underpinnings, making savage contact with the left shin, calf and ankle. Jays ended up 7-5 victors, but Gruber had a horrible bruise as a memento.

"My next at-bat, I noticed the ankle rolling away," Gruber said. "First thing I thought when I was in the box was, 'Oh-oh, here I go again.' Then I figured it was just time to accept being hurt. "

The next night, he was in the line-up as the Jays cakewalked over the Rangers 13-0. The ankle was tightly taped. "Tonight it was just tape, treatment and bear it. I made a vow they'd have to wheel me off once I got back in there."

It was a promise he kept.

# Glory Jays

## *Something Juan-derful*     10

Something wonderful, something wild.

Or perhaps that should be Juan-derful. As in The Great Juan, The Juan and only, Juan for the money, Juan singular sensation, Juan-ton soup. Juan can get carried away with this stuff.

If nothing else, the sudden emergence of Juan Guzman as the bulwark of the Toronto Blue Jay pitching staff made headline writers in local newspapers happy, as they merrily churned out Juan, uh, *pun*ishing caption after another. But their glee was nothing compared to that of the club brass who discovered within their own minor league system an anchor for their present and future baseball felicity.

The wonderful part was the strike-out arm that could send a ball whistling past hitters at speeds of well over 95 miles an hour. The wild part was the uncontrollable arm that could send a ball whistling past catchers at speeds of well over 95 miles an hour. He was the best of hurlers, he was the worst of hurlers: it was only a matter of inches that could make the difference on any given night. But in the late spring of 1991, fate and futility combined to bring about the union of Juan Guzman and the Blue Jays.

Futile was the verdict on Dave Stieb's chances for recuperating quickly from an ailing back problem that had taken him out of the rotation not long into the '91 season — and would keep him on the shelf for almost a full year. That had the Jays scrambling for an immediate replacement. It was with some reluctance that they turned to Guzman on their Triple A Syracuse staff. As a youngster, originally in the Los Angeles Dodgers system, he had continually struggled with his control and there was considerable doubt whether he would ever find the poise, the throwing discipline, to make it to the majors.

The Dodgers likely didn't think so. They traded him to the Jays on September 22, 1987 for infielder Mike Sharperson and few took notice of the transaction at the time. For Guzman, there was at least some cultural familiarity as a Blue Jay possession. He was a native of the Dominican Republic and Toronto had long scoured the baseball lots of that particular Caribbean island for future prospects. Under the scouting direction of Epy Guerrero, they had nurtured the talents of islanders such as Alfredo Griffin, George Bell, Tony Fernandez and Manuel Lee. It was in fact rather unusual that Guzman, who grew up playing on the streets of Santo Domingo with his pal Ramon Martinez, should have escaped the Jays' scrutiny in his youth, and been developed by the Dodgers instead.

Guzman entered the Jays' family at the Double A level, with the Knoxville farm team. He was third in the league in strikeouts there, in spite of his erratic control. He spent three years in the Southern League before being promoted to Syracuse, following a winter in Venezuela where he posted a 7-1 record with a 1.69 ERA. At spring training in '91, Guzman showed enough promise to impress pitching coach Galen Cisco who opined that the kid had "pretty good stuff," though nobody was paying much heed to this quiet newcomer to camp.

He was sent off with the Syracuse squad as the Jays concentrated on the real business of baseball once the '91 campaign got underway. But over the ensuing weeks, the news drifting up from the International League was that Toronto had a legitimate fireballer in their indentured underling. By mid-May, Guzman was leading that league with 34 strikeouts in 36 innings, although he had also walked 28 opponents. The men who called the shots in Toronto remained dubious. By June, however, they had little choice but to bring him up.

The mysterious righthander came to Toronto as an "insurance policy" for the ailing Stieb. In order to make room for him on the roster, the Jays put bumbling baserunner Kenny Williams (the fellow will go down in history for one particular night when he skedaddled from second to third to second to third to home all on the same play, decking third-base coach John McClaren in the process) on waivers. Williams was claimed by the Montreal Expos and Guzman was, presto, a Blue Jay. The 24-year-old had appeared in 12 games for the Syracuse Chiefs thus far that season,

11 as a starter, compiling a 4-5 record with a 4.03 ERA. But he had struck out 67 batters in as many innings, while walking 42.

On June 7, he made an inauspicious debut in Baltimore. He threw 97 pitches through 4 1/3 innings, giving up six hits and three walks while striking out five as the Orioles prevailed 6-4. Most of the hits were groundballs. "I was doing my best but the ball just kept going through the infield," said Guzman. "On the walks, I was just missing a little bit."

The walks, which had haunted him throughout his entire career, had hurt him yet again. But his other stuff had made a mighty impression on the Oriole hitters. Jose Mesa was so intrigued that he made a point of seeking out the guy who operates the radar gun. It turned out Guzman had the highest clockings of anyone at Memorial Stadium so far in the season — 95 miles per hour. Even his sliders were whipping across in the 88-90 range. Too bad not enough of the pitches were for strikes.

The Jays, still not convinced that they had a raw jewel in Guzman, were also experimenting with reliever Mike Timlin in the starting rotation. Who could blame Toronto for lacking faith in their young call-up, who had earlier been left unprotected and unclaimed in the December Rule 5 draft. Nevertheless, they continued sending him out there. In his next turn, again facing Baltimore, Guzman once more walked a trio, one in each of the first three innings, and every one of those free passes came around to score. Second game, second loss: 8-4. "He's a kid and he's gonna make mistakes," said Cisco. "But you can't beat yourself like that. You've got to make them beat you." Meanwhile, the news on Stieb remained disheartening, which demanded that Guzman be kept around. "That's all we've got right now," lamented manager Cito Gaston. "Guzman was great this past winter. We thought he'd overcome that stuff (too many walks), but he's been walking people in Triple A too. He's got a great arm. Hopefully, one of these days he'll get it together."

One of these days turned out to be immediately. The third time was the charm for Guzman and that charm didn't wear off straight through the year. He would not lose a game again until the very last night of the regular season. In the interim, he would become a godsend for the Jays, the boy from the barrio who would lead them out of the wilderness of their pitching woes. Given the opportunity, he may even have led them out of the wilderness in the American League championship series, but he was never given that chance. He would be assigned only one game in that five-frame pratfall. It was the only game the Jays would win.

But all that, while in the past now, was in the future then. Who could have predicted as Guzman took the mound against the Cleveland Indians on June 22, 1991, that he would rattle off 10 consecutive victories, a club record? There should have been more, too, lots more, if the bullpen hadn't let him down: 10 no-decisions in that stretch.

In the third game of his major league career, Guzman blanked the Indians 4-0. Afterwards, he tried to scoot out of the clubhouse before the reporters caught up with the big story of the night. Cornered, he was modest and perfunctory in his comments. "Everything's getting better. I'm working and getting used to the league." He recorded another shut-out his next time out, a 1-0 squeaker over 7 2/3 innings against the Twins at Minneapolis. His pitches were timed at between 95 and 97 miles per hour. In Seattle, he chilled the Mariners 5-2 with eight innings of three-hit heat.

And so it went. On August 27, Guzman finally managed to beat the Orioles too — the only team that had defeated him in The Show. Twice. He did it 6-1 in Baltimore with his first ever major league complete game. He had seen a lot of the Birds by now and he had not forgotten those first two disappointments. "Yeah, I remember. That was me before. Nervous. Trying too hard. Now? I got all kinds of experience now." Did he sound cocky? Perhaps. But he'd just struck out eight and walked nary a soul. Another first.

He had been worried, he admitted, after those two initial losses to Baltimore. "After those guys my first two times, I'm thinking how I don't want to go back to the minors. They tell me: 'Just relax, do the job.' Tonight, I showed what I learned — lots of fastballs first time (through the order), some sliders the second time, then mix it all up with some changeups after that."

Guzman was now, after 14 starts, 5-2 with eight no-decisions and a 2.97 ERA. Said Gene Tenace, who was subbing for an invalid Gaston: "Tonight, he really pitched, he didn't just throw. He might really be starting to develop." Talk about going out on a limb.

In September, he threw a nifty two-hitter against the Indians over seven innings, although the final result was in some doubt once the unstable (in relief of Guzman anyway) bullpen got in on the act. The Tribe assembled a late four-run charge after the starter departed. "I never thought the game would get so close," Guzman fretted, after the Jays had nailed it 7-4. "Geez, I was getting scared." With good reason, too. At that point, he had nine no-decisions in 17 starts. "This keeps happening to me. I don't know why. I've got nine no-decisions and we've got an excellent bullpen."

It was the same story his next appearance, when Guzman left the proceedings with Toronto leading the Mariners 4-2. Seattle rebounded for a 5-4 victory when the Jays' bullpen forfeited a bases-loaded walk in the bottom of the 11th inning. The run was charged to Guzman. "I feel if I can go six or seven innings and only give up two or three runs, I've done my job," a frustrated Guzman said afterwards. "We have a chance to win. But so many times the bullpen hasn't been able to do it. And we've got such a good bullpen. That's what makes it tough."

In Oakland, the following week, Guzman hung tough for eight innings, reluctant to turn over the ball. The Jays held on 3-2 and Guzman described the contest as his most satisfying start yet. "I had good control. Everything that I planned worked out." Equally impressive was that Guzman was showing maturity on the hill. He didn't fall apart after errors by Kelly Gruber and the usually reliable Robbie Alomar put the victory in peril. The win kept Toronto 1 1/2 games up on the Boston Red Sox. The rookie was now 8-2 with a 3.13 earned run average. In 18 starts, he had averaged seven innings and allowed more than three earned runs only three times.

Number nine came against the Minnesota Twins, as the Jays shaved their magic number for claiming the division to seven games. He gave up three hits over eight innings, walked another three, and struck out nine. That tied the Blue Jay record for consecutive victories by a starter. On October 1, he claimed sole possession of that honor with a 5-2 dismissal of the California Angels at the SkyDome, as the Jays clinched no worse than a tie for the American League East.

It seemed for the longest time that Guzman would never lose. But he did, in his last starting assignment of the regular season,

3-1 to the Twins at the Metrodome. It was a meaningless game by then, since these two clubs were set to do battle in the playoffs within days. "Tonight, it's not important," Guzman sniffed. "The next one, that's important, and that's what I'm getting ready for."

By now, baseball savants — at least all those not employed in the decision-making suite of the Blue Jay franchise — were pulling for an early playoff appearance by Guzman. Why not have the kid start the championship series, the way he was throwing? Too radical an idea for Gaston et al, who opted to start Tom Candiotti. In the five-game dalliance that ensued, Guzman — who had continually bailed out his faltering club down the stretch — would be the only victorious pitcher for the Jays, the first rookie to win a playoff game since Charles Hudson of the Philadelphia Phillies beat Los Angeles in 1983. Before his appearance in Game Three, he described his simple approach to his assignment: "Like always, I don't overthink. I find my release point and I throw the ball over the plate. I try to get the first guy out; I try to get the second guy out; I try to get all nine guys. Then I try to get all nine guys the whole game."

His routine did not change one iota. In the days preceding the start, Guzman stuck to his work-out regimen, which included getting to the ballpark earlier than anyone else so he could spend an hour running stairs. The lonely figure bounding through the stands had become a familiar figure by then. On game-day, he marched to the mound and confounded the Twinkie hitters through 5 2/3 innings before Gaston lifted him for Tom Henke with Toronto leading 3-2. This time, the lead was not squandered by the relievers as the Jays added two more runs for a 5-2 final in the other team's ballpark.

Guzman had been described earlier as something wonderful and something wild. On that playoff night, he had brought both personalities to the park. He also brought a scowl, some grit and a complete disdain for the pressures of playoff baseball. In case there were any skeptics left, that performance, which gave Toronto a 1-1 split in the series, marked the complete emergence of a future star from the chrysalis of youthful obscurity. With the perspiration dripping from his nose and the damp tendrils of his moussed perm flopping in springy coils over his brow and down the nape of his neck, he looked rather like that other Minnesota glamor dandy, the rock singer Prince, in mid-concert sweat. Brim of his cap drawn down low to shade his eyes, grimacing at the batters, with smoke flaring from his nostrils and from the tips of his fingers.

For a poor kid, who had grown up on the dusty streets of Santo Domingo, this was his moment of glory. Afterwards, he remembered the boy he had been, one of five children born to a construction worker and housewife, reared in a house that didn't even have indoor plumbing until recently. It was the house where Guzman still lived, when he wasn't playing summer ball in Toronto and winter ball in Venezuela.

"That first time I picked up the ball, it felt...natural. I knew I had the ability, the natural talent." He had started as an outfielder but switched to pitching, by his own volition, at age 13, which made him back-up to a childhood buddy by the name of Ramon Martinez, still one of his closest friends. Pretty soon he was thinking of nothing else. "My parents were worried. They wanted me to continue to go to school. But finally they said, do what you want to do. I could sign this contract and I could try to have a career. I could always go back to school, but maybe I could not go back to baseball. I thought I could make it. But never in my wildest dreams did I think it would turn out like this. Me, starting in a playoff game, as a rookie. I think the Lord has been with me."

He wanted the ball again, on three days rest, to pitch Game 5. It was not to be. Candiotti got the nod and took the loss. When the free agency offers came in, he also took a walk to the Dodgers.

In the off-season, Guzman was runner-up to Minnesota second baseman Chuck Knoblach as American League rookie of the year. The Jays were fortunate that their young phenom was not eligible for arbitration. Just imagine what Toronto would have had to pay if Guzman was earning a salary commensurate with his contributions. His estimated salary for last season was a paltry $220,000.

At spring training, a year ago, the expectations for Guzman were lofty. He was a prisoner of his own unanticipated excellence; at least, he would have been, had he been made of weaker stuff. Mused Cisco one day: "It was really something, that stretch of his. I don't remember too many bad innings. It'll be strange if he loses three or four in a row and people have to start asking what's wrong with Juan Guzman. It's almost like he made us forget he's human."

Guzman understood this but he was not rattled by it. "It's like I tell the little kids in the Dominican this year. I tell them baseball's like school — the more you work, the more you learn. And I work hard too. What I did last year was good but I don't want there to be just one year. I don't just want to be here two years. I want to be here a long time."

A long time may be a difficult frame of reference from the perspective of a pitcher only in his sophomore campaign in the majors. But Guzman started up where he had left off six months earlier. One day, in spring training, he almost threw a no-hitter in batting practice, of all things. During the winter respite, he'd also had time to think. And one of the things he'd thought about was all those no-decisions from '91. What he wanted, in 1992, was to be the master of his own fate. That meant staying out on the mound into the late innings of a ball game and to hell with the team's penchant for giving its hurlers the hook after 100 or so pitches.

"I want to throw 230 to 250 innings this year," he announced one afternoon. "I want to be able to go nine innings." He was well aware of the conservative-minded pitching professors on the club but he was insistent. "I think I can change that. As long as you're not tired, still throwing good, then they're not going to take you out. When you work hard, you get more consistent. And your arm doesn't get tired." To that end, he was fiendish about his training. On top of his regular workout and extra running, Guzman had taken to dropping by a local health club almost daily to work up an extra sweat. "I feel good. I don't have any pressure on me. Now I just need to get ready, throw hard, do my best. That's all."

Gaston started the season by slipping Guzman into the third spot in the five-man rotation, behind Jack Morris and Jimmy Key. With Morris the ace on the staff — how else to describe a guy who was lured away from the Twins for $5 million a season? — it was determined that Guzman's righthanded fastballs and deadly sinkers would make a nice contrast following Key's lefthanded breaking stuff.

Some bugaboos notwithstanding — Key's stuff was mostly stiff throughout much of the year — the plan worked. In his first game of the '92 campaign, Guzman polished off the Tigers nicely through seven innings in Detroit, as the Jays took the game 3-1 and the series 3-0. However, he had to get past a rocky first frame to do it. "Yeah, the first," said Guzman. "I get out of the first inning, I'm fine." (This would become a mantra as the season progressed.)

On April 14, Guzman prevailed in his second start although on this night he looked immensely hittable — he gave up eight hits and three runs over six innings — as the Jays doubled up the New York Yankees 12-6. "It's not the way I wanted to pitch," Guzman admitted. His next tango, in Boston on April 19th, felt like deja-vu. He came out of the game after six innings with a 2-1 lead on a dull performance during which he allowed four hits, issued five walks and threw two wild pitches. While he was showering, the Sox rallied for a 5-4 victory. The bullpen couldn't hold it, again, but it wasn't as if a stellar Guzman start had been wasted in the process.

Whatever had been bothering Guzman was no longer a problem when the Kansas City Royals came to town. His running fastball and tricky off-speed stuff handcuffed the Royals as the Jays nosed out a 4-3 victory, thereby improving their best-ever start to 14-4. Guzman's bid for a complete-game shutout was spoiled in the ninth by an RBI double off the bat of Wally Joyner, which brought out Tom Henke. That would be the same Joyner whose line drive to left had earlier broken off Guzman's opening string of 12 consecutive Royals set down.

The Gooze had said he wanted those complete game starts but in Milwaukee, next time out, he pumped out a season-high 128 pitches through seven shutout innings before giving way to Duane Ward with a 1-0 lead. The latter, on a horrendous evening, forfeited three runs and the game in the eighth. For his part of the affair, Guzman had walked four Brewers but he'd also stranded another quartet of runners at third. He was getting himself in trouble but he was also getting himself out of trouble.

Ward atoned for his miscues in Oakland on May 5, when he picked up Guzman again in the seventh. Toronto was leading 2-1 when Guzman walked himself into trouble, putting runners on second and third. Enter Wardo, who induced a pop foul from Rickey Henderson to end the threat. Kelly Gruber then sealed matters with a three-run blast in the eighth to secure a 5-1 Toronto victory. "That was a big relief," said Guzman, referring to Ward's cool rebuff of the A's. "No matter what has happened in the past, I know we've got a good bullpen. I have faith in them." Then, referring to all those blown leads in the past, he added: "Maybe now they are trying even harder for me."

Guzman capped that grueling 11-day road trip by throwing another corker of a game at Anaheim, where the Jays dumped the Angels 4-1. The win, which halted a two-game losing streak for Toronto, also marked Guzman's first complete game victory of the season and was only the second in his major league career. In doing so, and improving his record to 5-0 on the year, he conceded only four hits. His fastball was clocked on the radar gun at 91 to 95 miles per hour but Guzman still figured that day's effort was merely his second best of the campaign, preferring an earlier confrontation with the Royals as his personal gem. Cumulatively, he had allowed only nine runs in the seven games he had started, pitching a total of 50 1/3 innings. His ERA had dropped to a minuscule, and league-leading, 1.61. Although Jack McDowell of the Chicago White Sox was the most successful pitcher in the American League, 7-0 in seven starts, Guzman, with his two no-decisions and far less effective run support (58 versus 34), was viewed as a worthy equal.

The city of Toronto was learning something about Guzman as well. He was not as bland, as diffident, as might originally have been thought. That perception was due largely to an unwillingness to discourse extensively in English, a language he knew well enough but felt self-conscious about using in his first year with the Jays. Interviews were by necessity superficial encounters, barely scratching the surface of his character. It was all very quick and trifling: reporters didn't have the time or patience to analyze this baseball nova; Guzman was always in a terrible rush to get away from the park, often the first dressed and out of the clubhouse after a game. With journalists, Guzman could also appear cocky, brash, but this was more a case of dispassionate self-assessment than vanity. He remained pretty much the same off the mound as on it: totally cool.

His pitching was more cold than cool when he got the ball again on May 16 with the Mariners visiting the SkyDome. Despite the Jays spotting him to an early 3-0 lead on a monster home run from Dave Winfield, Guzman was unsure and sub-par on the afternoon, though he left with a 5-3 lead in the seventh. David Wells then obliged the opposition by coughing up a three-run homer, thereby costing Guzman another decision. Afterwards, Gaston excused his starter's weak contribution, which had included six hits and four runs. "He's entitled to have a day like

that. He couldn't get his fastball over, or his slider. He was kind
of a one-pitch pitcher, only a changeup, and then he couldn't get
that over."

The two leading moundsmen in the American League,
Guzman and McDowell, went mano-a-mano in Chicago the
following week. By the time it was over, it was McDowell who
had been taken to the mat, roughed up for nine hits and six runs
over 6 2/3 innings, as the Jays went on to a 6-2 decision. "Yeah,
a little bit easier than I expected," Guzman acknowledged. "But
not because of Jack McDowell. Jack McDowell don't hit. Those
other guys, though...I never faced Chicago before, either." He
had, in fact, held the White Sox to just five hits over eight innings,
and struck out seven — running his total to 62 on the year, just
four behind Boston's Roger Clemens.

The Jays' starting crew was now averaging almost seven
innings per outing, led by Guzman who had a 7.18 average.
Seven innings is exactly what he contributed in his next assignment, when the Jays blanked those same White Sox in the
SkyDome 3-0. Actually, Guzman left the game in a scoreless tie,
the first time in 10 starts through the season that he had departed
without a lead. Ward would eventually be credited with the W.
But it was Guzman who twice struck out former Blue Jay George
Bell, once with the bases loaded. That was in the first inning when
Guzman, still falling victim to his early inning wobblies, walked
the bases full. Then he bailed out of the mess by striking out Bell
with a wicked 3-2 changeup, and followed that by inducing a
ground ball out from Dan Pasqua. No damage, no problem. And,
in spite of his early difficulties throughout the season, he was still
the only Blue Jay pitcher not to concede a run in the first frame.
It may have been scary at times, but he always managed to pitch
himself out of the jams.

Guzman had been the Jay's top pitcher in both April and
May. June began on a more sour note after the Twins swamped
the Jays 11-3 at Minneapolis, pounding Guzman for seven runs
over a season-low five innings. It was his first loss in seven
decisions. "What I think," remarked an unbowed Guzman, "is
that you can't win them all." Not original but not untrue either.
The slender ERA, meanwhile, plumped out to 2.58 from 1.88. He
didn't have his deadly arsenal in New York the following week
either, but he still gave up only one run and four hits in seven
innings as the Jays edged the Yankees 2-1.

If there was anything unusual about Guzman's performance now it was that he was winning games he probably should have lost, a direct reversal of his fortunes from earlier in the season and the previous year when the bullpen had not come to the rescue. He was still pitching well, just not as well as everyone had come to expect. Yet he was able to regroup in time to save himself from disaster on the mound, and his teammates were coming through with timely hits. Against Boston in Toronto on June 14, he showed the erratic tendencies of old, but he still left the game in the seventh with a three-run lead. This time the victory did not escape him as the Jays blew out the Red Sox 6-2. "You have to have some luck and today we were lucky," observed Gaston. "Even though Guzman struggled, he still gave us a chance to win." How did he struggle? Well, he got three routine fly balls in the first before getting embroiled in a 34-pitch second, during which he walked in one of Boston's runs. It was actually John Olerud who saved the day, with a three-run double in the sixth that broke a 2-2 tie.

Guzman admitted to reporters that he was having difficulty getting untracked these days until the third or fourth inning. From that point on, he had become almost unhittable. But his teammates had to come up with sterling defensive plays or sudden off-setting offense to keep Toronto competitive until Guzman found his niche in the mid-innings. It happened again in Kansas City on June 20 when the Royals got their single run and all five of their hits off Guzman in the first two frames. Nothing after that, though, as the Jays cruised to a 6-1 final. "That's just normal for me," Guzman joked. "They're going to start keeping me out of the game until the third inning."

In Cleveland, the next week, Guzman was far more poised and never in trouble as the Jays squashed the Tribe 6-1. He struck out six, walked none and lowered his ERA to 2.13. All the Indians could dent him with were a couple of bunt and infield singles. But it was back to no-decision status against the Texas Rangers in the SkyDome on July 1 — Canada Day — in spite of giving up just two runs and five hits over eight innings, while striking out nine. The Jays were eventual 3-2 victors but no official credit went to Guzman. "I'm used to no-decisions," he told reporters. "It doesn't bother me." Some of those gathered 'round even believed him.

He was the club's player-of-the-month for June, with a 4-1 record, a 2.65 earned run average, and a staff-leading 31 strikeouts.

As a matter of course, he was also putting up the kind of numbers likely to snag him a spot in the upcoming All-Star game, an eventuality made even more probable when he and the Jays blanked the California Angels 3-0 in early July. During that encounter, Guzman tied a career-high stat by whiffing 10 batters which gave him a '92 strikeout total of 115, three more than Roger Clemens. In the process, Toronto's righty also overtook Boston's righty as the league's earned-run leader, lowering his ERA to a lean 2.01.

So it came as no surprise when Guzman, just barely a sophomore, was named to the All-Star team by coach Tom Kelly. The only startling part about that selection was that he didn't start the game in San Diego. That privilege fell to Kevin Brown. Guzman was not upset. "It's unbelievable," he said, recalling how he used to watch the All-Star spectacle on TV in the Dominican. "All my hard work has paid off. I feel proud of myself and happy. Everything's getting better and better."

Guzman lost his last pre-All-Star encounter, 3-1 to the Oakland A's, but who could quibble with a line-score of three runs in seven innings? Still, when he got to San Diego with maties Joe Carter and Robbie Alomar, Guzman remained the league leader in ERA, strikeouts, and opposition average against. "I've dreamed of this since I've been in baseball," he said with wonder upon his arrival at Jack Murphy Stadium. Actually, he croaked it, the result of a raw throat condition that had developed during the long flight from Toronto. "I'm not sick," he insisted. "I just can't talk."

It was an interesting game for Guzman, who followed Brown and Clemens to the mound. At the very least, you couldn't say he bored the crowd in his third-inning cameo, allowing two hits and a walk but then stiffing the National League by forcing the next batter to pop out with the bases loaded. Ho-hum.

When regular play resumed, Guzman ran his record to 12-2 while his team knocked off the Mariners 3-0 in Seattle. Now his earned run average was down to a flat 2.00 and there was much talk about Guzman becoming Toronto's first-ever 20-game winner. At this rate, what could possibly stop him?

The answer to that was injury. On July 23, Guzman took himself out of a game against the A's in Oakland. He departed in the third inning, complaining of muscle tightness in the back of his right shoulder. He had given up three hits and three walks in his brief appearance, though the Jays made 9-3 casualties out of the Athletics. The soreness Guzman had experienced was bothersome to him, and his club, but initial reports were upbeat. Relax, nothing to worry about, don't trouble yourself, was the message to Toronto fans.

For Guzman, this was another first in his career — the first time he had ever been betrayed by his strong, fiercely conditioned body. He didn't know quite how to react to the situation as he headed back to Toronto, still not convinced he would have to miss his next scheduled start. But there was a stab of anxiety when Guzman casually mentioned that the pain was similar to a tightness he had felt in his back through the later innings in each of the two starts previous to the Oakland game. So perhaps it wasn't just a sudden flare of agitated muscles that would respond immediately to a brief rest.

An examination by team physicians revealed that Guzman had strained muscles in the back of the right shoulder. Or, to put it more clinically, he was suffering from a strain in both the latissamus dorsi, which supports the shoulder, and the tres minor, one of the four rotator cuff muscles. Those are alarming words when mentioned in the same breath as pitching: rotator cuff. Ironically, the man tagged to replace him in the starting rotation, if only for one turn, was the now recovered (but perhaps not altogether) Dave Stieb.

The Gooze swallowed his medicine and took the prescribed hiatus from action. He was back at his sentry post, 60-feet 6-inches from home plate, on August 3 at Fenway Park. It was to have been a headliner match-up, Guzman versus Clemens. But the anticipated showdown was no-contest. Clemens and his Sox rolled to an easy 7-1 decision and Guzman was toast after just 4 1/3 innings during which he was tagged for six earned runs on four hits and four walks. As if all that wasn't trying enough, Guzman was humiliated when Billy Hatcher stole home with the game's second run. Most ominous of all, he was still hurting. The layoff had made little difference. His fastball was still there but the other pitches, particularly his changeup, were pure hell on his back. "Coming back like this was tough. I was trying to work on something different because of the pain in my shoulder. That's why all the walks."

A couple of days later, Guzman woke up in extreme pain. It became apparent to one and all that he would not be throwing anything, except maybe fits, for a while yet. What was also becoming obvious was the likelihood that the Jays, anxious for a stronger foothold in the AL East, had allowed their young reliable to come back before he was ready. Nor was Gaston overly sympathetic when he ambled onto the field to remove Guzman in that encounter with Boston. The two men stood on the mound, jawing and gesticulating, though most of the pantomime was provided by Gaston. What was he so mad about? Well, one version of events had it that the manager had called for a changeup to Wade Boggs which Guzman had refused to deliver. It hurt too much.

If Toronto had been rash in getting Guzman back in the saddle, it was a mistake that would not be repeated, even as the Jays stumbled through early August. And even as they watched a fairly healthy lead over Baltimore and Milwaukee shrink to a precious few games. "I think I'll miss one or two starts," predicted the eternally optimistic Guzman. "I got to be 100 percent ready the next time I go out there."

In his absence, the other starters sagged under the pressure, while most of the hitters appeared to take the rest of the month off, bats in tow. On August 4, Guzman was put on the 15-day disabled list and millions of Toronto fans began to chew on their fingernails. A precautionary MRI on Guzman's shoulder did not show any further damage to the rotator cuff. All he could do was rest and devise a modified exercise regimen that would help to strengthen the particularly stressed-out muscles in his shoulder. But on the day when he was scheduled to start throwing lightly, he was unable to do so because of continuing soreness. Now even Guzman was anxious and nervous about throwing.

The Jays got their indisposed hitter an appointment with an expert in Alabama who specialized in sports injuries. After checking him out, the orthopedic specialist ordered Guzman to lay off the arm for another couple of weeks. That doctorly advice came on August 17. Two days later he was throwing off the mound, if still at a modest 70-percent capacity, and pronounced himself pain-free. With an anxious Pat Gillick on hand as a spectator, Guzman appeared in a game with his former Triple A club, the Syracuse Chiefs. In three ragged innings he surrendered six singles and two earned runs. It was the first time he had pitched in a game situation in 20 days and his handlers limited him to a ceiling of 75 pitches. The fastballs were up to 92 miles per hour and the sliders and changeups were still there. Guzman pronounced himself fit for major league duties that weekend, but Gillick was not entirely persuaded. Now he needed insurance for the man who had come to him as insurance. Accordingly, he scooped up David Cone from the New York Mets. "If Guzman comes up lame on Sunday, you're a hell of a lot better off having David Cone sitting there," said Gillick.

Guzman rejoined Toronto on August 30 at the SkyDome to take on the Milwaukee Brewers, one of only two clubs he had never beaten (the other being the Texas Rangers.) In his absence, the Jays had gone 10-14 in games won and lost. In games that had been started by either Jack Morris or Guzman, the Jays were 35-13 on the season. With other starters, they were 38-43. In order to clear a spot on the rotation, the club optioned lefty reliever Bob MacDonald to Syracuse for the second time that year.

Milwaukee had just taken two straight from the Jays as Guzman came out to do his business that Sunday afternoon. They had also shamed the Jays in the process, first with a 22-2 imbroglio and then by stealing eight bases to mess up Cone's debut as a Jay. Finally, with Guzman back in place, sanity prevailed at the SkyDome. The Jays prevailed too, 5-3, although Guzman — held to a strict pitch count — was limited to four innings. More critical than the two doubles he forfeited, or the single walk, was the fact he fanned three, threw first-ball strikes to 13 of 16 batters, and hit 94 miles per hour on the radar gun. He even pulled the irritating changeup out of the bag on about 10 occasions, including once when he used it to fan Robin Yount. Most critically, he did it without feeling any twinges of pain. "It's all right," he assured the nervous Nellies. "I think I'm 100 percent."

Suddenly, the situation didn't seem so dire anymore. The Jays had salvaged a split with the Brewers and they would never have to meet them again, barring a tie-breaking division playoff game. When Minnesota came to town, Guzman was back in the groove of the rotation albeit a little fitful as he gave up five hits and four bases on balls. But he also struck out nine in the five innings allotted to him under the continuing, if expanded, pitch limit. The Dr. Jeckyl/Mr. Hyde nature of his pitching persona was most evident in the first inning, in which he struck out the side but also allowed a run on two hits and a walk, used up 31 of his allotted pitches, and took 20 minutes to do it. The 7-3 Toronto victory was Guzman's first since July 18 and improved his record to 13-3 on the year.

He may not have entirely figured out the Brewers but Guzman finally discovered the winning combination necessary to deflect the Rangers when the Jays ventured to Arlington Stadium in September. It was a make-up game and Guzman got the nod, as well as the 7-5 win over Texas, but his pitching was not of Juan-caliber. He threw a ridiculous 99 pitches over the five innings he lasted, while allowing three runs on eight hits and two walks. The bullpen saved this one for him, over a long haul. Afterwards, the Gooze had no time to analyze his performance for the media. His girlfriend, who didn't speak English, had been scheduled to arrive that day from the Dominican Republic. She hadn't made it by the prescribed time and Guzman bolted from the clubhouse to look for her as soon as he had dressed.

It was more of the deliberate, dawdling stuff against Cleveland, back in Toronto, where Guzman coughed up three runs to the Tribe in the first inning. In that frame, the righthander took about 30 minutes to serve up 28 pitches, each one delivered in molasses fashion. The Jays nevertheless rebounded for a 5-4 final and Guzman got his 15th W of the year. But even he acknowledged that he was becoming infamous for his slow, excruciating, first innings. "I've tried everything I can think of, but that's just the way I am. I have the problem all the time. Last year, same thing. I feel loose enough but I need time to make adjustments to the mound. It's not the same in the bullpen, warming up. I need the game to find my release point, to find the rhythm. I can't work quick if I don't find the release point." Fortunately, once he did find it, he was on cruise control. After giving up three singles and two walks in the adventurous first against the Tribe, Guzman conceded just four more singles the rest of the way, on another 68 pitches, and faced a minimum dozen hitters over his final four frames.

A curious irony was developing. By mid-September, Guzman led the majors in winning percentage. American League hitters were batting a measly, league-low .209 against him. He sported the third-best ERA at 2.49 and the fourth-most strikeouts, in spite of his time on the disabled list. And yet there was a sense that something was off about the rehabilitated Guzman; that this was not the smooth pitching machine of late '91 and early '92. He was not only lugubrious in his delivery to the plate through the early innings, he was not his overwhelming self. His lackadaisical pace was also having a negative impact on the Toronto fielders, who were having trouble acclimatizing themselves to the pace of the game behind their slow-starter.

The Rangers, on a return date to the SkyDome, took advantage of Guzman's hesitancy (and a crucial Devon White error), as they piled up a 7-0 lead, although they had to fight off a resurgent Toronto squad before nailing down their 7-5 win. Guzman departed with five runs on the board and the bases loaded with none out in the fifth. "Just not my day," he understated.

A dismissive remark but there was something definitely amiss with Guzman. It wasn't just the interminable length of time it was taking him to throw in the first inning. The man who had challenged Clemens for the AL lead in strikeouts had just one strikeout in each of his last two games. In New York, on September 26, he seemed to have relocated his stuff — most of it; his slider was still absent without leave — but his six-inning effort was wasted as the Jays were nipped 2-1. The second consecutive loss for Guzman was the first time that had happened since his first two career starts, more than a year earlier.

Then again, a two-game career losing streak is an enviable low water mark. And that's where Guzman ended it; the losing, that is. So it was appropriate and serendipitous that the young man who had rescued the team in some of its darkest hours should also be on the hill the day the Jays clinched their fourth division title. Moreover, it wasn't a corrupted victory, it wasn't a pitching struggle. It was a *fortissimo* effort that Guzman offered on October 3, one of his best turns ever: eight innings of one-hit baseball in a 3-1 victory over the Detroit Tigers at the SkyDome. Only a leadoff single by Mark Carreon in the sixth frame tainted an otherwise splendid performance. "He looked like a guy on a mission, didn't he?" marveled Cisco. "Like he wasn't going to be denied."

What was at stake, besides the division championship, was the opening assignment in the playoffs. Guzman, who had arguably earned that honor in 1991, didn't get it then. And, with Jack Morris capturing 21 victories in his first campaign as a Blue Jay, Guzman didn't get it in 1992 either.

# Gl⦿ry Jays

## *The Swing's the Thing*

*11*

---

John Olerud is an oddball. Then again, maybe the only oddity about Olerud is that he is so darn *ordinary*. Not as a ballplayer, of course. The mere fact the kid matriculated directly from college ball to the major leagues with nary a night in the rough 'n' tumble environs of the minors makes his experience extraordinary. That his unassuming personality remained intact in the process is the strange part.

The enigma that is John Olerud has become something of a metaphysical question around the Toronto Blue Jays. He exists at first, therefore he is, no? But that would be too simple. The canvas of his character appeared so blank, such virgin territory, that strangers rushed in to fill the void. Surely there was more substance here than met the eye? Passions roiling beneath the unruffled surface perhaps? A quirky temperament lurking behind a tepid veneer? Dark secrets waiting to be revealed in a flash of illumination?

Nah.

In three years and a bit of watching John Olerud, there had been no sudden epiphany. The question — what makes John Olerud tick? — had been inverted to: Does this guy tick at all? How can any 24-year-old, and most particularly one thrust into the limelight of The Show, be so unflappable? Indeed, Olerud's equilibrium, the constancy of his disposition, had generally translated as vagueness. Vacuity. Vapidity. Vatever. He played first base, on occasion, as if he had been disengaged, unplugged, short-circuited. Earth to John, Earth to John...And then he would redeem himself with that sweet swing.

The swing's the thing. That's what caught the attention of Toronto scouts, the beagles who are paid to scour the nooks and crannies of the continent — and outlying islands — where boys play ball. In Olerud, a lumbering giant with lead in his feet and gold in his bat, they espied a natural resource that needed no further refining in the baseball mills of the minor league hinterland. So confident was the Blue Jay brass about Olerud's impending greatness that they were able to trade home run king Fred McGriff to the San Diego Padres before the 1991 campaign began in order to make room for the (relative) newcomer at first base. Besides, the previous winter's outfield experiment in the instructional league had not been a resounding success. If there was ever an athlete unfit to patrol the expanses of distant green meadow, it was John Olerud.

The defensive demands at first base are far less imposing than they might appear, though Olerud has managed to oftentimes turn his residency there into an unexpected adventure. One game this past season in particular comes to mind. Toronto and Minnesota tied at two apiece, Duane Ward on the mound with one out. The SkyDome denizens, no doubt fretting over traffic congestion and the last suburbs-bound commuter train, have already started to head for the gates. Hey, they can always find out the score when they get home. But Olerud's mental synapses seem to have followed them to the exits.

At the plate, Kirby Puckett's come-backer tips off Ward's glove and scoots far enough away that he can scramble safely to first. That brings up Kent Hrbek but Ward's mind is still on Puckett. Olerud's mind, on the other hand, is circling Pluto. With play still in progress, the first baseman — never much of a conversationalist — picks this moment to gab with his Twins' visitor. Ward, figuring to keep Puckett close, tosses over to first. Olerud never saw it, never expected it. The ball sails into space, where it was fortunate not to make contact with Olerud's fluttering brain. By the time the first baseman retrieves it, Puckett has beetled all the way to third and the Twins' dugout is convulsed with laughter. Ward can't believe it. Olerud is just stunned, a not uncommon condition. Thoroughly discombobulated by now, Ward gets Hrbek to pop foul for an out but then plonks Brian Harper in the ribs. Chili Davis slaps a single past a diving Manuel Lee to bring Puckett home, Gene Larkin singles to cash in Harper, then Greg Gagne executes a running bunt that Ward fields but underhands past the now attentive Olerud. That cashes in two more runs. Final score: Twins 6, Jays 2.

Afterwards, Puckett reconstructed events for reporters: "Just asking him how he was doing," he said of the chit-chat with Olerud. "I was standing there and the next thing I knew, I hear 'sssss' going by my head." Minutes later he offers a more detailed version of events. "I looked up to get the sign from the third-base coach and then I had my head down. I look up again and all of a sudden, the ball came flying by me and Olerud both. It's lucky the ball didn't hit me or him in the face. The way Ward throws, we'd be dead by now." Puckett also admitted that the close encounter of such a bizarre kind had been a first in his career. "You'll never see that again in a hundred years, I'll betcha."

Olerud was sheepish. "Very foolish," he agreed. "I wasn't expecting it but I should've been. (Ward) likes to throw over early and try to get the guy jumping off the bag. I wasn't even looking at the mound. Ahh, yes, I was talking." Ward's recollection of events was wry: "They were in deep conversation over there. If you find out what they were talking about, let me know." Manager Cito Gaston didn't know whether to laugh or cry. One thing he didn't do was tear a strip off his abashed first baseman. He figured the public humiliation had been sufficient. "That's never going to happen to him again." And, yes, that was one for the blooper video. "First time I've ever seen it," the skipper continued. "A couple of the coaches said they had. Not me. But it's like I keep saying. Stay around this game long enough and you're bound to see everything."

But we are getting ahead of ourselves. By the time this incident took place, last May, Olerud was well into his third year as a Jay. By season's end, even he could laugh at it. Well, maybe laugh is too strong a word. Olerud never laughs from the belly. He smiles a lot, chuckles occasionally, never broods or utters a harsh word. He is a polite, well-reared young man. The term dispassionate comes to mind but that would probably be unfair. He does not appear to feel things very deeply and whatever he does feel he rarely shows. It just does not register, at least not on the barometer of emotions common to most sports, where athletes soar and plummet on a day-to-day roller-coaster of success and failure. Olerud remains as he always is: placid. It is just his way. But maybe that's what happens to a fellow who comes face to face with death at the age of 21.

This is no exaggeration. Olerud, an outstanding athlete at Washington State University at the time, suffered a brain aneurysm in 1989. And, for six weeks, he didn't even know it. The trouble began with a series of brief, violent headaches. Then, as he was preparing to do some running at school one January day, he suddenly collapsed. Olerud was subjected to a barrage of tests that revealed nothing untoward. But his father, himself a minor league ballplayer turned physician, would not accept this clean bill of health. His obstinacy likely saved his son's life. "After the tests didn't show anything, it was my dad who wanted me to see one more specialist. They tried a different angle and found the aneurysm. There's something about doctors I guess. Extra cautious or something."

What the experts discovered on closer examination was a subarchnoid hemorrhage, a bubble in a blood vessel at the base of the brain that was leaking into the spinal column. Olerud submitted to a six-hour surgical procedure that involved peeling back the skin, extracting a chunk of skull and attaching a metal clip near the aneurysm. He still carries a scar that curls up from one ear, across his brow, down to the other ear. It is most visible when he steps out of the shower after each game, his light brown hair damp. "I guess, looking back, I was pretty stupid not to have been more scared. But there wasn't anything I could do about it. I had to trust the doctors. It's a helpless feeling, like being at the mercy of another person."

At the time of his operation, Olerud — who stood 6-foot-4 and weighed 205 pounds—had been *Baseball America* magazine's NCAA player of the year, following his sophomore season at Washington State in 1988. He was a lefthanded pitcher/first baseman with a lovely short stroke and quiet hands. He earned All-American ratings at two positions, pitcher and designated hitter, in '87-88. The season before his affliction, he had won the Pac-10 triple crown (.464-23-81) while going 15-0 with a 2.49 ERA and a conference-leading 113 strikeouts as a pitcher. But after his illness many doubted whether he would be able to return to baseball. Olerud harbored no such doubts. The surgery took place on February 27. Astonishingly, he was out of the hospital in five days and back working out two weeks later. By April 15, he had returned to the line-up at WSU. In 27 games, he batted .359 with five homers and 30 RBIs. As a pitcher, he was 3-2 with a 6.68

ERA in six games. Fortunately, the Jays were not interested in him as a pitcher.

Though rated the No. 2 player in the June draft, the major league ballclubs shied away because of his questionable (in their opinion) health. Toronto selected him in the third round, 79th overall, ignoring Olerud's warning that he would return to campus for his senior year. The Jays, flashing a four-year guaranteed contract worth up to $800,000 with incentive clauses factored in, managed to dissuade him. Olerud said what tipped the scales in favor of turning professional was Toronto's promise to bring him to the majors as a September call-up in '89 — just for a taste of the big-time, in the middle of a pennant drive.

Olerud, who had spent the summer in the hard-nosed Alaska League, where he became the first player to hit .400 in that loop, showed up at the SkyDome on August 28 — the same day his classes were to begin at university. Snapping photographs to record the event were his mother and his father. The latter, a dermatologist, had played seven years of minor league ball, putting himself through medical school in the off-season. On September 3, with the Twins safely in command of what would ultimately be a 9-4 victory over Toronto, Olerud made his first appearance in a game as a Jay. Since the college-style aluminum implements are not allowed in the majors, he didn't even have his own bats and had to borrow a bunch of ash sticks from his teammates. No matter. He hit safely his first time out — a hard grounder to the right side.

Olerud was pleased but not ecstatic. This initial success revealed a low-wattage response that would become typical over the ensuing years, even as his new teammates slapped him on the bum with congratulations. As he would say over and over again to out-of-town reporters as they picked up on the miracle-Jay story: "Going through something like that puts a lot of things in perspective. You have a lot more patience. You learn to really appreciate things, to be happy at just being able to experience those things. So, if I go through a bad period in baseball, I know it's not the end of the world."

The fans liked what they saw too, though what they saw was rather unusual — a ballplayer who never removed his batting helmet, even when he played defensively at first base. This was a precaution his father had demanded and one Olerud would forever maintain. It has become part of his regular uniform and these days he even wears it in the clubhouse when he's doing nothing more dangerous that slurping a bowl of soup.

His sometimes deafening calm was a puzzle to his teammates. Here was a gentle giant who didn't drink or smoke or curse, never demonstrated excitement or depression, ego or temper. When he signed his then-record contract, he didn't splurge on hot cars and fine threads as might have been expected from a baby-phenom. Manager Gaston had to urge him to buy a few more sports jackets, at least, for traveling. "Me," said Olerud, "I'm just used to jeans and sweat pants."

At his first spring training, in 1990, the veterans tried to have some fun at his expense, which is the normal indoctrination process for rookies. One prank involved stuffing about a hundred rolls of toilet paper in his locker. When Olerud was confronted with the mountain of tissue, he simply shrugged his shoulders and reached for his uniform. The vets realized quickly that Olerud was a disappointment as a victim. They would never get his goat and that took all the fun out of the hijinks. They left him alone and salivated over his swing.

Olerud started the year as a Jay and stayed that way. He has never played so much as one inning of minor league ball. In his first full campaign, Gaston employed him mostly as a designated hitter, filling in occasionally behind McGriff at first. He had long since discarded the notion of continuing as a pitcher though the organization maintained they had left that decision up to him. It was a wise choice.

At the beginning of the season, Olerud was close to being an everyday player as the Jays designated hitter and McGriff's caddie at first base. After the All-Star break, his active duty was cut back drastically. First Gaston elected to use him only against right-handed starters and then, as Toronto tried (unsuccessfully) to stave off the Boston Red Sox in the pennant race, almost not at all. He ended the year with just 358 at-bats in 111 games, 14 home runs and a .265 average.

Immediately after the season was over, the Jays dispatched Olerud to Dunedin, where he put in a month trying to learn the outfield in the Florida Instructional League. The thinking was that he might be reconstituted as a left fielder to replace the departing George Bell. It was a difficult adjustment. "When balls are going over your head or through your legs, it's not much fun," he admitted. He didn't have to worry about it for long. When he arrived at spring training in February, he had inherited the everyday first baseman's job, following the trade that sent McGriff and Tony Fernandez to San Diego.

Olerud still had a lot to learn and he was a pliant pupil. On many days, after everybody else had gone home, he would linger for hours. Long shadows would fall across the grass, the ground crew would appear with their rakes and hoses, and still he stayed. Long-limbed, slightly knock-kneed, a little less than graceful — but reluctant to leave the cage as long as there was someone around to lob pitches. Afterwards he'd gather up the balls around the batting cage and deliver them back to whoever had been throwing BP, with a hopeful look on his face. As if to say, some more please? With his eager freckled countenance and his sweet disposition, it was hard to say no to this Blue Jay Opie. (Actually, his teammates had taken to calling him Ollie.)

"I've always been that way, pretty calm," he explained. "Baseball's a game where everyone's always saying you've got to stay on an even keel as much as you can. Not get too excited, not get too upset. Maybe I'm a little bit too much on an even keel. I do get excited sometimes, you know. I just don't show it where a lot of people can see me. It's more behind closed doors. But I have a friend who's always said that I'm just north of comatose."

It would be an up and down sort of year for Olerud but the Blue Jay braintrust was patient. He batted just .156 in May but rebounded in June, hitting .271. In July he was up to .342 and came within a single of hitting for the cycle in a game against the Boston Red Sox when he collected a career-high 4 RBI. He was patient at the plate — his critics would say moribund — but his discerning eye earned him 68 walks, a club mark. As the season wound down, he went on a career-high 11-game hitting streak and finished third in fielding among American League first basemen. His numbers at the end read: 17 homers, 68 ribbies and a .256 average. That was closer to what the organization had expected of Olerud but he wasn't quite there yet.

Olerud recognized that and he was determined not to under-achieve as he headed to Dunedin in '92, where he signed a new contract that brought his yearly wage up to the $400,000 level. In the off-season, he had embarked on a strengthening program, working out three times a week and packing another 15 pounds on his lanky frame. He talked about "raising the intensity level" of his game, too.

"Cito has said that he wants me to be more aggressive this year and I definitely agree with that. I've been too selective early in the count. I've been getting behind, and then they would come with the tough pitch. My first year, I really didn't know quite what to expect and I was happy with my numbers. Last year I felt like I would do a lot better. I had been around the league and I knew the pitchers. I was more relaxed and comfortable. Then I got off to a slow start and it shook me up. It proved to me that you've got to work hard at it. Being comfortable doesn't mean you are going to get results. It was a good experience and I hope I learned from it.

"I think I've got to make adjustments. I've got to figure out how they are gonna pitch me to get me out. The pitchers are always changing. If you hit a particular pitch, then they'll try something else. And if somebody gets you out with a particular pitch, pretty soon everybody is throwing it."

He still had that lovely swing but even he was starting to get sick of hearing about it. "It's a nice compliment that everybody thinks you've got this great swing and all. But people are going to get pretty tired of a short, sweet swing that keeps hitting .250." He was also slow of foot which was one of the reasons he had hit into so many double plays the year before. The conditioning coach, Rich Knox, had him doing base-running drills and by the end of spring training Olerud had quickened two-tenths of a second. He had also dedicated himself to improving as a first baseman. "I still have a lot to learn out there. There's throws in the dirt that I should be digging out and they usually just charge the error to the guy making the throw. There's definitely some balls I should have got."

The stage was set for a more mature, more potent John Olerud. And on opening day in Detroit, his solo home run and 415-foot double in Toronto's 4-2 victory suggested that happy days lay directly ahead. In the three-game series, he reached base safely in 10 of 13 plate appearances. Then he stumbled. On April 19, he committed his first error following 78 clean games. It was a critical misplay on a routine ground ball and figured prominently as the Jays fell 5-4 to the Red Sox. A few days later, he was the only starter not to get a hit as Toronto climbed back from a 3-

0 first-inning hole to tip the Cleveland Indians 13-8. In the middle
of this two-week fallow period, he went an appalling 1-for-30 at
the plate and again there was uncharitable talk about his *dimness*
— there goes John again, lost in a personal fog.

There was much bemusement on the last day of April when
Olerud somehow conspired to steal his first base in the major
leagues, as Toronto fell to the Brewers in Milwaukee 3-2. In fact,
that little piece of larceny was attributable more to Candy
Maldonado messing up a hit-and-run then Olerud suddenly
sprouting Mercury wings on his feet. Maldonado had gone down
swinging with Olerud on the move but the latter still got credit
for a purloined base. "I asked the ump if I could take the base,"
Olerud joked afterwards. "He knew why. I kind of figured that's
the way I'd get one. Either that or on, say, a 3-1 count and the hit-
and-run, the ball skips away from the catcher. It's still nice to
have. I don't have a zero in that column any more and here it's just
one month into the season and I've already set a career record."

Olerud was supposed to be the everyday first baseman but,
essentially, the Jays were going with a platoon of Olerud and Pat
Tabler. (Nobody was calling it such at the time.) By the end of a
personally disastrous early May road trip, his average had settled
down at .226. On May 12, against Oakland, he rediscovered his
errant home run stroke when he knocked a Dave Stewart forkball
over the padding in right-centre with one on and two out. It was
only his second since opening day. "You've got to keep believing
you're going to get your swings," he said, after the Jays dismissed
the Athletics 3-0. "Tonight, I was just happy I was able to
contribute. I really haven't been doing my share."

It wasn't just an aberration either. The very next evening,
Olerud whacked a bases-loaded two-run double with two gone
in the seventh to help cap another sweep of the A's. The outfield
had been playing him to go the opposite way. Earlier in the game,
Olerud had doubled and scored the 2-1 go-ahead run in the
fourth. He breathed a sigh of relief, which is about as demonstra-
tive as Olerud gets.

Unfortunately, his travails were not yet completely over. His
aforementioned humiliating encounter (or non-encounter) with
Duane Ward's toss to first on May 18 was followed by another
miscue a few nights later, also against those Twins. In the first
inning, on a potential double-play ball to short off the bat of
Pedro Munoz, Olerud failed to grab Robbie Alomar's relay from

second. That allowed Gene Larkin, who had been hit by a Todd Stottlemyre pitch, to score all the way from second. Jays eventually nosed out Minnesota 8-7 but Olerud's defensive deficiency was apparent. (He did redeem himself with a second-inning tater.) In Chicago four nights later, Tim Raines opened the scoring with a bunt single that scooted between starter Jack Morris and Olerud. Or, as one reportorial wag put it: "...between Morris and the bag at first, same thing." As if that weren't bad enough, Olerud had the fans at Comiskey hooting after turning a double play and flipping the ball to the umpire as he started to walk off the field. There were only two outs.

Could things get any worse? In a word, yes. Back at the SkyDome on May 26, Olerud was standing around the batting cage prior to Toronto's encounter with Milwaukee. Actually, he was standing with his proboscis practically *in* the cage. You'd think after all this time he would know better than to press his face up against the netting while someone else was taking batting practice. But oh no. A ball off Manny Lee's bat hit him squarely on the shnozz. There was blood spurting everywhere and for a while it looked a lot worse than it actually was. Dazed and bleeding, Olerud was helped off the field and taken to Mount Sinai Hospital for x-rays which revealed a displaced fracture. He returned to the SkyDome in time to see the Jays wrap up their 5-4 win over the Brewers and vowed never to do something so stupid again. "I think this will cure me of that bad habit."

Olerud missed two games, came off the bench to pinch-hit in a third and was back in the line-up on May 30. Two nights later, he laid down a letter-perfect sacrifice bunt, the first of the year for him, as the Jays disposed of the Twins in Minneapolis 7-5. In the eighth, off reliever Bob Kipper, he also accounted for his fourth homer. And now he really had turned a corner on the season.

Against Boston on June 14, Olerud broke a 2-2 tie with a three-run double against Danny Darwin in the sixth, as the Jays motored to a 6-2 victory. It was a big hit in many ways for the struggling young man. After the previous day's loss, he had spent a long time watching video replays of the game in general and himself in particular. "I noticed that my weight was back on my heels. I worked on staying on my toes and moving towards the pitch. Last time (Darwin) faced me, he made me look silly on a high fastball. I thought he might try to do the same thing." When Darwin came in with a fastball away instead, Olerud adjusted neatly. "When your balance is good, you should be able to take the outside pitch to the opposite field or be able to turn on the inside fastball. I had good balance."

In Texas, a solo home run off Jose Guzman helped spark a six-run second inning as the Blue Jays wiped out a 2-0 deficit on their way to a 16-7 pasting of the Rangers. Four nights later in Cleveland, with their own J. Guzman on the mound, Toronto beat up on the Indians 6-1, and Olerud led the way with two round-trippers. It was more of the same from Olerud, this time in a losing cause, as the Jays closed out their series 7-6. In that game, there was a scary moment as Olerud fell head-over-heels into the photographers' box while chasing a foul ball. That brought Gaston running out of the dugout in alarm, but his first baseman had landed on his helmet and there was no damage.

By mid-July Olerud was giving every indication that he was finally living up to the Jays' high hopes for him. As a pinch-hitter in a confrontation with the Mariners in Seattle, he came off the bench in the eighth and drove in the go-ahead run with a ground ball after Brian Fisher had balked Toronto runners to second and third. The final tally was Toronto 7, Seattle 2. The following evening the Jays came up on the short end of an 8-6 engagement and the first baseman had a mini-slump relapse. Olerud, who hails from just down the road in Bellevue, had dozens of family and friends on hand. The audience must have unnerved him because he was 1-for-6 at the plate with three strikeouts and he stranded six runners in scoring position. "We just didn't get it done," he said after offering a weak pop to short right-centre with the bases loaded to end the affair. "Leaving all those guys on base really hurts." Forty-eight hours later he righted himself with a three-hit performance as Toronto doubled up the Mariners 8-4.

Opening a three-game series with the Angels in California, Olerud connected with his 10th tater of the season in a 5-3 Toronto loss and was 2-for-5 the next day, which gave him eight hits in three games. He was also 15 for 30 against the Angels on the year but that didn't stop Gaston from sitting him out in favor of Tabler for the third game in the series match-up. He appeared as a pinch hitter in the waning moments but was unsuccessful as the Jays bowed out of Anaheim 5-4. Moving on to Oakland the next night, Olerud delivered three singles as the Jays dominated 9-3. That marked his third three-hit game in four starts but the bad news was that he strained his left hamstring trying to get out of the box on a foul chopper in the second inning and wound up leaving the game in the eighth. After sitting out most of three games (just one pinch-hit appearance) he returned to full-time activity with a single to centre in a losing cause against Kansas City at the SkyDome.

The pulled hamstring was still not completely healed as the Jays convened in Fenway in early August. This time Olerud lasted only as far as the second inning. He had just smashed a pitch off the wall and had tried to leg it out for two bases but was tagged out. "I thought the play was going to be close at second and I really turned it on. That's when I felt a sharp pain. But I don't think it's any worse than what happened in Oakland. It's definitely not a blowout (of the hamstring)."

Gaston sat him out the next night as the Jays were eclipsed 9-4. The following evening he was a spectator for most of a very odd encounter with the Red Sox which saw starter Todd Stottlemyre, Robbie Alomar and Cito Gaston given the heave-ho for a variety of disputes with the umpires. In the eighth inning, with the Jays trailing 4-3 and the bases loaded, Olerud limped to the plate and lined a two-run single to left-centre off reliever Jeff Reardon. (Back in August, Reardon still had the reputation as one of the toughest relievers in the game.) "I'm looking for a pitch up," Olerud later explained, since a sacrifice fly would have tied the contest. "I don't want a ground ball that I have to leg out." But the ground ball did just fine as Toronto held firm at 5-4.

His occasional bat was coming in handy but the Jays were missing him on a day-in, day-out basis even though Tabler was performing adequately as his replacement. Up to that point Olerud had been Toronto's best bat on the road with a traveling .324 average. Olerud would stay out of the fray for six games before returning to face Baltimore in Toronto on August 10 and contributing a pair of singles as the Jays doubled the Orioles 8-4. That performance made him an even .300 hitter on the season, and he would hover around that mark down the stretch, ending the '92 campaign at .284.

Facing the Indians in Cleveland on August 14, Olerud absolutely crushed an offering from starter Rod Nichols for his 11th tater of the year. That three-run shot helped catapult the Jays to a 9-5 final. But there was a lot of thwack left in his bat which he proved in Milwaukee a few nights later with yet another monster of a home run as the Jays cavorted to a 12-1 decision.

The two teams tangled again back in Toronto with decidedly different results. On August 28, the Jays matched a 91-year-old major league record of goofy baseball when they accorded the Brewers 31 hits in a 22-2 farce. "It was incredible the way the hits continued to compile," Paul Molitor said afterwards. "I told Olerud one time at first that you can never figure this game out. He just shook his head. They weren't too talkative out there." The next night, Olerud watched helplessly as the Brew Crew stole a team-record eight bases in 10 attempts on their way to dumping the Jays 7-2.

Toronto had gone through a dog days of summer swoon, a not uncommon affliction for the team in August. They had started the month with a 4 1/2 game lead on Baltimore, six on Milwaukee. They finished it with the Orioles nipping at their heels, just 1 1/2 lengths off the pace, and the Brewers prepared to pounce from 4 1/2 back. But Olerud was having personal success. The injury aside, he had posted a season high 10-game hit streak from August 2-19, batting .444 (12-for-27). September opened just as promisingly. When the Jays hosted the Twins on the 4th, and inhospitably dumped them 16-5, Olerud chimed in with four hits, a first-ever quartet for him. His growing self-assurance was obvious. After Toronto blanked the Royals 5-0 in Kansas City, with Olerud collecting a pair of first-inning RBIs, he said: "Everyone feels confident that we've got the kind of guys who can turn things around pretty quick." He had become one of those guys.

A week later, in Texas, he duplicated his recent four ribbie performance — three of them via his 13th homer — as the Jays dusted off the Rangers 7-2. He did it against one of the toughest righthanders in the American League, Kevin Brown, who had been going for his 20th win. There were more spectacular dramatics in store, however, when the Jays returned to Toronto to face the Cleveland Indians on the 17th. On that night, it was Morris who was looking to climb to the 20-victory plateau. He didn't make it. Gaston pulled his starter after nine innings and 116 pitches. That brought Duane Ward aboard, who would get credit for Toronto's 7-5 win in the 10th frame. But it was Olerud's first-pitch homerun blister to deep, deep right centre that made it possible. That had the 50,408 SkyDome patrons leaping out of their seats and his teammates leaping out of the dugout. Even the

normally impassive Olerud gave a little hop as he set out to lope
around the bases, his arms raised, well, waist-high.

"I'm not too good at that stuff," he chuckled afterwards,
referring to his less-than-boisterous display. "It needs work. All
I was thinking about was touching the bases." The four-bagger
was Olerud's 15th on the year and raised his RBI total to 62. His
average had climbed 61 points to .291 since his pitiful May. "I
don't want to think about statistics until the year is over," he
demurred. "But I've definitely been swinging the bat better in the
last few months. I just want to finish it up strong. Even when I was
hitting around .230, I felt I was better than that. So you push it a
bit, put the pressure on yourself. Now, the last three or four
months being as good as they were, one at-bat isn't going to hurt
you." He had committed himself to a more combative style and
he had followed through. "I've been working on being aggressive since spring training. But I go through streaks where I'm too
aggressive and swing at bad pitches and streaks where I lay off
good pitches. It's a great feeling to come through, get a big hit like
that. Down the stretch, that's what you hope for."

Riding that high, the Jays went out and whomped the Rangers 13-0 the next night. Olerud contributed one itty-bitty RBI and
then he was walked in with a run when Brian Bohanon gave up
a pass with the bases loaded. It seemed like the affable Ollie
couldn't fail for trying. The happy buzz of his home run in that
Cleveland 7-5 affair had imbued the team with confidence.
"Olerud's home run gave us a good feeling," said David Cone,
after he had held off the Rangers 1-0 in gritty combat at the
SkyDome. "If we'd lost that game, it might have been a tough one
to overcome. We might have produced an opening for Baltimore
or Milwaukee. Since then, we feel like we will do whatever it
takes to get the job done."

Going into Camden Yards for a key series that could have
decided the claustrophobic division one way or the other, the
Jays edged the Orioles 4-3. Olerud lined a two-run number off
Rick Sutcliffe to spark the three-run fourth. Moving up the
Eastern seaboard to New York, he even showed a whiff of speed
when a Kelly Gruber dribbler up the middle died in the grass and
Olerud scrambled all the way to third. Toronto prevailed 3-1.

A week later, at home against the Tigers, the Toronto Blue
Jays nailed down their fourth division title in 16 years. The final
out was a towering pop-up to John Olerud. He must have
jumped, oh, two centimetres.

# Gl⚾ry Jays

## Cito Stands
## for Winning                                            *12*

---

Cito Gaston is one of the few managers who looks good in a baseball uniform.

This is one of the sport's many affectations — dressing up the boss in jock's clothing. Frankly, no man over the age of 40 should ever wear clingy double-knit jersey pantaloons. It ain't fittin', it just ain't fittin'.

But it's a good fit for Gaston, physically and philosophically. He is one baseball manager who identifies with athletes. He has spent most of his adult life as a player and that is where his loyalties still lie. Gaston treats his hired hands with the kind of respect he was rarely accorded in his own career. That is the key to Cito Gaston's managerial style.

His approach has not been universally appreciated in Toronto. Gastonic attacks have evolved into a sort of recreational activity in town. "Cito-bashing has become such a popular sport, the bashers are thinking of hiring their own commissioner," wrote *Star* columnist Milt Dunnell, who went on to nominate Fay Vincent for the job. Of course, that was before Gaston's Gang won themselves a World Series, but it will be interesting to see how long the goodwill lasts.

With Gaston at the helm, the Jays had secured two American League East titles and missed another by just a couple of games, before 1992. Yet the abuse to which he was continually subjected on radio call-in shows suggested that Gaston had managed a collection of bottom-feeders since taking over the reins halfway through the season in 1989. He may treat his own players with solicitude, but he has not always been extended that same courtesy.

Perhaps that is just a manager's lot in the world of professional sports. Gaston has said repeatedly that he understands this. It's nothing personal, he claims. But he has often taken it very personal indeed. Personal enough to freeze out certain reporters, personal enough to keep the door to his office closed after too many games, especially the bad ones, personal enough to tell off the fans on occasion. This is the dichotomy of Cito Gaston: He pretends that it doesn't hurt but he never forgets a slight. He still remembers one SkyDome patron who always sat just around the corner from the dugout. "He's been on my butt all season," he complained to Dunnell last October. "And he doesn't know a damn thing about baseball."

On another night, a leather-lunged critic was actually ejected from the ballpark by custodians because of his screed, aimed mostly at the manager. Gaston had not asked for the fan's removal but the subtext to the whole episode was that the skipper had to be protected from the patrons who paid his salary. It also provided more ammunition for Gaston's critics. Nyah, nyah, Cito can't take it.

Gaston could have been forgiven for gloating last fall. But he didn't. Victory was the sweetest revenge. That plus a substantial raise and a new two-year contract from a franchise that had never offered its field managers any more security than a year-to-year umbilical cord. "I was definitely wanting to get paid," he told reporters in a press conference from his home in Dunedin, Florida. "The two years is something that's good, although they can call it in any time they want to. But it does give you some security and, for some of your players, it lets them know you're going to be there for a while."

He has been there longer than he ever expected. When Jimy Williams was sacked in May of '89, Gaston, at that time the club's hitting instructor, was appointed interim manager. The Blue Jay brass insisted that he was not in the running for the permanent assignment as they scouted around for a replacement. Indeed, Gaston maintained that he didn't want it either. On the last day of May, he was given the job for keeps, or at least as permanent as these things get in baseball. It had been one of the few silly episodes in the club's history of even-handed corporate management. They had hedged and obfuscated, they had made it clear that Gaston was a caretaker until something better could be found, and then they made themselves look as if nothing better had been found. This did not augur well for Gaston's long-range tenure as the man in charge.

Yet his wardship of the club, from the inside-out anyway, has been largely serene. The Blue Jays are not a fractious assembly of egos who make their manager look bad by demeaning him in public. In those instances where Gaston has appeared inept as a dugout sage, it has been his own doing. He is a cautious, even unimaginative, manager. He is loyal to his veterans, to a fault. He eschews the more creative formulas for producing offense: the aggressive running game, the pinch-hitters. He rarely alters his line-up and he doesn't platoon players. But it is his handling of his pitching staff that has tried the patience of the fans and self-appointed experts. It is telling that once, when TV analyst and former pitcher Jim Kaat criticized Gaston's handling of a game situation, the manager responded by saying that Kaat "was a pitcher — not a player." It's a fine distinction and one that spoke volumes about Gaston's own prejudices.

During the World Series, Jack Morris suggested that Gaston was more a veteran's manager than a rookie manager. "Cito respects you as a person, expects you to know your role. I respect him for being able to turn his cheek some times, when I know things bother him."

In a decade as a major league player, Gaston enjoyed just 10 days on a club that played over .500 ball — when he was shipped, at the very end of his last season, to the Pittsburgh Pirates. It had been a lean career, on hopeless squads, and maybe that has forever colored his view of the world.

He gives the impression of a laid-back, calming influence in the oftentimes feverish environment of baseball. And he looks the part, tall and strong and methodical in his movements. The face is impassive, with high cheekbones and flat-lidded, almond-shaped eyes. It's a noble visage. His voice, with its faint echo of a Texas twang is so low that reporters have to lean in forehead-to-forehead in order to catch his quotes.

He says he's a man who doesn't want to stand for anything, certainly not for causes that come in capital letters. Like being the First Black Manager in Toronto, the Fifth Black Manager in major league history, the First Black Manager in the World Series. He said he hadn't even realized that, until reporters brought it up. "I don't see color, I'm just trying to win a game."

He agreed with Morris' assessment of him, though, about his faithfulness to the veterans. "I was treated badly by certain people, certainly not by all the people that I was involved with. In this game, you meet good people and you meet bad people. I guess I learned that everybody has feelings. If you treat them like you like to be treated, it makes you a better person and it will probably make them a better person.

"When I played, if you didn't have a couple of hits, a lot of managers didn't speak to you, they didn't talk to you or, sometimes, even look at you. I can give you a good example. When I was playing in San Diego, Bobby Tolan and I were platooning in right field. He got hurt sometime in June, I think, and I played for a week. We scored 13 runs in the week and I drove in eight of them. On the eighth day, I was sitting on the bench. So I was confused about why I wasn't playing. Things like that."

He was born Clarence Edwin Gaston on March 17, 1944, into a family that would eventually expand with five daughters, but just the one son. His father was a truck driver, his mother a housewife and occasional waitress, his grandfather a preacher. He gratefully gave up the name Clarence when a childhood friend re-christened him Cito because Gaston reminded him of a Mexican wrestler who went by that moniker. "I've always said, if your name's Clarence, you wouldn't mind being called Cito."

It was a hard-working family in a hard-edged town. "Not quite middle-class. More on the poor side." He was a powerful but gentle boy, a youthful version of the man he would become. Though a Baptist, he went to Catholic schools. "I loved that. They taught us good values to live by, about the rights of the people. We were even taught to make the sign of the cross whenever we heard an ambulance."

In the 1940s and 1950s, there was a social and racial order of things. There were whites and there were blacks and there were Mexicans and everyone knew their place. For young Gaston, that was at the back of the bus. "There were times when we were segregated. I remember sitting in the black section in the movie theatres and riding in the back of the bus."

But San Antonio was nowhere near as bad as South Carolina, where Gaston went after an all-star sports career at Holy Cross High School. "We'd roll into some towns and I couldn't get off the bus to eat. The black players couldn't stay overnight with the rest of the guys. We'd have to stay in the black motels out in the country."

He says he bears no ill-will against his teammates from that period, but he has not forgotten the shame of it. "They did what they could. They'd buy me a hamburger and pass it through the window. They'd say, 'Sorry Cito, we know how you feel.' But they didn't, not really. They couldn't." He insists there is no residue of resentment. "People are just ignorant. A lot of these racists who are Catholics and born-again Christians, who pretend they're so religious. I don't know. It seems to me, if there's a heaven or a hell, there has got to be some black people there too. I'm not angry about it now. It's over, in the past. My parents didn't raise me to spend my life hating people."

But he recalls something else too, the 1966 season, when he was playing for Batavia in the New York-Pennsylvania League. He was leading the league in home runs, RBIs, and batting average — the kind of numbers that encouraged visions of a triple crown title. Towards the end of the season, he was vying for the triple crown laurels with another player. He recounted the story to the *Star's* Jim Proudfoot: "The guy I was head-to-head with hit a fly to left field, where the man flat-out dropped the ball, then kicked it around a while. Error. No doubt about it." But the fellow was given credit for two RBIS when two runs scored.

The race for the batting championship remained tight, right to the wire. "I was two percentage points ahead of that guy from Jamestown and our last three games were against that club," he continued. "In Jamestown, I was 4 for 4 and he went 3 for 4. Back in my place, I'm 3 for 4 and he's 4 for 4. Now we're finishing up in Jamestown. We each get an early hit. Now we're finishing at bat, he pops to second. The ball comes down, hits the fellow's glove and bounces out. Up on the scoreboard goes the verdict: Hit. And their boy's the batting champion."

Proudfoot commented on the poor officiating in the minor leagues. "No, that's not it at all," said Gaston. "This was racism, pure and simple."

As a youngster, Gaston worshipped Hank Aaron. Then, when he was traded to Atlanta, they were teammates. "I actually got to share a room with him at spring training. I couldn't believe it." It was Aaron, too, who brought Gaston back into baseball at the end of his playing career, after he had played winter ball in

Venezuela and Mexico. "I was sitting at home with a cast up my leg and Hank Aaron calls me. He's trying to talk me into coming back as an instructor but I wasn't interested. He phoned me three times before I agreed to go to the Instructional League in Sarasota." He was a roving hitting instructor before coming to Toronto in 1982 under Bobby Cox, who had been fired in Atlanta. When Cox returned to the south, Gaston stayed on as hitting instructor under Jimy Williams. He was also a rare Blue Jay in that he lived in Toronto during the off-season. (He had married a Canadian, his second wife, who wasn't much of a ball fan. After the '91 season, they sold their house in Toronto and relocated their home-base to Dunedin.)

Gaston found some of the managerial realities distasteful. On several occasions, he would talk wistfully about his hitting instructor days, which were less combative, more leisurely. Even as late as last fall, during the World Series, he was telling reporters that he missed having time to spend with his family, that he longed for barbecues in the backyard and a settled domestic life. But he didn't get out — managing can get in your blood, even when you try to resist it.

In many ways, he had changed. He had hardened in the job, or it had hardened him. There was one infamous night where he engaged in a war of words, and gestures, with David Wells on the mound, in full view of 50,000-plus spectators. It was not an attractive sight but it also served notice — Gaston was the man in charge. What was peculiar about it is that Gaston was loath to chastise his players, unless it was behind closed doors. But Wells' childish behavior had invited the public scolding. And his back woes in 1991 had made Gaston a far less patient man. Eventually, he would end up in the hospital, turning over the managerial duties to bench coach Gene Tenace. The Jays were 19-and-14 under Tenace. When Gaston returned to the dugout, Toronto had a 2 1/2 game lead in the AL East, the same margin they had enjoyed on the day Gaston had left.

Gaston was second-guessed no end for the way he handled his pitching staff in the playoffs against the Minnesota Twins in '91. It seemed as if his job was hanging by a thread but the Jays re-signed him to another one-year contract nonetheless. It may have been a vote of confidence but a battery of critics shook their heads. Some clucked that Toronto would never get to the World Series with Gaston in charge. This created the most curious scenario as the team convened in Dunedin for spring training last year: Gaston had one of the most enviable records in baseball — two AL East titles in three attempts, 235 victories against 182 defeats for a .564 percentage — yet anything less than a World Series in '92 would have been considered a personal failure.

Throughout the year, Gaston continued to manage his way. He stuck with the veterans with whom he identified. He allowed Candy Maldonado to claim the left fielder's job over Derek Bell. He granted Dave Winfield's wish to play in the outfield, if only on an irregular basis. He kept Jack Morris on the mound even as the bullpen pined for work. He retained his Duane Ward-Tom Henke closing combo when it seemed as if their order should be reversed. He was an ardent defender of Manny Lee at shortstop and Devon White at lead-off.

The fans ranted but his players loved him for it. And, in the end, they made him look like a genius.

# Gl⚾ry Jays

## *Where It All Begins* 13

Pat Gillick is a staunch disciple of baseball according to the Old Testament: Thou shalt not have too much pitching.

But the Toronto general manager, the creator of all things bold and Blue Jay, has also learned the hard way that too much is never enough. Arms fall off, arms go limp, arms suffer rotator cuff damage, arms get sore elbows, arms don't have a leg to stand on. On occasion, Gillick must have wanted to throw up his own arms in dismay at the constant erosion of million-dollar limbs that were never designed to throw little white balls at speeds of up to 95 miles an hour.

He hasn't, of course. All Gillick has done is quietly go about his business of acquiring replacement parts as the need arose — only to watch too many of those proxy pitchers, acquired at substantial cost late in the season, decamp to other teams in other ballparks once their itinerant employment had been concluded: Bud Black...Tom Candiotti...David Cone...

But Gillick is still out there, pitchin' for pitchers.

That's where it all begins, on the hill. As the 1992 season got under way, the Jays appeared richer than most in that position, with a complement of starters that included Jack Morris, Juan Guzman, Jimmy Key, Todd Stottlemyre and David Wells, the reliever who had been promoted from the 'pen pending Dave Stieb's return.

Key, the 30-year-old Alabama southpaw, was second only to Stieb in time served as a pitcher with the Jays — eight full seasons and 103 victories. He had a career ERA of 3.41, had appeared in two All-Star games and had recorded 12 or more wins in each of the previous seven years. Unlike Stieb, Key also had a reputation for winning critical games (playoffs notwithstanding) — though he had been the loser on the last day of the 1987 season, 1-0 against Detroit, when the resurrected Tigers clinched the division over the El Foldo Jays.

An elegant pitcher, with a quiet delivery and precision control, Key was, historically, the most reliable starter of the bunch. He was also on the final year of his contract, which often spurs athletes to higher levels of achievement in the hope that they will be compensated accordingly come deal-making time.

But '92 was mostly a horror for Key. He lost pretty and he lost ugly. He lost by one run and he lost by 20 runs. (Most of those weren't charged to him but he was still the losing pitcher of record.) He lost when his teammates performed beautifully and when they performed hideously. He was star-crossed and he was snake-bit.

In the off-season, he fell off a ladder while changing a bulb at his home and severely sprained his ankle. How's that for getting off on the wrong foot? He was in a cast for weeks and had to undergo rehab before reporting to Dunedin last spring.

Southpaws are a rather mystic breed in baseball. They are expected to be a little bit addled in temperament. Key, with his even-handed nature, was an exception to the rule. But then he wasn't even a real lefty. "I eat righthanded, write righthanded, golf righthanded. I don't know why that is."

Why? Why? Why? Key would be asking himself that question a lot throughout the year. Why were all these nasty things happening to him? How did he lose his release point? Where did his breaking ball go? Can't anybody here play this game when it's *my* turn on the mound?

Key had pitched three successive season openers, from 1987 to 1989, and won them all. He started the home opener for the Jays last April but it was Pat Hentgen who got the W. The game began at 1.45 p.m., the first hit off Key came at 1.55 and the first homer at 2.02. He did settle down and worked seven innings but by the time Toronto had mounted a 4-3 comeback, Key was already in the showers. "It was a struggle for me all day," he said. Little did he know.

Key *et al* beat the Yankees a week later, 2-0, but got no decision in Boston next time out. Jays prevailed 6-4 in 13 innings and this time it was reliever Bob McDonald who was credited with the win. Against the Kansas City Royals later in the month, Hentgen again took over from Key, who had departed in the sixth with

Toronto trailing 4-3, runners on second and third, one out. Once more the combative Jays made a winner out of the rookie, coming back for a 6-4 final.

In Milwaukee on May 1, the Brewers surmounted a 3-0 deficit by stinging Key with back-to-back homers. Hentgen rode in on his white charger again but this time the magic didn't work. Facing the Mariners next in Seattle, Key was the beneficiary of 12 Toronto hits, including two home runs, which is what it took to dump the homeside 12-4. His third W of the season came in a tidy 3-0 effort against the Athletics in Toronto. Key issued four free passes but shaved his ERA from 3.70 to 3.23. He hadn't walked more than three in any outing since the start of the 1990 season.

The Mariners got one back at the SkyDome, clipping the Jays 3-2. All three Mariner runs came from single homers off Key. In all of '91, Key had only one start in which he gave up as many as two four-baggers. Thus far in '92, he had served up back-to-back homers twice. (There was at least one Key in town who was winning. A horse called Key 22 — the owner had named him for the pitcher — got to the wire first at the Woodbine Race Track.)

The Jays traveled to Chicago for a weekend of baseball under brutal weather conditions. The wind howled and the icy rain eased up to an annoying drizzle as Key took the mound against the White Sox. In fact, he pitched rather well considering the circumstances. Still, it was for naught as Toronto succumbed 5-2. "It wasn't the cold — I can handle the cold — so much as the wind," said Key, who had walked three and given up a troika of runs over six innings. "Mostly it was right in my face, but it was blowing all over the place. One time you'd kick up and the wind would blow me back. The next time, it wouldn't. It throws you off. The three walks, for instance."

The Jays avenged that loss in Toronto the following week. Key persevered for seven innings and conceded just one run. Toronto took it 2-1, yet the laurels this time went to David Wells. In his last four starts (27 innings, a 2.33 ERA) Key had given up just seven earned runs but was 1-2 in that stretch because his teammates had scored only four runs while he was on the mound.

He had to be almost perfect to win a game. Actually, *almost* just didn't cut it. Against the Orioles in Baltimore on June 5, Key was near flawless in a 1-0 loss. He gave up just two measly hits before running into problems in the bottom of the eighth when

Brady Anderson beat out a high chopper and Mike Devereaux slashed a single to right-centre. Key was good but Oriole starter Rick Sutcliffe was better.

The Jays hosted the Tigers on June 16 and it looked like Key was cruising. The long ball had stopped hurting him. He was working on a three-hitter into the sixth frame when Mickey Tettleton scored a deuce with his 15th home run of the year. Detroit 4, Toronto 3.

Before the season had begun, Key told reporters that he was anxious to hang around the mound into the late innings. "I'm going to try to stay in longer this year. I think I'm strong enough to go 120 or 130 pitches." Facing the Royals in Kansas City on June 21, Key lingered for the full nine yards, his first complete game of '92. He struck out five and didn't walk anybody. Yet he still lost, 2-0.

It was no decision but four runs forfeited against the Cleveland Indians in another losing cause before the Blue Jay bats woke up in support of Key, 10-1 over the California Angels and 6-0 over the Mariners. The latter was Key's first shut-out of the season, his second complete game, and Toronto's seventh consecutive victory. The southpaw was now even up at 6-6 and Key figured his sporadic season was back under control.

Uh-uh.

Against those Mariners again, he served up another trio of home runs, two of them by Lance Parrish, who had recently been picked up on waivers. But this was a team effort of ineptitude by the Jays who stranded a club-record 17 runners on the bases. Moving into Anaheim, Key surrendered three more round-trippers to the Angels and the Jays went down 5-4. "Homers are usually the result of bad pitches, so there you go, six bad pitches," observed Key, in reference to his last two games. "These last two starts, I've lost my release point on a consistent basis." He now led the team in gopher balls with 17 in 134 1/3 innings.

He improved to 7-8 on the year as the Jays dismissed the Royals 6-4 in his next assignment but Key had to throw 90 pitches through six innings in order to do it. He was equally spotty the next time he ventured to the hill, against the Yankees at the SkyDome, but it was under-utilized Mark Eichhorn who got the 7-6 decision. Key had thrown only 55 of 106 pitches for strikes over six and now sported a 6.68 ERA in his four outings since the All-Star break.

His much-vaunted control was nowhere in evidence when the Jays visited Tiger Stadium. Skeeter Barnes — yes, Skeeter Barnes — whacked a three-run homer off Key and the Tigers rolled over the Jays 7-2. In the process, Key allowed all seven runs (six of them earned) on eight hits through just 5 2/3 innings, but on 119 pitches. Two of those runs came in the first inning — opponents were now hitting .322 off Key in the first frame.

Things got worse. With the Orioles in town, Key was purely awful and the Jays were equally stinky as the team was pounded 11-4. Key lasted only 3 1/3 but by then Baltimore was already up 5-3. "Again, I'm throwing some good pitches and some bad ones. When I throw the bad ones, they hit me."

In Milwaukee, the Jays saw to it that Key would not have to endure another thrashing. They connected for 15 hits off a half-dozen Brewer pitchers and annihilated the Crew 12-1. Key, who threw easy through eight, gave up just three hits and the one run. What had gone right this time? Key couldn't explain it. "I've been working on my mechanics for the better part of three weeks," he told reporters. "When you start pitching badly, you start searching for answers. Basically, we went back to some old tapes, then made a few small adjustments to my wind-up."

At the Metrodome in Minneapolis, Key pitched well enough to lose: four hits in seven strong innings, but one of those a single homer to Lenny Webster in the fifth. Twins on top 2-0. "I don't know if you can call it consolation, but it does feel good to put together good games back to back," said Key, searching for silver linings.

And then we come to...what's this?...must be a typo. 22-2. Twenty-two. To. Two. XXII-II. We were there. We saw it. We saw it and we still don't believe it. The Jays were clobbered, moidered, by the Brewers, the very team they were trying to stave off in the AL East. Key was hung for that baboon of a game too but, sheesh, it was just 3-0 when he departed after 1 2/3. (It seemed like a bright idea at the time.) "The good thing about games like this is that it only costs you one loss," he noted.

His next outing was easier on the eyes but the verdict was the same. A sturdy Key allowed five hits over eight innings against the White Sox and he still ended up getting stiffed 3-2. Two of his pitches had been redirected as home runs but what really cost the Jays was Robbie Alomar getting thrown out at third after Joe Carter had cashed in Devon White in the first. John Olerud hit into a double-play and what could have been a big inning fizzled into a slim 1-0 lead that Toronto couldn't hold. "The most frustrating year I've ever had," Key mumbled.

He didn't know it then but the bad times were finally over. "I'd pitch good and lose, I'd pitch bad and lose," he had complained. Then, in Kansas City, Key blanked the Royals 5-0, a complete game gem. At Arlington, he didn't allow a runner past second base in the first six innings and the Jays prevailed 7-2. At the SkyDome, he shut out those same Rangers through seven for a 13-0 final. In Baltimore, he limited the Orioles to four hits and two runs over six and Toronto won 8-2. When the Jays dusted off the Boston Red Sox 5-2 on September 29, Key had his fifth win in a row and squared his record for the season at 13-13.

It had been a long, meandering road back to respectability. And there was one more tiny rut to jangle his nerves: a 64-pitch, two-inning cameo on the last regular game of the season, a meaningless encounter over the Tigers that the Jays would eventually pull out 7-4. "It was a game to get over with and that's the way I pitched," he said.

Key had righted himself but the damage had been done. He was left out of the starting rotation for the playoffs. The veteran was disappointed but stoic. And, in the World Series, Key would make a profound difference in the Blue Jay saga. He had saved the best for last.

Todd Stottlemyre was left out of the starting rotation in the post-season as well, though he too made significant contributions — albeit out of the bullpen. In other, more unpleasant ways, his 1992 season also paralleled that of Key. It was not what he had expected.

The son of New York Yankees pitcher Mel Stottlemyre, Todd had come to spring training eager to prove that he had put his erratic, tempestuous pitching demeanor behind him. The 26-year-old was in better physical shape than he had ever been before, thanks largely to a training regimen overseen by his physical fitness-conscious wife, Sheri.

However, Stottlemyre's athleticism was never the problem. It was the head, not the body, that had betrayed him in the past. Like Dave Stieb, Stottlemyre was infamous for his explosive temperament on the mound. The game would get under his skin and then he'd blow. These mini-rages would never last long — in the clubhouse afterwards he would appear regretful and chastened — but the brief spurts of fury would often cause damage to himself and to his team. For a relatively young man, he was also an old-fashioned pitcher. Stottlemyre was never bashful about getting his message across on the mound: brush-back pitches were sometimes so obvious that even a visually-impaired umpire couldn't miss them.

It was politically incorrect baseball.

The Jays had shown much patience with Stottlemyre, who was nurtured within the organization from the minors through to the majors. Too patient, some might argue. But in 1991, he had posted a 15-8 record with a 3.78 ERA and the most starts (34) in the rotation, in what was only his second full season as a starter. He was no longer just a kid with promise — he appeared poised to be taken seriously.

Coming off his best season as a major leaguer and eligible for salary arbitration for the first time in his career, Stottlemyre agreed to a new contract with Toronto: $1.25 million, or roughly four times what he had made the previous year. In 1991, with no bargaining leverage, Stottlemyre had his contract renewed at $315,000 and was not happy about it.

Like others in the Blue Jay pitching fraternity — and no doubt provoked by the acquisition of workhorse Jack Morris — Stottlemyre told reporters that he wanted to pitch into the late innings too. "I want the ball every four or five days and I want to go as long as I can," he said. "I feel I'm capable of pitching 230-240 innings." In '91, he had come close with 219 innings, another category in which he led the Toronto pitching staff.

Then he went out bass fishing one afternoon in Florida and almost scuttled his season. He was packing up his gear, ready to return to his home in nearby Tarpon Springs, when he reached up to take off his hat. And impaled his index finger with a fish hook, so deeply that the barbs sank below his skin. Doctors spent two hours removing the lure. "The doctor had to stick a bunch of needles in my finger to deaden it," he explained to *Toronto Star* reporter Tom Slater. "Then he pulled the hook out. He told me it was a 50-50 deal. He might have had to push the hook all the way through the finger but he got it out clean." Fortunately, the freak accident had involved the left hand, his glove hand. Pitching coach Galen Cisco was not mollified. "Geez, it could have been disastrous."

Disastrous could also describe Stottlemyre's first pitching assignment of '92, in the opening series against the Tigers in Detroit. His teammates had spotted him to a 8-1 lead but Stottlemyre, who had waltzed through the first four innings, was chased with two out in the fifth. In his truncated appearance, he had surrendered four hits and seven walks. Before he departed, the Tigers had closed the gap to 8-4. The Jays ended up 10-9 victors in that messy encounter but the win went to Tom Henke. "I'd feel 10 times worse if we'd lost but, basically, I feel like I let down the other guys. They got me a lead like that and I don't do a damn thing with it."

This was typical Stottlemyre. Even on the nights when he stunk out the joint — and there were many — he never hid from reporters or offered cheap excuses. He would lash out at himself long before the writers got in on the act.

In his next turn, against the New York Yankees, Stottlemyre accomplished one of the objectives he'd set for himself. He turned in a complete game. He also lost 5-2. Through eight innings, he had held the Yankees to just three hits, retiring 10 of the first 11 Pinstripes he faced. But in the ninth, with the score tied 2-2, he imploded: single to Roberto Kelly, double to Mel Hall, home run to Danny Tartabull.

His first win of the year came in Boston, where the Jays edged the Red Sox 2-1 at chilly Fenway Park. Stottlemyre worked seven tidy innings, limiting Boston to the one run on only three hits and three walks. His next time out, against the Cleveland Indians at the SkyDome, he finally became a career .500 pitcher, with a 41-41 record. "That's right, I'm back to 0 and 0 again," he joked with the scriveners. It wasn't exactly a resounding achievement. Toronto won 13-8 but Stottlemyre had afforded the Tribe all of those runs in his 6 2/3 innings of work.

A far finer performance was offered against the California Angels on April 29 when Stottlemyre and Jim Abbott battled it out from beginning to end; one throwing from the right, the other from the left. But it was Stottlemyre who was rewarded with a 1-0 verdict after Abbott walked home the winner in the bottom of the ninth. This marked Stottlemyre's first career complete game shutout. He had allowed seven hits and fanned five. "That was fun," he enthused later. "It was especially fun because every pitch was so meaningful."

The two combatants, Stott and Abbott, did the minuet again 10 days later — Stottlemyre had a 7-3 win against Oakland in the interim — and it was another beauty. The results, however, were reversed. Abbott hung tough through seven and left with a 2-1 lead, which is how it ended. Stottlemyre went all eight innings and allowed only six hits, but took the loss. "I'm sick of that guy," he kidded with reporters, referring to Abbott. "No, really, it's fun to pitch against him. It really gets your juices flowing. He's tough, a great competitor."

The final score was the same against the Mariners a week later. Toronto was nipped 2-1 and Stottlemyre, who went seven innings — giving up both runs on just three hits — absorbed his third loss of the young season.

There was a lot more scoring, not to mention fireworks, when Stottlemyre and the Jays tangled with the Minnesota Twins at the SkyDome. The Twins played head games with Toronto, and in particular with their moundsman, by having the umpire con-tinually check the ball for imagined irregularities. Jack Morris, from the bench, provided some verbal dickering of his own. But it was Stottlemyre, fuming in the dugout over some tight pitch-ing by Scott Erickson, who eventually led the charge that pro-voked a bench-clearing brawl. Fired up by the roustabout pro-ceedings, the Jays rebounded for an 8-7 win.

It was more of the same against the Milwaukee Brewers less than a week later, and again Stottlemyre was one of the leading protagonists. In this case, the shenanigans began in the fifth inning when Joe Carter tried to charge the mound after being hit with a pitch by Jaime Navarro. He was thrown out for initiating the fracas that ensued. Stottlemyre held his own temper in check, at least until the sixth when he nicked Paul Molitor — who had dinged him for a two-run homer earlier in the game — with a pitch. He had been warned and now he was gone. For those still interested in something as banal as the score, the Brewers doubled up the Jays 8-4.

No decision for Stottlemyre next up against the Twins, though the Jays out-dueled Minnesota 7-5 at the Metrodome. At Yankee Stadium, he allowed just three hits and one run in six innings as the Jays walloped New York 16-3. But he faltered against the Red Sox when Boston came to pay a call, conceding three home runs including back-to-back shots in the second inning as the Beantowners prevailed 5-3. "I'm not taking any-thing away from the Red Sox," Stottlemyre told reporters. "But I guess my mistakes just end up in the seats."

His mistakes against Kansas City on June 19 ended up in the seats and just about everywhere else as the Royals pounded the Jays 11-4. All the runs were scored off Stottlemyre who lasted just 4 2/3 innings. His escalating ERA was finally given a break, if one could look at it that way, because soreness in his right arm and left knee took Stottlemyre out of the rotation, to be replaced by David Wells. Apparently, the soreness had been bothering him for several weeks. He was placed on the DL on June 20 and stayed there till July 16. When the impatient starter was reactivated, he was elated. "I feel like Christmas came early," he said. Nor was he concerned about how he might be utilized. "Starter, relief, I don't care. I'm just glad to be back."

With Stieb staggering and David Wells not much of a solu-tion, Stottlemyre was inserted back into the rotation. In his first return assignment he was shaky, giving up three runs (two earned) over the first two innings before settling down for five innings of seven-hitter. Toronto fell 5-3 to the Angels at Anaheim but the loss was hung on Pat Hentgen. "I felt like a rookie all over again," said Stottlemyre. "I was looking forward to this. I was excited but I was also a little rusty and my command was a little off. I still did a couple of things I wanted to do. I had good concentration, I had good focus. If I can keep doing that this second half, I'll have a chance to win some ball games."

Not immediately. With Stottlemyre on the mound through six, the Athletics shut out the Jays 6-0 in Oakland. The Toronto bats were noisier against the Yankees, when Stottlemyre finally won a game, 13-2, on July 31. It was only his second victory since May 4. Over the all-star break, he had gone home to Yakima, Washington, and thought about his predicament. "At this point, I'm just trying to put in as many good innings as I can and not worry about anything else. I've put the first half of the season behind me."

It was still a struggle, though. Against the Red Sox in Boston, he lasted 2 2/3 innings and left with Toronto trailing 4-3 before the Jays bounced back 5-4. His departure was not his idea, or the manager's. The pitcher had been sent packing — his second ejection of the season — after a chest-to-chest dispute with umpire Jim Joyce.

Stottlemyre wasn't alone in his misery. With the exception of Morris, all the starters were getting banged around. Against Baltimore in Toronto, he battled for seven innings, longer than any Toronto starter had gone in nine games. The hitters did their part too and the Jays won 8-4 to maintain a three-game length on the Orioles.

With that effort, Stottlemyre had squared himself at 7-7 on the season. The next day he was handed a five-game suspension for what had transpired a week earlier in Boston. Pending his appeal of the suspension, he continued to pitch for the Jays. And perhaps that wasn't such a brilliant strategy because he lost to Cleveland and Minnesota.

But facing the White Sox in Chicago, Stottlemyre was almost perfect. In what was arguably his finest effort as a ballplayer, Stottlemyre had a no hitter going into the eighth before Dan Pasqua lined a one-out double up the gap in right centre. The pitcher's reaction? "Oh poop!" That was all the Sox could manage, though, as the Jays smothered Chicago 9-0. The complete-game — ninth of his career — dropped Stottlemyre's average below a fin.

Five days later, facing Chicago again at the SkyDome, he provided more of the same. Almost. Five hits in another complete game which Toronto won 9-2. "It's been very tough to mention my name and the word consistency in the same sentence," he admitted to newspaper chroniclers afterwards. "But Galen (Cisco) has been working with me a lot on my approach, and my last two starts I've just tried to get strike one and be real aggressive." Those two victories were the Jays' first back-to-back complete games in more than three years.

Against the Twins, Stottlemyre bowed out after 7 1/3 but he got the win nevertheless as the Jays polished off Minnesota 4-2. On September 16, Stottlemyre struck out a season-high eight Cleveland Indians and didn't allow a walk—though he hit a man with a pitch — and he still fell to 10-11 on the season as the Jays lost 6-3. Former teammate Glenallen Hill dinged him for a three-run homer.

Meanwhile, the Orioles remained in pursuit. Stottlemyre, 6-0 against Baltimore over his career, got the opening assignment in a three-game series at Camden Yards. In spite of a two-hour and 42 minute rain delay, which required him to warm up twice on the night, Stottlemyre supplied 6 2/3 innings of four-hitter and the Jays squeezed out a 4-3 win. He still owned the Orioles and Toronto now owned a six-game lead over Baltimore.

Stottlemyre also announced that he was dropping the appeal of his suspension. The day after knocking the Orioles out of the race, he began to serve his penance. When it was over, at the end of the month, he found himself relegated to the bullpen because Cito Gaston was already finalizing his rotation for the playoffs. How ironic, then, that the displaced starter earned his final victory of the year in the last regular-season game, a meaningless 7-4 encounter with the Tigers which saw the Jays send seven pitchers to the mound for brief warm-up exercises.

It was his 12th win against 11 losses. If nothing else, after a yo-yo season, Todd Stottlemyre was a better than .500 pitcher.

For David Wells, the numbers alone don't tell the story.

Boomer, as he is known, also had a schizophrenic season. But his effectiveness on the mound was only part of the story. He began '92 as a starter, was shunted to the bullpen after Dave Stieb returned to the rotation, was retrieved from the relief corps when Stieb blew up and a couple of other starters came up lame, then was returned from whence he came after the Jays acquired David Cone. Versatility is one thing, vacillation by your masters another.

Wells, a doughy southpaw with an irreverent sense of humor, had been used primarily as a reliever since sticking with the club in 1989. He had never been pleased about this. In his mind, he was a starter — and the club has made use of him in that capacity on several occasions. He was a one-man B-Team for whenever the club found itself short of first-inning arms. This fall-back characterization had become something of a tease for Wells: the opportunity was extended just often enough to keep him hopeful.

As was his custom, Wells made his feelings known to Blue Jay management last March at spring training, even though he was aware that kvetching was not going to hasten his promotion from the bullpen. "I'll moan about it, all right, and they know I will too. But what kind of choice do I have? If that's where they say they need me, that's where I gotta go. What? I'm gonna do something stupid and mess up $2 million (his new contract)? I'll be the waterboy here for $2 million."

He'd been a full-time reliever in '88, '89 and through the first two months of 1991. (He also ended the year back in the pen.) "As a reliever, you spend a lot of your time spectating," he observed. "In some ballparks, the bullpen is so far away that you can't even get into the game."

When the '92 campaign began, and with Stieb still on his rehab assignment, Wells contentedly took to the mound as the starter against the Orioles. He four-hit Baltimore through seven strong innings—not counting the three batters he clipped, a new club record—and the Jays prevailed 3-1, for a perfect 6-0 record. On the way to the shutout, Wells had survived a nervous fourth when he loaded them up on a hit batsman, single, pop-up, pop-up, four-pitch walk and near-homer to Chris Hoiles that died on the warning track in left. "I'm notorious for giving up the long ball," said Boomer (which is not the genesis of his nickname), pointing out that he had been mauled for a team-high 24 round-trippers the year before.

In Boston, the Jays and the Red Sox slogged their way through a rain-delayed marathon that took six hours and 35 minutes to complete. Wells left after one of those foul weather-induced halts but he still took the rap for the 1-0 loss as Roger Clemens shut down the Toronto offense.

It seemed a particularly unfair way to bow out of the rotation. With the return of Stieb, Wells was back in the familiar environs of the pen. On April 28, the two of them combined to hand California a 9-5 victory. The score was 4-1 when Stieb gave way to Wells who promptly coughed up another five runs. In fact, he pitched for the cycle: single, double, triple, homer. Throw in a walk too.

His first save, again picking up Stieb, came against Seattle more than two weeks hence, when the Jays trimmed the Mariners 5-4. But two nights later, Ken Griffey Jr. rifled a three-run homer off him and Wells not only blew the save but was charged with the loss as Toronto fell 7-6.

A middle-reliever, which is what Wells had reverted to, doesn't often have a dramatic impact on a game. It's a role that offers neither the grandeur of a starter nor the glamor of a closer. It's marginal, sporadic baseball, which is why Wells continued to chafe as the days grew longer and the nights grew warmer. But he had learned a lesson along the way: big boys don't whine.

Finally, in late June, Wells was relieved from his reliever duties. With Stottlemyre on the shelf, Boomer was seconded as a starter again, allowing two runs on seven hits in six innings as the

Jays squeezed the Texas Rangers 3-2 in Arlington. Then he got blown out when the two teams met again at the SkyDome: nine runs in only 2 2/3 innings as the Jays were overwhelmed 16-13. Gaston, for one, indicated that the experiment would continue but Wells' grasp on the starting job seemed tenuous. Another game like that and he'd be back . . . you know. Instead, he and Mike Timlin combined on a three-hitter as Toronto dumped the Angels 6-2. "That last outing got me down," he admitted to reporters. "This one was not only important for the team, but it was important for the organization to see me go out there and pitch the way I'm capable of. They'll probably have to make decisions when some of our guys come back from injuries. This is where I want to be and I think I showed them this is where I should be."

Alas, he showed the Jays something else entirely when he took to the mound again against Oakland. The A's won 5-1 and all the runs were scored off Wells, dropping him to 4-4 on the year. He then scrambled through six innings to get the win as Toronto doubled up the Mariners 8-4 in Seattle, contributed seven innings of three-hit shutout ball when the Jays breezed past the Kansas City Royals 3-0, but served up a trio of home runs (eight runs in all) to the Red Sox who pummeled Toronto 9-4 at Fenway. At least he had a legitimate excuse for that dastardly encounter — Wells had spent the previous 48 hours in close communication with the washroom after eating a bad tuna fish sandwich. The problem, what with injuries and an over-worked bullpen required to pick up the faltering starters in early innings, was that Gaston was running out of arms to call upon. The manager needed Wells in the pen as much as he needed him to start.

Against the Tribe in Cleveland, Wells scaled the heights to heave his mighty bulk over the .500 mark (7-6 on the season), persevering through 5 1/3 tougher-than-you'd-imagine innings, as the Jays dumped the Indians 9-5. But what transpired next in Milwaukee shouldn't happen to a dog.

Wells was hung out to dry, left twisting in the wind, abandoned and forsaken as the Brewers clobbered Toronto 16-3. Blow-outs in baseball are a fact of life, happens to all teams, can't dwell on them. Blah-blah-blah. But a pitching line of 13 earned runs in 4 1/3 innings? What kind of a manager would fail to rescue a pitcher, as soon as possible, from such a horror? Had Gaston no heart? Was he trying to destroy the guy? Was this personal?

Gaston, naturally, denied any sinister motives. He said he was trying to spare the exhausted pen. "Sometimes you got to stand in there and take your lumps." But these weren't lumps. This pitching line was Himalayan: 11 hits, four walks, two hit batsmen, 13 earned runs. Nobody could remember ever seeing such a thing before. And Wells said he wouldn't forget it either.

"They had a field day," he observed, standing by his locker, braced for the reportorial onslaught. "It's embarrassing for me. I'm MVP of the day for those guys. But I know our 'pen's been used a lot lately and, if I have to take one for the team, I'll take it." The best he could find to say about the night was that it was over and he had survived. "Now, I'm low man on the list, though," he added. "Now, it's the next guy's turn."

But when his next turn came around, the results were only marginally more palatable. He lost again, if not in such spectacular fashion, 6-3 to the White Sox. All six runs were forfeited in Wells' 4 1/3 innings of work, though only three were earned.

So much for starting. It was Wells-as-reliever when he next surfaced, bringing up the rear (and giving up three runs) in Milwaukee's 22-2 Murder At The SkyDome on August 28. At least his ineffectiveness was lost in the general gore of the evening. A few nights later, he offered a neat 1-2-3 ninth inning mop-up job against Chicago, Jays winning 9-3. It was a brief outing but a huge relief, no pun intended, for the beleaguered Wells.

For six days he rested, collecting his thoughts and his equilibrium in the 'pen. When Gaston motioned him into the game against the Royals on September 7, the score was tied 4-4 in the 12th inning. Curtis Wilkerson lashed a two-out single to left, scoring Brian McRae, and it was game over. "Some things that shouldn't happen, happen," Wells sighed.

Another long, very long, rest for Boomer ensued. When he tentatively stuck out his neck on September 16, with the Tribe in town, former teammate Glenallen Hill chopped it off — a 451-foot homer that rattled the glass surrounding Windows, the restaurant beyond left-centre field. That finished off the scoring at 6-3 for the visitors.

Wells got into three more regular season games and didn't give up another run. It was small comfort.

David Cone began 1992 as a New York Met, ended it as a Kansas City Royal, and in between managed to squeeze out a World Series ring as a Toronto Blue Jay.

But his tour around the continent was only the tip of the tumult Cone experienced in a year that saw his name linked with sexual scandal almost as frequently as it was invoked by baseball. This is the flip-side of celebrity: there's no place to hide from the scrutiny of public examination when one's private life explodes in salacious headlines.

Cone has never denied that he was drawn to the neon lure of New York City. Some people are not cut out for life in the fast lane but Cone reveled in it during his tenure in the Big Apple. He was a boy from the Midwest who loved the rhythms of the most cacophonous metropolis in the world. He thrived on the juice of New York. And why shouldn't he? He was young, handsome, single, the strike-out king in the National League. And he had more depth than is usually found in professional athletes, who are too often incubated from the harsher realities of life away from the ballpark.

In 1991, as the Mets struggled through their worst year since 1983, Cone was a lone beacon of excellence. His 241 strikeouts — including 19 in a victory over the Philadelphia Phillies — gave him the NL title for the second straight season, and tied him with Roger Clemens for the major-league lead. All that in spite of a mid-season slump during which he almost came to blows with former manager Bud Harrelson during a game at Cincinnati. He finished the year with a 14-14 record.

Then a New Jersey woman claimed that Cone had raped her in a Philadelphia hotel room, on the very eve of that game in which he fanned 19 Phillies to tie the NL record. Police said they could not confirm that a crime had been committed.

The woman's claims hung over the pitcher's head through the winter, even though no charges were filed. The unsavory atmosphere did not prevent Cone from seeking, and getting, a record $4.25 million in salary arbitration, following a 5 1/2-hour meeting, a $1.9 million increase from his '91 stipend of $2.35 million.

Then came the disclosure that Cone had allegedly lured two women into the Shea Stadium bullpen, back in 1989, and masturbated in front of them. This information, still unsubstantiated, was included in a $8.1 million suit, filed in New York State Supreme Court, and was an amendment to a suit filed by three women the previous September, accusing Cone of harassment and slander. The women also alleged that, later in the '89 season, Cone went to a Montreal hotel room where two of the women were staying, climbed on to their bed and masturbated.

It should be stressed, yet again, that Cone has never been charged with a crime. The civil suit claims have yet to be addressed in court either. But the New York media pounced on the information, revealing Cone's name and that of three other Mets who had been implicated in sexual escapades. In response, 31 Met players signed an agreement at spring training last year, in which they vowed not to speak to the media. Of course, the news blackout was soon rescinded.

Against this titillating backdrop, Cone continued to pitch well for his team. On August 27, when the Blue Jays traded for his services through the pennant stretch, Cone sported a 13-7 record, 2.88 ERA and was leading the National League with 214 strikeouts. All this with a perfectly dreadful, exorbitantly overpaid ballclub.

Cone seemed, on the surface, as atypical as it was possible to be for a Blue Jay recruit. He did not fit into the Canadian team's profile. He was an exotic bird. But general manager Pat Gillick, fretful over the team's pitching status as the pennant race tightened, concluded that Cone was not only the solution to his problem but available. In spite of the fact that the right hander was eligible for free agency at the end of the year — this scenario had been damaging to Toronto in the past — Gillick extracted him from the Mets, sending rookie infielder Jeff Kent and highly-touted prospect Ryan Thompson to New York. That was a lot of youthful talent for a 29-year-old who was expected to return to the bosom of Gotham — the Bronx ballpark this time — when the season concluded, World Series or not.

"It's disappointing to be leaving the Mets," Cone told reporters in a telephone hook-up after the trade was announced. "I feel like I'm leaving a sinking ship and I feel bad about that." But, oh my, he was surely looking forward to playing with a big-time contender. The Toronto media, by the way, could hardly bestir itself to question Cone about the sexual controversy. "The status is, everything is on the back burner," Cone explained, surprised — as he admitted to a New York writer later — that the controversy elicited only minimal interest from the Canadian scribes. "We have a very strong case but it's in my lawyer's hands and when the time comes, I'll have my say." He also observed that Toronto fans "didn't get a boring character, that's for sure."

His first night in a Blue Jay uniform, Cone charted pitches as the Brewers pummeled Toronto 22-2 at the SkyDome. Even the Mets had been spared that kind of humiliation. The following afternoon, in his Toronto debut, Milwaukee stole a team-record eight bases in 10 attempts. Cone also issued seven free passes in 6 2/3 innings as the Jays fell 7-2. "Not what I was looking for," he said. "I'll get better."

If the pitching rotation remained intact, Cone would have six more opportunities to show his stuff as a Jay -- at $130,102 per. In his second outing against the Minnesota Twins, he survived two shaky innings and a 3-0 deficit before his teammates rallied for a 16-5 victory. He conceded that he was trying too hard to impress his new masters. "The first game, I held 'em to one touchdown. Tonight was a little better." His personal line-score was less-than-intimidating: seven hits, three walks, a hit batsman, a wild pitch, five runs. But it still amounted to his 14th win of the season and first ever in the American League.

He should have savored that offensive support. He would not enjoy similar largesse again. From here on in, Cone had to earn every single W, the hard way.

Returning to his hometown of Kansas City, Cone blanked the Royals and the Jays won 1-0. It was the first time he felt confident enough with his new battery-mate, Pat Borders, to use his wicked backdoor slider. As Cito Gaston told reporters: "If David can do that well in front of friends and relatives, I think he's over the hump. He should be able to relax now."

He was almost as stingy when the Jays hosted the Cleveland Indians. However, Jose Mesa — one of two young righthanders the Jays had given up for Mike Flanagan in their unsuccessful division drive of 1987 — was more miserly still and the Tribe beat Toronto 2-1. Cone gave up just five hits over eight frames, but one of those was a home run by ex-Jay Glenallen Hill.

Cone was hardfisted again when the Rangers visited the SkyDome. He combined with relievers Duane Ward and Tom Henke to stonewall Texas as the Jays eked out another 1-0 win. It was another display of gritty pitching by Cone, who struck out the side in the third inning after serving up a lead-off double. "That was probably my best bit of pitching," he said afterwards. "Striking those guys out was a turning point for us. It was scary because I couldn't make a mistake."

He insisted that he was fitting in well with his new teammates, that they had made him feel welcome. But, on the field, they had responded by scoring 21 runs for him in five games — and 16 of those came in one single contest.

When Toronto traveled to New York, Cone was trailed by the media hordes. What everybody wanted to know was this: Would he be coming home in the near future, or what? Cone is that rare breed of professional athlete; he actually likes reporters. He luxuriated in the intense media scrum. He was good-natured yet coy about his future plans. Toronto was a fine place to play ball, he told the scribblers. But New York was...New York. "Toronto's probably the closest thing to New York you can find north of the border. But New York gets in your blood. Sometimes you have to get away and get your sanity back but New York never goes away."

On the day he pitched at Yankee Stadium, he said that it was strange driving out to the Bronx and not making the turn along the way to Shea Stadium. He didn't lack for direction on the mound, though, holding the Yankees to four hits in seven damp innings as the Jays slogged out a 3-1 victory. "I'm still kind of pinching myself (that) I'm here, on this side of town, at this time of year."

On September 30, Cone faced off at the the SkyDome against his former Met teammate and friend Frank Viola, now with the Boston Red Sox. Matt Young had been scheduled to start for the Bosox, but Viola approached manager Butch Hobson and asked if he could have the ball. He was eager to get involved in the pennant race, even though it meant pitching on only three days' rest. Besides, he wanted a shot at old pal Cone.

It was a masterful evening of baseball between two grudge clubs that have traditionally viewed each other with fear and loathing. Now, one was in dogged pursuit of a division championship, the other was simply trying to wrest a degree of respectability from a season of mastery. As Viola would say afterwards: "The best thing about the night was playing in a game that means something; our season was over a long time ago."

Viola was hungry and bloody-minded and almost perfect. Through eight innings, in fact, he *was* perfect. Not a single Jay could weasel even a cheap little blooper out of the mustachioed southpaw. Viola, known as Sweet Music in the silly nomenclature of big league ball, played a dulcet melody until late into the night. Finally, with Devon White leading off the ninth, the pitcher hit a sour chord and the centre fielder hit a clean single. But that was it.

Viola's best previous low-hit game had been a two-hitter in 1986 while pitching for Minnesota. And no Sox pitcher had thrown a no-hitter since Dave Morehead did it against Cleveland on Sept. 16, 1965.

Cone was nearly as impressive, allowing only four hits. But one of those was a fourth-inning homer to rookie John Valentin. That was all the scoring in this late summer jewel of a game.

It is impossible to say whether the Jays would have won the division without the contributions of David Cone. At the very least, they would have won different. He was an uncharacteristic addition. But he was one hell of a character.

# Glory Jays

## *The Tom 'n Duane Show*       14

They are wallflowers at the ball. Or ballgame, rather. They take their seats in the loge box, far afield from the action and the busy nonsense of the dugout, segregated from their teammates as if by writ of punishment or quarantine. They are a secluded few, partitioned in their otherworldliness.

They are the bullpen.

What a curious designation and one peculiar only to baseball. They are not substitutes for starters in the normal sense. Some of them — the closers, the short men — may very well be the most valuable players on their clubs; even, as was the case for Dennis Eckersley last year, the most valuable player *and* pitcher in the league. Yet they spend most of their time *spectacting*, as David Wells described it. They sit and they gab and they strike up friendships with the fans, in their own parks anyway. Oftentimes, they arrive at their pews late, straggling out from the clubhouse between innings, meandering to their enclosure while their teammates are already seriously engaged in the battle at hand. And then they can do nothing but wait for the call, for the invitation to the dance.

What do they do in there through six, seven, eight, innings, which is the routine period of idleness for relievers if all goes according to plan, and the starter isn't being blown out of his underwear? Tom Henke, the Toronto Blue Jay closer of record since 1985, shed some light on the mysteries of the bullpen during a conversation last fall. Folding his six-foot-five frame onto the bench in the dugout, he waxed expansively on life, fishing and the Zen of the 'pen.

"Well, we spit sunflower seed shells to see who can hit the outfielder," he revealed. "And we play a lot of word games. Twenty questions, trivia, that kind of stuff. Like who was Arnold Ziffle?" Arnold Ziffle? "Didn't you ever watch Green Acres?" Henke continued, shaking his head at another example of reportorial ignorance. "He was the pig."

When it came to baseball trivia, Henke admitted, his colleague Duane Ward was the undisputed champ. "But on movies and cartoons I've got him beat. I've got four kids so I still watch a lot of cartoons."

Then you've got your fishy fish tales. Lots of those get repeated ad nauseam in the bullpen. Henke proceeded to recount his favorite close encounter of the scaly kind. "Back in '88 it was, a bunch of us went up to the Severn. Let's see, there was me and Mike Flanagan and Jimmy Key and Todd Stottlemyre. We were in two boats and I bet we must have caught about 300 fish in each one. You could drop your line over the edge of the boat and they'd fight to get hooked." Not that the intrepid moundsmen concluded their angling adventure with any evidence of this gargantuan haul of bass. "Nah, we always throw the fish back, never keep 'em. What, you don't believe me?"

What they don't do in the bullpen, Henke added, is chow down on hotdogs and other ballpark fare, even though their nostrils are constantly assaulted by the odor of stadium gastronomy. "Nah, Sully (bullpen coach John Sullivan) won't allow that. But I just might have one today. Who knows, we might just break all the rules today."

In fact, no rules were broken on that particular afternoon which just happened to be the final regular season game of the '92 campaign. Henke didn't get in to the contest and neither did Ward. Since Toronto had already captured the American League East Division championship 24 hours earlier, most of the Blue Jay regulars were given the day off.

This did not come as a surprise, of course. But then there are very few surprises in how manager Cito Gaston deploys his troops and in particular the bullpen brethren. From starters-to-Ward-to-Henke, in a situation where Toronto has the lead. Henke never comes to the mound (okay, almost never) unless the Jays are in front. This is classic closer cant. Dogma.

Certainly, it had been Toronto's modus operandi for the last couple of years. One inning for Henke following one or two innings for set-up man Ward. And, when necessary, when more interim help was required, just pick from the rest of the arms as needed: Mike Timlin, the strapping sophomore whose arm was blown out the previous season from injudicious over-use; Pat Hentgen, another kid who got a couple of starts in 1992 and several wins in relief; David Wells, alternating duties as reliever and starter; Mark Eichhorn, an ex-Jay acquired in late July from the California Angels; and whatever other arms happen to be passing through the organization at any given time.

But, essentially, it had been the Tom 'n Duane Show in Toronto.

What is surprising is that this juxtaposition of arms and egos worked so well for so long. Ward demonstrated last year — as he did during Henke's ailing periods in 1991 — that he was eminently qualified to shoulder the responsibilities of the closing assignment. Yet he didn't pout or whine when he was held back, relegated to the Number 2 job in the relief crew. He bided his time and, in 1993, that time has finally come.

For this serenity in the 'pen, most of the credit has to go to Henke. He is not a saint but he is rather admirable. He is *likable*. And, as he pointed out in spring training last year, he had done nothing the previous season to lose his job in '92.

The Terminator, as he was hastily christened when he came up to the Jays in the summer of '85 — he had spent several years in the Texas Rangers organization before that — Henke led the American League with eight saves through August his first summer in Toronto. For that, and his folksy disposition, he was an instant hit in town and continued to enjoy the affection of the fans throughout his tenure in Toronto.

Still, there were rumors last spring that he was about to be demoted to the chorus line ranks of the bullpen. If not that, then maybe the Jays would trade the 34-year-old, and his $3.6 million salary, to some other club. Henke wasn't buying any of it. "I don't think I did anything last year (1991) to lose my job," he insisted. This was true. Despite tendinitis and two stints on the disabled list, he had still racked up 25 saves in a row, a major league record. He had also finished the year first in AL save percentage, with .914 (32-35). "Cito has already told me that it'll be the same as last year. I'm gonna get the majority of the saves. Duane will get some. We're going to share the load. I think I'm mature enough to handle that."

He had toughed it out in spite of severe arm soreness in the final weeks of the '91 campaign, playing when he should have been resting, taking two cortisone shots and returning to the fray to pitch in the playoffs. It was gutsy but, in retrospect, not wise. "You work so hard to get to the big dance and you don't want to miss it," he said, simply. "Sometimes pride and stubbornness just take over."

So now he and Ward were, according to the baseball chroniclers, supposed to be battling it out for the closer role. Except it was one of the most genteel duels you could imagine. "Some people think me and Duane are mortal enemies but we're not," Henke told anybody who would listen last spring. "It's a good competition. It keeps us both sharp. You have to have that competition to keep that edge."

There was an irony there, too. Henke knew exactly what it was like to be in Ward's action-itchy shoes. In the mid-80s, as the hotshot new centurion on the block, he took the closer job on the Jays away from Bill Caudill. He remembered how classy the latter was under similar circumstances.

"He knew I was taking his job. But every time I had a bad game or something, he was there to help cheer me up. Or to let me know what I was doing wrong. I had a good role model to learn from."

There had been others, of course, who helped fashion this generosity of spirit in Henke. Mostly, there had been his family: his parents and the eight brothers and sisters who still make their home in the tiny town of Taos, Missouri, which is where Henke resides in the off-season with wife Kathy and their four kids. "We never had a whole lot growing up. But Dad and Mom instilled a lot of good values in me that I try to practice now. I've always liked to help people, regardless of whether it's baseball or just going out and helping my neighbor do some farmwork when I'm at home.

"I feel I've helped a lot of people coming up in the minor leagues. I take young guys in and let them stay with me until they can find a place, stuff like that. I had guys do the same for me when I was coming up through the minors. I had guys give me spikes when I didn't have enough money to buy a pair."

The big guy with the broad shoulders and the sorta goofy countenance has always been a genial, steadying influence on the field and in the clubhouse. He's a bricklayer when he's not a ballplayer and that kind of solid grounding has kept him *normal*.

To really know Henke is to visit the town and the family that created him. Taos, a rustic burg with a population of 700, is nestled in the Ozarks, about a two-hour over-the-speed-limit drive down the blacktop from St. Louis. This is deep Henke territory, where all the residents still have a proprietary interest in their most famous native son. For a long time, before satellite dishes and video cassette recorders became more popular, Henke's stats and game-story results would be posted daily on a special bulletin board at Eiken's Food Store and Hardware, a backwoods version of Peking's Democracy Wall.

It's a Roman Catholic enclave, settled by German immigrants in the late 1800s. Henke and his many siblings grew up in a cramped log cabin just down the road, a sort of log-house that has been reinforced with stone and mortar over the years. Henke's mother played the church organ, his father worked for many years as a supervisor at a toolmaking company, and the large brood was raised on Missourian common sense and one-pot dinners. It was an idyllic childhood for the Henke kids — all of them healthy, robust and *big* — as they fished and hunted and played sports.

Several years ago, Henke's mother Mary Jane told a reporter that she rather expected Tom, who was deeply religious, would dedicate his life to the church, not baseball. "He liked to pray. I always thought he was going to become a priest."

A priest? The Terminator? Yet there remains about Henke a placidity, a kindliness, that suggests he would have made a fine clergyman had he not been tempted by the siren song of baseball.

So there was tremendous sympathy for the big closer last spring, particularly among reporters who had covered the Jays through all the years when too many of the players were not particularly lovable or amenable to the press. But the Blue Jay administrators showed their hand early when they refused Henke's request for a contract extension before the '92 season began. That would have forced the team to protect Henke in the expansion draft last November. His age and his recent arm problems precluded such a commitment.

Their reasoning seemed to be justified when Henke, a notoriously slow starter anyway coming out of spring training, had to
get more cortisone squirts last March, which sidelined him for a
couple of weeks during the Grapefruit League tune-up period.
Henke told reporters that it was not in his nature to hang on, a
pathetic shadow of his former self, if it looked as if his career was
coming to a close. He just wasn't convinced that this most recent
episode of tendinitis signaled that end. "I'm a realist. I'm not one
of those guys who feels he can pitch forever. I'm not gonna be
trying to hang around, hanging onto a job. But this, heck, I'm
really optimistic about it. I've had worse, lots worse." He also
acknowledged that, being in his mid-thirties, he had to accept
that pitching would no longer be an effortless activity. "I know
I'm getting towards the age where I've got to pitch with pain."
Yet he was still toying with the idea of re-introducing the long-
discarded slider into his pitching repertoire. This did not sound
like a man contemplating retirement.

In the end, the status quo was maintained. If nothing appeared to be broken, then the skipper would resist any urge to
tinker. Henke's paramount position in the bullpen was his to
keep or lose.

That was the word coming out of Dunedin, anyway. But in
his first three appearances of '92, Henke preceded Ward onto the
mound and the latter had converted each chance into a save. On
April 14, Gaston announced that he was reverting to the old
routine. "Wardo's not the closer anymore," he told reporters.
"We've switched. Tom Henke's going into that now." No further
explanation was forthcoming. But closers are a rather delicate
breed, like hot-house orchids, and they have to be handled with
a certain psychological tact. One had to assume Gaston knew
what he was doing.

The night after Gaston's bulletin, against the New York
Yankees, Henke delivered a 1-2-3 finish for his first save of the
season as the Jays won 2-0. Given his manager's clear support,
Henke was a much relieved reliever. Yet there was something
different about the man on the hill. It was as if the ground had
shifted slightly, tilted fractionally, and he was no longer as
dominating, as sure-footed, as he had been in earlier days. In
subsequent months, it would appear that Henke had lost some of
his menace and hitters were no longer as intimidated by his once

devastating forkball. There was always a feeling, on any given night and regardless of the situation, that with Henke pitching, something *bad* could happen.

Against the Red Sox in Boston on April 19, it did. The Bosox, trailing by three runs in the ninth, strung together a messy collection of bloopers and bleeders and — abetted by a John Olerud error — managed to claw back a 5-4 victory at Fenway Park.

"Everything went wrong," Henke admitted, after delivering four runs (three unearned) on three hits and a walk for his first loss of the year. After the first Boston run was scored in that wretched inning, Gaston had the option of yanking Henke in favor of David Wells, who was warmed up and ready. But he stuck with his closer-of-record because that is how Gaston operates. He had already declared that Henke was his short man and he was keeping his word, even if the circumstances cried out for an amendment.

A week later, Juan Guzman left a game against the Royals with a 4-1 lead and two out in the ninth. On came Henke, with Wally Joyner on second, to face George Brett. The wily batsman greeted the closer with a two-run homer. Henke then got Kevin McReynolds on a line drive to dispel any fantasies of a comeback victory. But he had made the outcome far less certain than it should have been, especially for Guzman.

No getting around it. Henke was not the decisive Terminator of old. Against the Mariners in Seattle, the tying run made it as far as third before Henke nailed down his fourth save of the season, as the Jays squeezed past the home-side 8-7. Against the Brewers he served up a ninth inning home run to Darryl Hamilton before locking up his seventh save, Toronto prevailing 5-4. "I thought it was a fly ball when he hit it. Luckily, it didn't hurt us."

Luck was becoming an increasing factor in his appearances which is not how it's supposed to be done. The fans were noticing too. They began to boo Tom Henke, so much so that Kelly Gruber scolded them for their fair-weather support, with disastrous consequences for the third baseman.

Facing the Twins in early June, Henke held on to a 5-3 lead by surviving a shaky 10th inning and a line drive off the bat of Kirby Puckett that landed directly in Candy Maldonado's glove. Luck. In Baltimore, he secured save number 11, but only after giving up a leadoff single, inducing Billy Ripken to pop-up on a bunt attempt and then benefiting from Pat Borders' throw to second, which nailed Mark McLemore stealing. Luck.

On June 24, in Texas, Henke pitched the ninth for his 13th save. It was his 413th appearance for Toronto, breaking the pitching record he shared with Dave Stieb. He struck out Brian Downing with a runner on second to end the game. Two weeks later, against the California Angels at the SkyDome, he earned his 200th career save, the 13th pitcher in history to do so, though these stats are a relatively recent preoccupation. "I'm glad to get it out of the way because I've been thinking about it for the last couple of weeks," he said. "Hopefully, I'll get another 100 and make it 300."

Later in the month, good fortune smiled again. With Toronto leading the Athletics, Henke had blown his bid for his 16th save in the top half of the ninth, but in the bottom of the inning Maldonado delivered the blow that drove home Robbie Alomar for a 4-3 Toronto final. Against the Kansas City Royals on July 28, he recorded the final four outs to post his 17th save but not before allowing an RBI single by Gregg Jefferies in the ninth, and then fanning George Brett.

In mid-August, Toronto doubled up the Orioles 8-4 but Henke again forfeited a couple of runs in the ninth. August was also a dreadful month for the starters which meant the Ward-Henke combination was not getting the amount of work it needed to stay sharp. Henke, in particular, has a propensity to lose his edge after long periods of inactivity. Still, he got his 22nd save against the Minnesota Twins, despite a leadoff walk in the ninth followed by a single and a Manny Lee throwing error.

The Jays were struggling, or at least it was as close to a struggle as the club would come in this fruitful season. Gaston even tried to change the alchemy on the team by inverting his Ward-Henke combo. That made no difference when Chicago dumped the Jays 6-3. Neither short man conceded a run but by then the final tally was already on the board. The manager had utilized them both in a losing cause.

Two nights later, facing the Brewers, Henke's first pitch of the night was redirected into the Toronto bullpen but he persevered for a 5-4 win and save No. 23. Two weeks later on, he was up to No. 27, again in Arlington, closing for winner Juan Guzman but allowing two hits in the ninth. Still against Texas, 48 hours later, a warmed-up Henke had to sit down without having seen any action when a late-innings spurt by the Rangers narrowed the gap to 4-2. Ward, who had worked the eighth, finished it off and the Jays won 7-2. Some of Ward's long-repressed frustration may have shown when he told reporters: "It's nice to go back out there and get a save for a change." He had not been given the opportunity since racking up No. 10 in early August. "It's like a bit of a reward for doing a good job."

The tag-team functioned well through September. By the third week, Henke had six saves in six appearances while Ward countered with a win, a save and four holds in six games. When Toronto traveled to Baltimore for a much-hyped three-game series — and the AL East still very much a three-way race — the Jays showed their grit by taking two, including the opener, a 4-3 marathon that lasted almost six hours because of a rain delay of two hours and 42 minutes. In that one, the Orioles got runners at first, second and third in the ninth before Henke nailed down the final out and his 31st save by popping up Mike Devereaux on a hanging forkball right down the middle. "Smooth as silk," he said afterwards, tongue firmly in cheek.

On October 2, Henke struck out Mickey Tettleton for his career-high 34th save and the Jays defeated Detroit 8-7. That was the irony of it: his most saves ever and yet the accomplishment was tinged with doubt.

The following afternoon, when Toronto dismissed the Tigers 3-1 at the SkyDome, the Jays clinched their fourth American League East Division championship. In the glow of that achievement, and with all hands celebrating, the specifics of the game itself were almost immediately forgotten. But something significant happened that night. It was the changing of the guard.

In the ninth inning, with Toronto leading 3-0, Henke came to the mound. It was fitting that he should be there, in the heart of the action, with the Jays and their fans poised to rejoice. But he couldn't do it. He couldn't finish off the Tigers. One-out singles to Travis Fryman and Cecil Fielder, followed by a walk to Mickey Tettleton, loaded up the bases. Henke got Rob Deer on a pop-up but then rookie Scott Livingston worked him for an RBI walk.

This was too hazardous for Gaston. He pulled Henke and sent in Ward. Dan Gladden cracked a towering popper and the game was finally over, 3-1.

"It would have been fun to finish it," said Henke. "I didn't get it done." Then he offered a lame joke. "Ah, I just wanted to get Wardo some ink."

It didn't seem to mean much at the time. In retrospect, it meant everything.

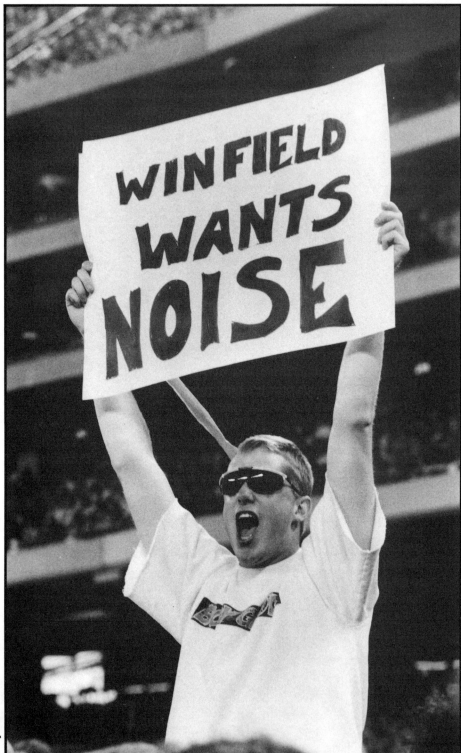

# Gl⦿ry Jays

## *Five Games that Mattered*

One hundred and sixty-two games. Ninety-six victories. Sixty-six losses. At the end of the regular season, a four game lead over the second-place Milwaukee Brewers in the American League East.

Looking back, every victory seems crucial. If not for this one or that one or the one over there, there may have been no division title, no American League title, no World Series. In fact, there were some games that mattered more than others, some wins that did save the day and maybe even the year. These were distinctive episodes that said something about the Toronto Blue Jays, about the team they had become and the team they wanted to be.

It's all open for debate, of course, a diversion for spectators. It amuses us and makes us feel clairvoyant to look back. Nevertheless, here are short recaps of five games that deserve to be remembered:

Tuesday, June 2: Toronto 7 at Minnesota 5
The Metrodome is always noisy and always inhospitable to visitors. So the short ceremony that preceded the game was downright bizarre, as the Twins franchise honored a pitcher from the opposing team. Jack Morris, roundly censured for abandoning the Twins after leading the club to a World Series championship the previous fall, was greeted with more jeers than cheers when he came out to accept the club's 1991 Most Valuable Player award.

That done, an unabashed Morris made his way back to the dugout and Todd Stottlemyre took the mound for the business at hand. Motivated perhaps by the brief appearance of their former teammate, now the enemy, the Twins took out their resentment on Stottlemyre, who had lost his last three decisions. Minnesota built up a 3-0 lead on four hits in the first, abetted by Kelly Gruber's hurried throw to John Olerud at first which allowed leadoff hitter Shane Mack to reach second on the error, then added another run in the second.

It seemed like it was over before it had barely begun. But Stottlemyre settled down and the Jays got one back in the third, another in the fourth, and two to tie up the game in the fifth. In the eighth, John Olerud belted a solo home run, his fourth, off Bob Kipper — who had come on in relief of Pat Mahomes — to put the Jays in front 5-4, but not for long. Kirby Puckett, 4-for-6 on the night, doubled and scored in the bottom-half.

It stayed deadlocked until the 13th when Olerud — who had also scored Dave Winfield with a sacrifice fly back in the fourth — combined with Derek Bell and Gruber for some timely offense at the expense of loser Gary Wayne. (All three Jays involved had been much maligned of late. Bell, batting .140 coming into the game, had taken extra batting drills prior to practice that afternoon, using a shorter bat and swinging with one hand on balls tossed up by hitting instructor Larry Hisle. It must have helped; he later connected for a double in the third.)

Gruber doubled, Olerud laid down a sacrifice bunt and Bell got the RBI with a long sacrifice fly. Shortstop Manuel Lee then singled in Pat Borders for the insurance tally. The win went to rookie Pat Hentgen, who had come on after four scoreless innings by David Wells, and now had a surprising 4-0 record for the year. Tom Henke pitched the 13th and nailed down the save, his 10th.

What was most impressive about this comeback victory for Toronto was that it was the second night in a row they had beaten the Twins in extra innings. (The previous evening, Devon White's inside-the-park home run in the 10th had lifted the Jays to a 5-3 win.) It was also their third extra-inning game in the last four days and the Jays had produced five consecutive wins with their final at-bats. Said Henke: "These are character-builders."

Tuesday, July 7: Seattle 3 at Toronto 4

Aesthetics don't count in baseball. Which is fortunate since this contest was as homely as they come. One run on a wild pitch, another to tie the game on a bases-loaded walk. So what? This isn't figure skating. Ugly form does not translate into demerits.

Pat Hentgen, the rookie who had been living a charmed life on the mound by scooping up a series of unexpected wins in middle-relief, was sent to the hill in only his second major league start, against Seattle's Rich DeLucia who would be close to brilliant through six shut-out innings.

For a guy with a 7.09 ERA in 12 games, DeLucia's subsequent performance could not have been predicted. He held the Jays to just three hits and tied a career-high with eight strikeouts. A close call was averted in the sixth when Devon White doubled and scrambled all the way home in what appeared to be his second inside-the-park home run of the year. But the ball had become trapped in the outfield wall and White was sent back to second base. Then Robbie Alomar fanned and Joe Carter popped out to first.

Hentgen, inserted into the starting rotation as a possible solution to the problems caused by Dave Stieb's continuing woes, was marginally less impressive than his counterpart. He allowed two runs on seven hits through seven frames.

With the Mariners leading 2-0, Seattle manager Bill Plummer decided that DeLucia was fading and called for Brian Fisher, purchased from the Triple A Calgary Cannons two days earlier, to start the seventh. The Jays promptly got one back, the uncomely way. After Dave Winfield singled, John Olerud walked and Candy Maldonado's grounder forced out Olerud at second. Fisher bonked one off the backstop which allowed Winfield to score and cut the margin to 2-1.

Duane Ward, taking over the chores from Hentgen to start the eighth, surrendered a solo homer to Pete O'Brien. But even though Seattle now had the 3-1 lead, they were the ones who looked to be on the ropes. With closer Mike Schooler unavailable because of a sore arm, Fisher continued to work without a parachute in the eighth. Manuel Lee flied out to left, Devon White flied out to centre. Then Robbie Alomar and Joe Carter both singled to put runners on first and second.

That brought Winfield to the plate and Fisher bore down, working a 1-2 count. Winfield tried to check swing on the 2-2 pitch and, judging by the TV angle anyway, apparently failed to do so. But the umpire saw it differently. Winfield, still alive, lashed the next pitch toward third where it bounced off third baseman Jeff Schaefer's mitt. That enabled Alomar to score.

Juan Agosto came on and walked Olerud. Jeff Nelson replaced Agosto and blew two strikes past Candy Maldonado but then delivered four consecutive balls which forced Carter home with the tying run.

Ward held down the fort in the top of the ninth and Pat Borders opened the bottom of the inning with a single off Nelson. Pinch runner Rob Ducey was moved to second on Lee's sacrifice bunt and Devon White slashed the game-winner up the middle. That made a 4-3 victor out of Ward.

The victory pushed the Jays' winning streak to six games and gave them with a four-game cushion in the AL East.

Thursday, August 13: Baltimore 2 at Toronto 4

The month of August was a trying time for the Jays. Not disastrous but decidedly uncomfortable. Largely a result of poor performances from their starters (with the exception of Jack Morris), compounded by injuries to Dave Stieb and Juan Guzman, Toronto's dominance in the division was threatened. The team's lead over the Baltimore Orioles had dwindled to just one game. This distressing turn of events had been accomplished face-to-face since the Orioles had just taken two out of three from Toronto at the SkyDome. If the Jays lost the final confrontation of the series, they would lose sole possession of first place and, psychologically, a lot more.

In order to stop the erosion, Cito Gaston turned to Doug Linton, a long-in-the tooth rookie who had been kicking around the minors for too many years. Now 27, Linton had struggled to come back from rotator cuff surgery in 1987, his first pro year. But other, younger, arms had passed him by in the organization over the interim. These were indeed desperate times.

Baseball loves melodrama. And, over the decades, the game continues to throw up scenarios that would make a corny Hollywood screenwriter blush. But this dreamy night, starring over-the-hill ingenue Doug Linton, would be such a tale.

Gaston had been hoping, at best, that the "kid" could get the Jays through six innings before turning matters over to the bullpen. In order to make Linton more comfortable, the manager also started Randy Knorr behind the plate instead of Borders —

Knorr had played in Syracuse with Linton and was a familiar batterymate.

The Orioles had their own fine rookie on the hill, Arthur Lee Rhodes. Joe Carter tattooed him in the first inning for his 26th homer of the season, a solo shot. In the second, Baltimore got one back on a leadoff home run by Glenn Davis but the Jays regained the lead in the bottom half when Knorr delivered Kelly Gruber with his first major league RBI. That's how it remained until the seventh, during which Linton set down 15 Orioles in a row. The Orioles then tied it up on a leadoff double by Cal Ripken, who came around to score on a ground out and sac fly.

Linton's teammates would not allow Linton to waste such a fine debut on a no-decision or worse. In the eighth, Devon White blooped a single to left and Alomar, after messing up two bunt attempts, rang one up the left-centre gap for a 3-2 lead. Rhodes was lifted for Todd Frohwirth and Joe Carter put down his first sacrifice bunt since his days as a Cleveland Indian. Alomar moved to third and scored on Candy Maldonado's insurance single.

The Jays, about to embark on a 12-game road trip, had split the series and secured a two-game cushion in the AL East. Linton, who gave up just three hits over eight, had his first major league win.

Some kid.

Thursday, September 17: Cleveland 5 at Toronto 7.

Somewhere along the line last year, the Cleveland Indians stopped being patsies. The Jays were reminded of this yet again when they sent out their ace, Jack Morris, who was hungry and looking for his 20th win of 1992.

You would have thought the chances were good, that the 50,408 fans at the SkyDome would come away from this encounter having witnessed the first such achievement by a pitcher in Blue Jay history. As it turned out, they would have to settle for an extra-inning victory that was extraordinary in spite of Morris' no-decision. The veteran came up just one, albeit prominent, inning short.

Morris was coasting along with a 5-3 lead through seven when Albert Belle, who had dinged him for a two-run homer in the first, connected with a one-out, two-run double in the eighth.

The damage could have been worse had not Alfredo Griffin executed a diving stop on a Carlos Martinez liner to start an inning-ending double play. Bloodied but still standing, Morris returned in the ninth and blanked Cleveland. However, Eric Plunk — the fourth Indian pitcher on the night — also stone-walled the Jays through the eighth and ninth. At the end of the regulation nine, having thrown 116 pitches, Morris was deemed to have had enough. Duane Ward took over and delivered a 1-2-3 10th.

In the bottom of that inning, Dave Winfield worked a one-out walk off Plunk that brought John Olerud to the plate. The first baseman, now batting .291 after a fitful start to the season — in late May, he was still plodding along with a .225 batting average — cracked a two-run bolt on the first pitch he saw to deep, deep right-centre. His 15th tater of the year gave the Jays a 7-5 final and Ward his seventh win. "It's a great feeling to come through, get a big hit like that," said the low-key Olerud, who had driven in 22 runs in his past 29 games. "Down the stretch, that's what you hope for."

### Tuesday, September 22: Toronto 4 at Baltimore 3

The Orioles, who had been shadowing the Jays throughout the summer, were five games back with time running out. They had set themselves a goal -- to sweep Toronto and regain much of the ground that had been lost in September. But the Jays, aware of their own reputation for swooning in the stretch, envisioned something else entirely. To that end, they sent Todd Stottlemyre (soon to begin serving a five-game suspension) to the mound. Stottlemyre had a 6-0 career record against the Orioles.

This would be a plucky, assertive affair for Toronto, a game in which the Jays showed their mettle, unfazed by a two-hour and 42-minute rain delay that forced Stottlemyre to warm up twice before getting in his 6 2/3 innings, and the victory that would square him at 11-11 on the year.

It was windy and wild and ferocious. Devon White opened the scoring in the first with a four-bagger off the out-of-town scoreboard on Rick Sutcliffe's fourth pitch of the night. The Orioles tied it in the third but John Olerud lined a two-run shot, his 16th homer, to kick-start a three-run fourth. That last tally was scored by Kelly Gruber who, after stealing second and third, was driven in by Alfredo Griffin's bunt, the first run bunted home by the Jays in '92.

Baltimore crept back within two in the seventh and Stottlemyre, who had surrendered just four hits and set down 10 in a row after his two-out homer to Mike Devereaux in the third, gave way to Duane Ward. The Orioles came even closer with their third run in the eighth, and almost their fourth. Brady Anderson was on third base when Cal Ripken sent a sharp two-hopper towards the same spot. Anderson, following orders from the bench, headed for home and Gruber's throw caught him at the plate for the second out. Glenn Davis followed with a single that would have tied the game had manager Johnny Oates not gambled earlier with Anderson.

Tom Henke trotted out to sew-her-up in the ninth but this proved to be another lively inning. The Orioles had runners on first and third with one out. No doubt regretting the eighth inning gamble, Tim Hulett was held back by third base coach Cal Ripken Sr. on Mark McLemore's fly to medium-deep centre. Finally, with the bases loaded, Henke got Devereaux to pop-up on a hanging forkball right down the middle and it was game over.

It was also 1.20 in the morning.

# Glory Jays

## *No Excuses,*
## *No Chokes*         **16**

Marla Maples, the actress and erstwhile lover of Donald Trump, once used her shapely posterior to promote a brand of jeans called No Excuses. For the Toronto Blue Jays, there could be no excuses in 1992 either. No turning of the other cheek if they got their backsides paddled yet again in the American League Championship Series.

They were still a relatively young organization, an adolescent member of the major league fraternity but in just 16 years of existence, the Jays had established a regrettable tradition of playoff incontinence. They were not in the same league of post-season self-mutilation as, say, the Boston Red Sox, but they were working on it. Not for nothing had they earned the sobriquet Blow Jays. In 1985, leading the Kansas City Royals three games to one, Toronto had sputtered and surrendered the series at home. In '89, the Oakland Athletics had picked them apart in just five games. And in '91, the most numbing collapse of all, the Jays had yielded meekly in another lumpish quintet to the Minnesota Twins.

When they were raw and inexperienced, it had been easier to accept these setbacks. They were callow recruits to the very real pressures of playoff baseball. Easier to applaud them for the tremendous strides they had made in such a brief time than to deride them for their shortcomings in the crunch. But that rationale didn't have much of a shelf-life. In 1989, the club blamed injuries instead, which was true, except that injuries are a fact of life in sport and the teams with real fortitude usually overcome these obstacles. Then again, the A's were an overwhelming ballclub in the late '80s. There is no shame in losing to a superior opponent.

In the most recent failure, the previous autumn, there had been no plausible alibis, no place to hide. The Jays had choked and let's dispense with the euphemisms. But the throat-slashing was not entirely self-inflicted. Jack Morris, on the mound for the Twins, had a little something to do with the end result. Now he was Toronto's most lethal weapon.

Well, you'd have thought so, wouldn't you?

Putting aside for the moment the Jays' distressing history in the playoffs, it should be remembered that the strangest things can happen in the pennant round, often have. This is the toughest challenge in baseball — getting out of the league championships alive. Some of the most entertaining baseball can be found here too, but who remembers that when everything is said and done? There is at least some cachet to losing the World Series. It means you were good enough to get that far, you had survived. Only one team can go home at the end of the year completely happy but there is considerable solace in finishing second. No ring of course, but you were there, you were on the field when it happened. You played until the very last second of baseball.

The Jays were a team ripe for victory in the fall of '92. Everyone was healthy, everyone was prepared. With expansion looming, and a heavy winter turnover of free agents expected, the face of baseball would mutate and the Blue Jay roster more visibly than most. When would such an opportunity come again?

In olden days, not-so-distant days, the Oakland A's had given the Jays fits. This was a team that had their number. Many fans, their hopes dashed in the past, were behaving like scaredy-cats on the eve of the playoffs. In Toronto, there were those who braced themselves for defeat because it was safer to contemplate failure than anticipate victory. These individuals were not necessarily fatalists. They just didn't want to be hurt again. It was a kind of psychic armor that they donned — better to gird up one's loins for the worst than leave the fleshy underbelly of desire exposed.

The A's shouldn't have set any hearts to pounding in terror. What were they doing at the top of the American League West anyway? Here was a collection of aging menaces and enfeebled athletes — a team held together with spit and glue and tenacity. Over the course of the season, 16 different players had gone on the disabled list, some more than once. At one point, the entire outfield was on the limp. Yet manager Tony LaRussa had brought his crew to the playoff circle once more, or they had brought him, as the case may be. The A's had won the World Series in 1989 and much of that roster was intact — with the notable exception of the cantankerous Jose Canseco, traded to Texas just two months earlier for Ruben Sierra, Bobby Witt and Jeff Russell. The A's didn't need to win, in the same way that the Jays did — there was no element of atonement — yet their yearning was no less intense.

Oakland may have been hobbled throughout the '92 campaign but the club, on paper, had matched up evenly with the Jays. Toronto had finished with a 96-66 record, topping the East by four games; Oakland had a 96-66 record, winning the West by six. The two clubs had split their 12 games against each other, 3-3 at home and on the road. One of these teams would have to rack up its 100th win of the year in order to claim the American League gonfalon — a century for a pennant.

In Game 1, the Jays had Jack Morris, the A's had Dave Stewart Morris was 37, Stewart was 35. A pitching battle for the ages, you would imagine. When the series opened in Toronto on October 7, the Jays were 3-2 favorites in the best-of-seven encounter. Chided Stewart: "A lot of odds-makers go broke."

There was a promise to keep before the real business at hand got underway. As the fans settled into their seats, a figure from out of the past appeared in the dugout. Moving slowly, deliberately — as if he had to think about what his feet were doing — he climbed the steps and walked onto the field, a tall man in an elegant navy suit. As recognition dawned on the crowd, the fans rose as one to acknowledge him. Years earlier, the passionate Damaso Garcia had burned his Toronto uniform in disgust. It had been a vicious gesture of discontent and he had eventually been sent away. But those rebellious days were long ago and he had been forgiven. Now Garcia was a 36-year-old invalid battling the ravages of chemotherapy following surgery to remove a malignant brain tumor. His body was weak, the hair on his head a sparse growth like the down of a gosling. But he smiled, and he waved, and he threw the ball. Alfredo Griffin, his long-time friend and former teammate, caught the ball and they embraced. "I feel like I've been through a war," said Garcia. Those are the real wars. Baseball is just a diversion.

But it's what 51,039 paying customers had come to see. What they hadn't reckoned on witnessing was Morris getting long-balled into the loss column. Mark McGwire, Terry Steinbach and Harold Baines all took him out of the park. Morris should have left the park too, or at least the hill, but manager Cito Gaston — ignoring the entreaties of the patrons — left his starter in there for the full nine frames. And the 4-3 defeat.

Yes, they booed Jack Morris. In this city, in this ballpark, that didn't happen often. Now the hired pistol had been shot right between the eyes.

It had all happened so quickly, in two separate explosive spurts. McGwire and Steinbach connected back-to-back for a 3-0 Oakland bulge in the second, but even this misshapen score was not overly worrisome. It was early innings yet and Morris had made a habit of getting himself out of similar scrapes throughout the season. His teammates regularly battled back for him — it was sometimes like a game within a game that they played: "Give up a couple and hold 'em Jack, we'll do the rest."

In typical fashion, Morris got stronger and stingier with his pitches as the game wore on. It seemed as if his largesse had been expended early and there would be no more goodies. Meanwhile, Pat Borders and Dave Winfield countered with solo shots of their own. "Solo shots don't bother me," said Stewart, he of the Death Stare eyes. "With guys on base, yeah, those homers pretty much get up under my nose, but solos — it's not okay, but it's okay."

LaRussa, putting hard-nosed baseball sense over goopy loyalty to an individual, pulled Stewart in the eighth, after his starter gave up a two-out double to Winfield. That brought Jeff Russell aboard but John Olerud smoked a single past his ear to centre, driving in Winfield and tying the score at 3-3. "Yeah, I thought that was a big run for us," Olerud admitted later. "We'd been swinging the bats good and driving the ball all over the field but we couldn't seem to get any runs. Then, everybody felt like tying it up would get us over the hump."

A hump is one thing, a cavern is another. Morris tumbled into the latter when he reappeared to start the ninth, much to everyone's surprise. "I figure Jack's pitched well enough this year to give him a shot to go out and win the game," Gaston would explain in the post-mortem. Leadoff hitter Harold Baines — who had stung Morris with a hard single to centre in front of McGwire back in the second — drilled a 1-0 pitch to right for the winning home run. It was his third hit of the night. "A slider over the plate," reported Baines.

At about the same time that Baines was providing this terse appraisal for reporters, Morris was sitting deep in his locker, an ice pack on his arm, a beer in his hand. He had heard the jeers, he said, but he wasn't cowed by the public. "I'm just glad they showed up." He was cool and calm, his angular face no paler than usual. "I made a bad pitch," he shrugged. "I made three of them, as a matter of fact." No, he wasn't disappointed, he maintained, even though he may have lost some of his post-season lustre on route to losing the game. "I'm happier than hell just to be lucky enough to be here. There are a lot of guys sitting at home who would love to be here. It's in the past. We've lost it. Tomorrow the sun will come up and we'll play another ballgame."

Technically speaking, he would not play in that ballgame of course. The next pitching assignment fell to David Cone, a latter-day Jay who had been pulled out of a hat in late August by general manager Pat Gillick. Cone was 1-1 in past playoff experience, with the New York Mets in '88. His only previous exposure to the A's was 2/3rds of an inning as a reliever with the Kansas City Royals in 1986. The advantage, in this strangers-when-we-meet situation, had to go to the pitcher, although Cone was not convinced. "It's a wash. They haven't seen me and I haven't seen them."

Talking heads on TV like to babble about pivotal games. In a 7-game series, they're all pivotal. But after losing the opener at home, Game 2 took on added dimensions for the Jays. Venturing to the coast for a three-game set, two-in-the-hole, was a disquieting prospect. Faint-hearted fans could already hear the rattling of playoff ghosts.

Cone, anxious to prove his worth (and, by the by, display his talent to potential employers for 1993) strode purposefully to the hill on that Thursday evening. For the next two and a half hours, he was brilliant. Fastball, slider, split-finger fastball: the A's were rolling their shoulders, swiveling their hips and hacking at the ball. Cone stiffed the Oaklanders on five hits over eight innings, striking out six while walking three. Another half-dozen stole on him but they wilted on the base-vines. The A's had threatened in the third and the fifth but Cone persevered and dominated. His finest moment came in the fifth when he froze Walt Weiss with a wicked slider for strike three. Weiss is still looking for it.

Some higher power must have been looking down on Cone with affection in that same inning. Willie Wilson, on the front end of a double-steal, had charged home with time to spare after Cone's 1-1 offering to Weiss caromed off Pat Borders' shin guards, then his chin, and bounded towards the Toronto dugout. Borders scrabbled after it and Wilson rounded third. Borders slid six or seven feet on his knees, keeled off the top step of the dugout and landed at his teammates' feet. Wilson crossed the plate. Meanwhile, the fleeing orb had stopped rolling. Borders could have made a play but wisely declined. Had he grabbed the cowhide, it would have been a live ball. Ignoring it, the ball rattled into the dugout, rendering it dead.

The pertinent rule is complex, but a simplified version reads thus: Two bases allowed on a ball thrown from the field, if it ends up in the dugout; one base on a ball from the rubber, regardless of whether there's a stolen base in progress. Wilson was escorted back to third, Weiss whiffed, inning over. The same predicament had befallen the Jays just a month earlier so the ruling was fresh on their minds. Several players later claimed they had shooed Borders away from the ball. He said he had heard nothing. "It was a last minute decision. I had no chance at getting him anyway."

The game had chugged along in a scoreless tie until the bottom of the fifth when, BOOM, Kelly Gruber whacked a two-run homer off Mike Moore. It was a toss-up who was more surprised, the man who hit it or the 51,114 men, women, and children in the ballpark who saw it. After all, Gruber had long since stopped being a power-hitting threat.

For a moment, Gruber stood at the plate and admired the trajectory of the ball as it arced into the left field bullpen. Then he chased Candy Maldonado, who'd preceded him with a one-out walk, to home plate. Two innings later, Gruber slapped a double and came around to score the third run on Manny Lee's sacrifice fly. The crowd responded accordingly. "For all Kelly's been through this year," said Cone, flush from his own achievement, "you just had this feeling he'd be the guy who'd step up some-time during this series."

Cone had departed to his own round of public approval in the ninth after a lead-off triple to Ruben Sierra. That brought Tom Henke trotting in from the pen. He surrendered an RBI-single forthwith to Baines and so long shut-out. The comebacker had traveled straight back through the box. "Not as quick as I used to be," said Henke. "I thought I had it, actually. Must be a hole in me or something."

The A's could do no more damage and the Jays evened up the series at one game per.

Earlier in the day, Gruber had talked to a reporter about his frustrations throughout 1991. He was still smarting over a late-summer meeting in Gaston's office that had been attended by president Paul Beeston, general manager Gillick and assistant GM Gord Ash. The message for the oft-injured Gruber was, according to sources, either get his heiney back on the field or go on the 60-day disabled list. He chose the former. Had he been forced to play against his will? "Even if I was, I wouldn't say," Gruber responded. Then he added cryptically: "Some things happened in there that I didn't totally agree with. But this is a business and I'm fighting just to do my job. If this were the end of the season, then maybe I'd have something more to say."

He had tried to shut out the derision of the crowd. "I'm a sensitive person. I was always taught to treat people the way you would want to be treated yourself. Those are the rules that I was taught to live by." On this afternoon, while driving to the ballpark, he'd had a stern conversation with himself. "I made three promises. That I would stay totally focused, that I would concentrate on what I was doing, and that I would give 100 percent dedication. That's the only thing that I have any control over."

He'd come out early to take extra batting practice with hitting coach Larry Hisle and roving hitting instructor Willie Upshaw. Whatever advice was imparted, it worked. "We were discussing hitting the outside pitch," said Hisle. "At this level, in my own opinion, mental confidence is a big part of one's success. What distinguishes the good from the great are the ones who have that mental toughness and I know Kelly has it. I keep looking back to 1990, when Kelly had that outstanding year. To have those results, over a long period of time, it can't be just luck. What I'm trying to do is find that one thing that will help him get back to that place. Having a great playoff and a great World Series can make up for a lot of the problems that he's had this year."

After the game was done, Gruber stood at his locker and stripped down as reporters clamored for quotes. He did not behave like a man who had been vindicated, he did not gloat, he hardly cracked a smile. Because of laryngitis that had developed suddenly that afternoon, he could barely speak either. Gruber was asked about the good roar of the crowd, this time, in a game when he was finally a star. He rolled his eyes. "Am I surprised?" he croaked. Then, using hand gestures, he described how Mike Moore had been pitching him in all night. "He stayed right in here," he rasped, pointing to his abdomen. The pitch he'd hit for a home run, on an 0-0 count, was a fastball "right on the bat." And, while he may have admired it earlier, he was taking no bows in the clubhouse. "It feels good to have a good game. I'm just happy to take some pressure off these guys."

But would the public's kindness last? Had Kelly Gruber finally been forgiven? He raised his hand and pointed upwards, a saintly pose, motioning to the fans. "You'll have to ask them."

They'd already gone. And the Jays were shortly on their way too, bound for northern California and the wrong side of the Bay.

There is one good thing about going into Oakland as the visiting ballclub. Eventually, you will be able to leave. Win, lose or postponed due to earthquake, the Toronto Blue Jays would not have to linger long in the city that Gertrude Stein was talking about when she said that there's no there there.

The mayors of Toronto and Oakland had made a wager on the series. If the Jays succumbed, Toronto's chief civic dignitary had promised a jar of maple syrup. If the A's bowed out, the Oakland mayor would send Toronto a vial of crack. Okay, that's a lie, but it was typical of the perverse humor floated by the newspaper hacks who had followed the teams to the coast.

Oakland was a curious place for a peripatetic ballclub to call home. The Athletics, who arrived in 1968 via Philadelphia and Kansas City, had tried mightily to fashion themselves into a community-oriented franchise. Since the Haas family had taken over the reins from oddball (some claim visionary) Charles O. Finley in 1980, they had rebuilt the organization into a baseball powerhouse that one could fairly describe, without undue hyperbole, as a dynasty. The team had proceeded to the World Series three times since 1988, winning it all in 1989.

At the same time, the club had made an admirable effort to include and be responsible to the 'hood. The team's Community

Fund oversaw 50 programs in the area, involving the East Oakland Youth Development organization, the Oakland Police Activities League, the Spanish Speaking Foundation, the Association for Retarded Citizens and the California Congress of Senior Citizens.

A key player in these activities had been Oakland pitcher Dave Stewart who was born, raised and continued to reside in the city — not five kilometres and an entire universe away in San Francisco. "My mom raised six kids in a two-bedroom house here," he said. "It's home. It will always be home." Stewart can be monosyllabic but he was always prepared to beat the drum for Oakland-town. "To me, it's just a matter of putting something back into the environment where I grew up. A lot of people are always putting the knock on Oakland and I don't think that's fair. It's just like any other place, where people work hard and try to raise their kids right. Sure, you're gonna get some bad areas, just like you have in any other city." But it's the bad areas that dominate the landscape and the folklore. Oakland is blue collar and no collar. It's high unemployment and almost mythic crime. Oakland is trouble.

Would the A's be trouble for the Jays? What Oakland did have, what Toronto lacked, was a history rich in baseball accomplishments. If you go back to the very beginning, and we do mean the embryonic stage of major league baseball, you are talking about a team (then known as the Philadelphia Athletics) that was born with the league itself in 1901. Those Athletics predated baseball as we know it. The A's won the first National Association pennant in 1871.

Ancient history too dusty? There's more recent glory, such as the relocated Oakland A's contingent that captured three straight World Series titles, from 1972 through 1974. Or the Bash Brothers crew of the late 80s and early 90s, who were still fairly sound. This current version of the club had something to prove too, that its era had not faded. They were no less hungry for another pennant as the series resumed at the Oakland-Alameda County Coliseum.

The front three hitters in the Oakland order — Rickey Henderson, Carney Lansford and Ruben Sierra — were a combined 1-for-21 in the first two games. Henderson was 0-for-six with a couple of walks and not a single stolen base. But only a Blue Jay fool would have been silly enough to write the A's off so

early. With three matinee games at home on tap, it was the Jays
who had reason to be apprehensive. Stuff happens.

The first problem was the field itself. A recent concert by
Guns 'N Roses and Metallica had badly damaged the outfield.
Whole patches had to be resodded and groundskeepers needed
3,000 pounds of grass seed to correct the problem. Three weeks
later, the grass was soft and springy.

Game 3 was a playoff record (for nine innings) three hours
and forty minutes long. That's cruel and unusual punishment
under a broiling California sun — earthquake weather, as the
mischievous locals took pleasure in informing the visitors from
far and away.

On a strange, strange day, it took all kinds to win a ball game.
But this was a strange, strange place: a place where the traffic
lights talked to you and they said, "Cuckoo, Cuckoo"; a place
where a university student had spent the past two weeks attend-
ing classes at nearby Stanford University in the buff and no one
had complained; a place where you could drink in the parking lot
but not smoke in the open stands.

No wonder then that it took a curious combination to secure
Toronto's 7-5 victory: A little man, a big man, an invisible man
and a Guzman.

The little man in question was Manny Lee, the much-ma-
ligned and often maddening Blue Jay shortstop who hits in the
nether regions of the batting order. On this afternoon, his two-out
triple in the seventh inning, scoring a deuce, propelled Toronto
to their eventual, nearly squandered, victory. As Devon White
put it after the game — this while Lee was in the unfamiliar
position of being sought for quotes by baseball correspondents
— "Manny kicked some A'ssss here today. Today, Manny was
the star."

A novel situation. "I feel, uh, exciting," offered Lee, who was
so overcome by his unexpected clutch-hitting prowess that he
mixed up his grammatical tenses. "The ball that I hit, I no hit it
that well." He gave the credit for this sudden outburst of power
to Larry Hisle. "He gave me confidence. Every time I go to hit, he
says, 'Manny, you can do it'. Last year, nobody told me nothin."

This year, Lee had been troubled by a sore left knee that had
caused him to miss 19 games through the stretch drive. At the end
of the campaign, there was speculation that he was still unfit to

return to the line-up. "When I thought I was 90 percent, I told Cito that I'm ready to come back. Now I think I'm 95 percent." At that point in the conversation, Lee broke out of the reportorial huddle. "I want to phone my family," in the Dominican Republic. "They were all watching me on TV."

Next up is the big man — Dave Winfield. He scored the seventh run on a day when the Jays needed all the insurance they could get. He did it on a wild pitch. But earlier in the game he had broken up a double play, then was almost called out at second base when he casually sauntered off the bag. That's because he thought he was out. "I took a step. Then I thought, nah, I'm gonna stay right here until they explain it to me."

The invisible man was Candy Maldonado, who drove in the first run and homered in the fifth off starter Ron Darling after the A's had rallied to tie the score at 2-2. (Robbie Alomar had homered in the second.) This was a guy with a brutal career post-season record. Going into the game, he was 8-for-68 (.118) in post-season appearances. He was also a guy who had fallen between the cracks in Toronto, in spite of muscling out hotshot prospect Derek Bell for the starting job in left field. You know Candy's around, but you don't much care.

After the game, Maldonado was whisked away to the inter-view room, where the really good guys are taken to be shmoozed by the press. It was a career first for him. "I got to go up to the press conference," he marveled. He'd never had a roomful of scribes waiting for him before. For whatever reasons, Maldonado had infrequently commanded attention. This, he maintained, was not a blow to his ego. "I've never been a guy that lives for the credit. I'm happy just being part of the success. When you get the big warm shake, the pat on the back from your teammates, that's what's important." Uh-huh.

The Guzman part, well, that would be starter Juan Guzman, who was not exactly outstanding but who would go down in the books as the winning pitcher nonetheless. "This is a big moment for us," he said. "Not just for us but for everybody." More sloppy syntax, but he was referring to the fans back in Toronto who must have had multiple conniptions during this protracted affair.

Guzman, unable to throw his slider or changeup for strikes, had turned over a 3-2 lead to Duane Ward when he departed after six. That margin was plumped out to 5-2 in the top of the seventh.

With Kelly Downs in to replace Darling, John Olerud had reached first on an error by second baseman Lance Blankenship. Then Borders singled Olerud to second and Lee tripled them both home.

In the home half of the seventh, Ward walked Henderson who stole second and then proceeded to third on an error charged to Lee. With one out, Sierra scored Henderson on a sac fly to foul territory in right. Baines singled, McGwire singled, Steinbach singled. By the time Wilson struck out, it was 5-4 Toronto and getting stickier by the minute.

Winfield, aboard on a pass, got one of those back in the eighth. He had made it to third on Olerud's single to right, then scampered home when Jeff Russell threw one by Maldonado all the way to the backstop. In the next frame, the A's nibbled again. After a brief appearance on the mound by Mike Timlin — leaving Weiss on second and Henderson on first with one out — Tom Henke took over. Lansford flied out to second and nobody moved. Weiss made it home on Sierra's single but Henderson was stranded at third when Baines grounded out.

In the ninth, Lee worked a leadoff walk from Jeff Russell and was driven in by Winfield's bullet, a line drive that almost made a soprano out of diabolical closer Dennis Eckersley. That's the way it ended, 7-5. The Jays had been outhit 13-9 by the Athletics, but Oakland had outfumbled Toronto afield, three boners to one. What had really hurt the A's was an unfathomable baserunning blunder in the fourth inning. Oakland, lookin' good, had already brought two runs across the plate to tie the game. The bases were now loaded, and there was nobody out. Mike Bordick ticked a soft liner towards right that Joe Carter caught easily and whipped to Borders. The catcher executed a half-pivot and crunched the lead-footed McGwire, who had been directed homewards by third base coach Rene Lachemann. Cheap double play. Weiss ended the inning by grounding out.

The Jays had played hardball. The A's had played dumb ball. While both had their moments of exasperation, Toronto had hung tough enough to take a 2-1 lead in the series. It wasn't pretty but aesthetics don't count. As Devon White put it: "The main thing is we don't want to hear anybody say CHOKE."

That is a word that would more adequately described what happened to the A's the next afternoon. How does a division-leading team blow a five-run lead with two regulation innings left to go in a crucial playoff game, especially with hardfisted closer Eckersley riding to the rescue? It helps if that aforementioned Eckersley taunts the opposition by shoving his finger up their nose. Figuratively at least. Actually, what he did was glare at the Blue Jay bullpen after striking out pinch-hitter Ed Sprague to end the eighth and "stop the bleeding", or so he had thought.

Let's wind the tape back to the beginning. Jack Morris on the mound for Toronto, Bob Welch for Oakland. Another uncommonly torrid day in Oakland. Dorothy, the scarecrow, the tin man and the cowardly lion are taking a tipsy turn of the ballpark before the game begins. Toto, too. Of course, he's stuffed, the other characters are merely stiff. Because it's never too early to get smashed on game day.

That pantomime set the scene and the tenor of the grotesque encounter that was about to follow. No, that's misleading. It was freaky but it was also breathless baseball. The kind that leaves you gasping for air, clutching at your heart, giddy with the wonder of it. Beautiful baseball, even with its many ugly, unbearable, somebody-please-end-this-thing moments. Backbone baseball, because that is what the Jays showed the cynics and that is how they beat the Oakland A's 7-6 and that is why they ended the day just one win away from the World Series.

Down 6-1 after six innings, seemingly dispirited, obviously stunned. And Jack Morris, the smell-of-money-pitcher, dispatched to the showers in the fourth frame after going single, single, single, walk, sac fly, double, intentional walk, unintentional walk, single. Oakland leads 5-1 after three and Olerud's second inning wrong-field homer suddenly feels long ago and far away.

Morris, no wizard yet again, gave way to a relief roster of Todd Stottlemyre, Timlin, Ward and Henke. Oakland managed only one run off them and it looked to everyone as if the jig was up, series tied at two apiece. But fasten your seatbelts, this was going to be a bumpy afternoon.

When Welch left the game after giving up a double to Alomar to lead off the eighth, the A's had a 6-1 lead. Jeff Parrett took over and Carter connected for a single RBI. Winfield singled Carter to third, which immediately brought The Eck loping out of the 'pen, long tresses flowing from beneath his cap. Olerud singled off Eckersley's first pitch, scoring Carter. Maldonado singled off

Eckersley's second pitch, scoring Winfield. Gruber flied out, Borders grounded to second, Sprague whiffed. And Eckersley gave the business to the Blue Jay bench.

The players started clucking and jumping and demanding of each other, Did you see that? *Did you see that?* "It was a little gesture and the guys responded," Winfield noted. "We got very, uh, vocal. It's a good thing the TV cameras weren't in the dugout." Morris, in the clubhouse, watched Eckersley's body language on TV and couldn't believe it. "He should know to let sleeping dogs lie. You don't wake 'em up. It's a cardinal sin in baseball."

The A's couldn't do anything in their half. They had hit the wall, used up all their runs on the day. Toronto had not. In the ninth, the Jays came out fuming. White led off with a single to left, and barrelled all the way to third when Rickey Henderson overran the ball. Then Alomar strutted to the plate in that puffed-out-chest way of his and launched a tater into the right field seats. Score: 6-6. "I have no muscles, but sometimes little guys can hit one," he trilled. Added Morris, referring to Eckersley's earlier gesture of defiance: "He wouldn't look over here after the homer, would he? Funny how that works. It's just Little League stuff."

It was stupid. Now Eckersley was stupefied. He had allowed just two of 31 inherited runners to score all year and now this? The Jays had slapped him around silly. And he had been responsible for it by inciting the enemy. "It was just emotion coming out. I thought I'd finally stopped the bleeding. We still had the two-run lead. I thought that was the game. But they (Jays) can say anything they want. They're happy, I'm sad. I don't feel like this very often. It's a weird feeling." He was shaken and incredulous. "Stunned. I mean, the way it happened. A 6-1 lead to begin with, that in itself is pretty amazing. I can handle this personally. I have to take the bad along with all the success I've had, but it's the team I'm worried about. I really let them down here."

They had gone down kicking. In their half of the ninth, with pinch-runner Eric Fox on third and one out, Ward got Steinbach to hit a ball directly at Alomar. The omnipresent second baseman — four hits, a walk, two runs scored, two RBIs and a stolen base on the afternoon — gunned down Fox at the plate, preserving the tie and sending the game into extra innings. In the 11th, with Downs pitching, Bell led off with a walk, moved to third on

Maldonado's bloop single to right, and scooted home on Borders' sac liner to left. Tilt.

The amazing comeback had rendered Morris' personal fiasco — five hits, five walks (one intentional) five runs — irrelevant. In the clubhouse, as his mates whooped and hollered, he sat alone, with his hands on his knees, fully dressed in black shirt and jeans. "It was a team effort," he said. "The only guy on the team that did the poorest is the one you're talking to right now. But I can't tell you that I didn't try my best, I didn't try my hardest."

Across the way, Winfield had a gap-toothed grin on his face and a drumstick in his fist. Barbecue sauce dribbled down his chin. "Trench warfare, man. But this team wouldn't roll over and it wouldn't quit. You guys saw no-quit, don't roll over, hardnosed baseball today. It was a wonderful game."

It was indeed warfare. Dirty, messy warfare. When it was done, the combatants were exhausted. There was Ward, who got the win, with his cheeks florid, wild look in his eyes. And Gruber, with the baseball black smeared across his face. He looked like Alice Cooper.

But back to Winfield, because so much of the Blue Jay prosperity could be traced back to him in '92. He was asked, as every Jay is always asked, about team inadequacies in the past and the ballclub's perceived lack of character. Winfield pointed to the avian logo on the front of his T-shirt. "This is the same logo as before, this is the same city as before. But we're a different bunch of guys now." The past, he meant, was not their fault and not their problem.

Had the Jays exorcised their demons? Could they finally bury that past? Did they even pause to recall what had befallen their Blue Jay ancestors in 1985 when Toronto was up three games to one in the playoffs? Did those Jays have anything to do with these Jays? Perhaps.

The next day, the Jays got Stew-balled.

Stewart, the mean-looking hurler with the pipsqueak voice, had never lost a league championship game. He still hasn't. The Jays, with Cone on the mound, were physically abused 6-2. In retrospect, it seems asinine to think that the A's would get swept three straight in their own ballpark. So the Jays couldn't beat Stewart? Who could? He delivered a complete-game effort, which meant no Oakland bullpen to ravage, no Icky Ecky to save the day for the Jays. But the Oakland fans had already lost faith. The game didn't even sell out.

The series was returning to the SkyDome. There was no dejection, no gloom in the Blue Jay locker room. It was quiet after the game but mostly because reporters had crept into the clubhouse on tippy-toes, expecting a solemn reception. "Somebody die?" asked Carter. Morris teased: "Let's not all just stand around here and do nothing." Okay, but do-nothing might more accurately describe Morris' contribution. "We're not robots," he countered. "If I had pitched a perfect game the other day and Dave (Cone) had pitched a perfect game today, we'd be busting champagne in your face, right?"

Cone had only made it into the fifth inning, with the A's already leading 6-1. He insisted that, no, he hadn't been tired, and pitching on three-day's rest (Gaston had gone to a three-man rotation for the playoffs) was not a strain. "I felt fine. I would not want to use that as an excuse. It is not a major factor at this point."

Cone was polite and composed as he stood at his locker, tie neatly knotted, hands clasped behind his back. He looked like a baby-faced political candidate fielding queries from the press scrum, occasionally nodding towards a reporter in the rear of the throng as if to say, I will entertain your question now. "I have no one to blame but myself," he began, overlooking some of the sloppy defensive play behind him. "Once I got into a jam, I couldn't make the big pitch to get us out of it. My downfall was not executing a good fastball early. That sets up all your other pitches."

He was particularly upset at himself for failing to back up a play at third, with Henderson running. "I was slow. I was trying to get back there but I just broke slowly. It was embarrassing." The A's had overpowered him in the fifth. Was he rattled, someone probed? Cone stared straight back at his interlocutor. "I wouldn't use the word rattled."

The players were glad to be going home to Toronto, even if they weren't coming back with a pennant tucked under their arm. "This is what we have been aiming for ever since spring training," said Alomar. "It's gonna be nice to play at home. We came here meaning to win two games and we did. We have the advantage now. We get to play in front of our crowd."

Someone asked Carter about playoff pressure and he waved his hands as if shooing away the oft-posed query. "We haven't let the outside pressure get to us all year. We believe in ourselves, in this clubhouse." Taking it all back to Toronto was a fitting conclusion. "It would be history."

Mike Maksudian, a utility backstop picked up along the way, heretofore noted primarily for his odd gastronomic tastes — he'd recently ingested a giant bug to cop a bet from his teammates — had offered himself as a sacrificial talisman. Actually, he'd offered his (lower) left cheek, on which had been tattooed a little red devil for luck. Now that's taking one for the team.

Devon White had some good luck going for him too. On the eve of Game 6, he was in a car crash while out test-driving a new Mercedes with his wife. The vehicle slammed into a pole and flipped into a ditch. Providentially, neither White nor his wife nor the dealership agent who had been driving were injured in the crack-up.

Still, there was a game to be played. One more game is all that stood between Toronto and its first ever World Series. Or Juan more game, since it would be Juan Guzman's turn on the mound. Gaston had some final words of advice for his pitcher, which he delivered in both English and Spanish: You be the boss. *Tu tienes el comando del juego.*

White, batting leadoff, came to the plate to face Mike Moore. Another sold-out crowd of baseball supplicants clapped their hands and pumped up their lungs. This was one day when the fans didn't need any coaxing from the JumboTron. White lofted a pitch to Henderson in left field. It should have been an easy out but it slipped right through Henderson's outstretched arms for a two-base error and the crowd hooted. Alomar struck out, but Joe Carter reached down for a fastball in the dirt that he blasted to straightaway centre and beyond. He had come damn close to calling that shot, too. Upset with his performance through the series — just four singles for 21 at-bats — Carter had tossed and turned in bed the previous night. He wanted, he *needed*, to contribute. When he got to the park the next afternoon, he announced to his teammates: Come on, hop on. "I'd been riding their backs through this thing. It was time they got on mine."

Carter had given Toronto an instant 2-0 lead. Minutes later, when Guzman took his place on the hill, he began to unload a barrage of pitches, including "one of the best sliders I had all year." The fans got the drift and leaned back to enjoy this one.

Henderson's error, Carter's homer, Guzman's heat: this was going to be easy. They knew, they just knew, how it was going to turn out.

Maybe it was even too easy. The Jays decimated and demoralized the A's 9-2, which shouldn't happen to any team, especially in the playoffs. You don't want to leave them laughing. Alomar, who would be selected Most Valuable Player of the series, ran his hitting streak to 11 consecutive playoff games and brandished his marvelous glove at the Oakland hitters every chance he got. The Jays chased Moore off the mound in the third, when they piled up four runs including another four-bagger for Maldonado.

Meanwhile, Guzman struck out eight over seven innings, including a pair to end both the fifth and the sixth innings with two A's aboard each time. Oakland got one off Guzman in the sixth and one off Ward in the eighth but by then it was too little too late. Henke conceded two walks in the ninth, which just prolonged the anticipation. Then a high flyball, Maldonado settling underneath it for the final out, and pandemonium. An ecstatic Stottlemyre tackled Henke to the ground. When he managed to get back up, Henke dusted himself off, trotted to the stands, and kissed his wife.

The Jays had cranked out nine runs on 13 hits. It had been a high impact joy ride. "Everybody said we'd choke in the end," crowed Alomar, fingering the rosary that he always wore around his neck. "We didn't. The monkey, we can take it off our back."

No monkeys here. Just 51,335 fans going ape in the stands, in the corridors, out on the streets. Toronto was going to the World Series, the World Series was coming to Toronto.

"This means a whole lot to this city and to Canada," said '85 veteran Dave Stieb, whose elbow problems had relegated him to dugout cheerleader. "The fans deserve it. I'm sure they're celebrating across this whole country right now, just the way we're celebrating in this clubhouse." Except probably not in their underwear.

"This is great for the organization, great for the city, great for the country," rhapsodized Key as Ward removed his colleague's cap, poured champagne into it, and replaced it on Key's perfectly round head. "We're going out to relish this tonight, party up, then come to the park tomorrow and get ready for whoever we're going to play next." Key, who had been through all of Toronto's playoff wars, had been left out of the rotation for the playoffs. That may be why it was taking so long for the reality of what the Jays had done to sink in. "Maybe tonight, when I'm lying in bed, I'll be able to believe that it actually happened."

In the eighth inning, Winfield had struck out but the crowd applauded him anyway. Since spring training, he had led the troops to this spot, this moment. He understood what this pennant meant, for him and for the city. "We're keenly aware that we don't represent just a city. We represent an entire country. Every team has its territory of course — maybe a state or a region. But hey, we've got all of Canada."

Leaning against a pillar, as if for support, was Henke, nerdy spectacles discarded and his eyes pink. "The fans deserve this because they've been there for us, year after year. It's just such a great feeling to bring them a World Championship, uh, I mean the World Series. What am I saying? We still have to win four more." He too was a veteran from those playoff disappointments that stretched back to 1985 and he took a moment to remember Jays gone. "I'll toast everybody tonight. Jesse, Lloyd, even George." Jesse Barfield, Lloyd Moseby, George Bell. "All the guys who deserved to be here. They put so much into this organization."

In another corner stood Guzman, all goofy and giddy, his baseball cap spun around backwards. The morning before, he had called his family in the Dominican Republic and asked for their help. "I told them to pray for me. I told them I needed to win this game." The prayers may have worked but he also put faith in his slider. "I knew I had good stuff right from the bullpen. I had my confidence the whole time and I knew what I could do. That's what I said to myself: *I'm going to do this.*"

Borders looked physically and emotionally drained. "We've got one more step to go. If we win the World Series, then I promise you'll see one jubilant guy." On this night, Borders was worried more about his glove, the one he'd massaged and oiled and moulded over the past three years into a leather extension of his arm. The one he had *broken* in the first inning. "A part of the leather just came flying off. I'm gonna have to take it in for some quick repairs." He was so anxious about the mitt, he passed on the champagne.

Later, when it was all over, when the bubbly had stopped flowing and the fans had finally vacated the premises to dance up Yonge Street, one Blue Jay reappeared on the field. He walked to the bullpen, picked up a ball and started throwing.

Jack Morris.

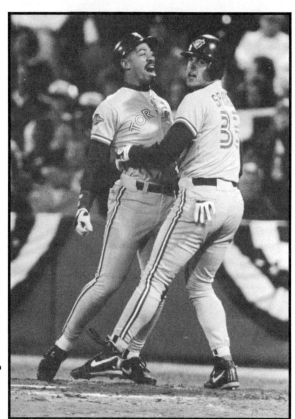

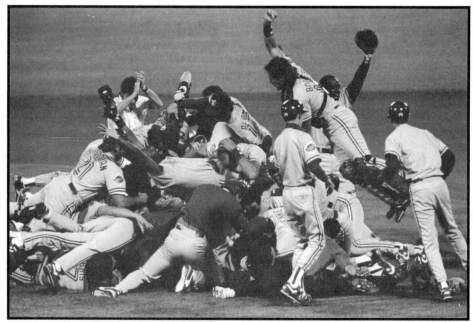

# Glory Jays

## *Finding Heroes in the Strangest Places*       **17**

Now what?

The Blue Jay juggernaut had finally trundled into the World Series but this was uncharted territory for most of the players and all of their fans. What did we know from the Fall Classic, north of the 49th Parallel? This was an American party and the upstart hosers had crashed it. We were parvenus at the ball, lumberjacks stomping on the dainty feet of crinolined ladies. Come the crispness of autumn and the Canadian soul pines for hockey, for the thwack and shudder of bodychecks against the boards and the pristine expanse of glistening ice. We carry curved sticks, not rounded clubs. It's the way we play, up here, in the Great White North.

Baseball is a sissy sport, you have to admit. Which may be why Toronto had embraced it so enthusiastically, so citified had we become in this most American of Canadian burgs. We wanted to be Canuck Doodle Dandies, even as we relished the thought of beating the Yankees at their own game. And for once this most quarrelsome of nations was united in a cause. We put aside the interminable bickering of French versus English and East versus West, of farm folk versus city folk and them-that-have versus them-that-want.

For a fortnight, it was all of us versus all of you.

We had resented Americans even as we had envied them. Because they took us for granted and treated us like the village idiot — politically, socially, economically. Now we were invading your turf, just as we had in the War of 1812, when the Redcoats torched the White House. The hostility was settled diplomatically with the Treaty of Ghent even though you Americans continued to claim a victory. But you always do, don't you?

There were more recent grudges too. Atlanta got the 1996 Olympic Games and Toronto got the shaft.

Now it was Canada's team against America's team, the Toronto Blue Jays against the Atlanta Braves. Or perhaps just our Americans and Latinos versus your Americans and Latinos. After all, there was no Canadian mixer in this Canadian Club. Rob Ducey, the lone Canuck Jay, had been traded earlier in the season. No matter. We had convinced ourselves that our players had sucked up some Canadian character along the way, by proximity or osmosis.

There was a shared history here too between the Braves and the Jays. Semaphoring at third base was exterminated Toronto manager Jimy Williams, who had been disgraced and deposed by his Jays in 1989. More acutely missed was Atlanta manager Bobby Cox, Toronto skipper in 1985 when the Jays had lost the pennant to the Kansas City Royals in seven games. He had been lured away by pasha media Ted Turner, sweet-talked into returning to the south. Some had never forgiven him. But Cox said he had only pleasant memories of Toronto. "I love that organization and the people that run it," he waxed poetic as the teams worked out at Atlanta-Fulton County Stadium before Game 1. "I wish we were still playing at Exhibition Stadium up there. I love that ballpark. It had a fast carpet and there was always a wind blowing out to right field."

He loved Exhibition Stadium? Nobody loved Exhibition Stadium. Exhibition Stadium was to a ballpark as the Kitty Hawk was to the Concorde. And what we remember most about that wind blowing to right field was Jim Sundberg's fly ball lofting to the wall back in Game 7 of the '85 series when...oh, never mind.

Everybody was making kissy-face on the eve of the World Series. "Coxie and I are friends," observed Toronto manager Cito Gaston, cutting in smoothly on the affectionate quadrille. He had been Cox's hitting instructor with the Jays and he had learned something, he said, watching the wily veteran at work. "You can't demand that people respect you. But perhaps you can get them to live by your rules."

Then there was Jack Morris. While Atlanta may have once defeated Toronto in a head-to-head contest of civic pride in the Olympics sweepstakes, Jack Morris had twice defeated Atlanta on the mound. That was in 1991, of course, when he had anchored the Minnesota Twins to a world championship against the Braves. Now he was Toronto's ace and what were the Braves gonna do about it, eh?

Oh.

Back to that in a moment.

Remember first the sensations of that Game 1 night, a chilly night in Dixie. But not too chilly for those of us used to seeing our breath hanging in the air on autumn evenings. From the vantage point of the blimp high overhead, the park was like a gaily-lit vessel floating out of the darkness. Pretty, but an illusion. At ground level, it was just another 60s-era concrete donut with peanut shells crackling underfoot and corroded fencing folded back at the gates.

The fans, oblivious to the aesthetics or lack thereof, pulled out their tomahawks and chanted their eerie mantra. Political incorrectness notwithstanding, it was difficult not to be struck by this aural assault as it swelled and rolled around the stands. Outside the park, members of the American Indian Movement maintained a silent vigil to protest what they considered a racist insult. There is no innocence anymore, only offenses to be taken and grievances to be nurtured.

Behind home plate, a clutch of Blue Jay wives hoisted Styrofoam "J"s but their valiant attempt to make some noise of their own was smothered in the general din of Atlanta mayhem. They were overwhelmed even though their ranks had been augmented by several hundred Blue Jay fans who had made the trek to the south. But there was southern hospitality on display too, or so the visitors from a bilingual nation thought: The electronic message board spoke French.

Morris, the Braves' nemesis, was warming up. He had disappointed in the American League playoffs but surely that was just a temporary anomaly, an aberration? Everybody is entitled to a bad game, even two — preferably not at this time of year. The fates could not possibly conspire to humiliate him again. Could they?

The previous afternoon, during a press conference, it was obvious that Jack Morris had already donned his game face — the ugly face, the one that curls its lip and sneers at reporters and casts a cold eye on the world. The one that says, beat me if you can, go ahead and try it. Perhaps his teammates, strangers to this whole World Series business, had looked to him for a clue on how to behave. Morris chose to project a nonchalant air, a been-there done-that cool. "It's another game," he shrugged. "Sure, I realize its importance but I can't approach it any differently than any other game."

One could only hope that Morris' diffident posture was a self-protective ruse because there is something inherently wrong-headed about such an attitude. If a World Series assignment is like any other game, then what's the bloody point? Was it just routine when he had persevered for 10 scoreless innings in Game 7 the year before? Was there no magic then, no superhuman effort in that obstinacy? Don't lie Jack.

Oftentimes, you find your heroes in the strangest places. That's one of the wonders of sport, in particular; that an also-ran, a spear-carrier whose name and face you hardly know can be blessed on any given day. On this night, in Game 1, fortune kissed Damon Berryhill on the cheek. He was a 28-year-old surfer from California who batted in the bottom of the Atlanta order and who had platooned behind the plate for most of the year until Greg Olson broke his leg in a home plate collision in mid-September. He'd hit a puny .167 in the National League Championship Series against the Pittsburgh Pirates and was considered an easy out. Certainly nothing for Jack Morris to fear in the sixth inning with the Jays leading 1-0, even if there were two men on base.

Toronto had got its run, its only run as it would turn out, on a leadoff homer from Joe Carter in the fourth. Atlanta had threatened early when Otis Nixon — who had missed the World Series in '91 because of a drug suspension — singled past short. He stole second, made it to third on a ground-out, but died there on a feeble whiff by Dave Justice. From then on, Morris rang up 11 straight Brave batters until back-to-back two-out walks to Justice and Sid Bream in the fourth. Morris gunned a bullet to the backstop and both players advanced but then Ron Gant struck out swinging and again Toronto was off the hook.

Morris was making Toronto boosters nervous but he had flirted with danger all season long and rarely been burned, as attested to by his 21-6 record. Now he was beginning to falter, seriously. He was trying to be too good with his pitches and, consequently, overthrowing. A pitcher with messed-up mechanics is a pitcher who should be given the hook. The Braves had left a pair of runners in each of the fourth and fifth, all four reaching on two-out walks and Morris had only thwarted Atlanta by unloading some pivotal strikes. Meanwhile, Atlanta starter Tom Glavine got tougher with each passing inning. After his mistake to Carter, he had set down a dozen Jays in a row.

In the sixth, Gaston did not go to the pen. Now Morris walked Justice, the fifth free pass of the encounter. Sid Bream drifted a single to left — in spite of some sticky moments due to the walks, this was the first hit off Morris since Nixon's leadoff single in the first. That brought the allegedly harmless Berryhill to the plate. He had only 10 home runs on the season.

Staying back on the pitch, he smoked a 1-2 offering. It was a bodice-ripper, an emphatic shot that cleared the fence in right field. The fans sprang to their feet, Berryhill was in seventh heaven, and Game 1 would shortly be gone with the wind as far as Toronto was concerned. That's the way it ended: 3-1 Atlanta.

Fiddle-dee-dee.

Berryhill's dinger — the first by a National League catcher since Gary Carter socked one for the New York Mets in Game 4 of the '86 Series — snapped an 18-inning scoreless streak in World Series play for Morris, all of them against Atlanta. "I guess I needed about three or four more, huh?" the pitcher cracked to reporters in the subdued Toronto clubhouse afterwards, where the players seemed more intent on lining up for their charred steak 'n' potatoes than dissecting the loss for the media.

If he had any psychic bruises, Morris was not about to show them to the interlopers. But he was reduced to repeating the banal phrases that he had recently uttered in the playoffs. "The sun's gonna come up tomorrow...probably."

This is how he described his "one bad pitch" to Berryhill: "Your basic, hanging, 390-foot forkball." When one addled TV pretty-boy suggested that maybe it hadn't been such a lousy pitch at that, Morris rolled his eyes and snapped: "How can it be a good pitch, man? It went 390 feet! You wouldn't even have thrown that one."

Morris did tip his cap, which of course he was no longer wearing, to Tom Glavine, who had confounded the Jays with a complete-game four-hitter. In the playoffs against Pittsburgh, he had been mauled — a 12.27 ERA with two losses. "I think Tom Glavine did everything humanly possible to win this game tonight." Then, apropos of nothing, Morris added: "That shows why pitching is worth more money than anything at this time of the year." Perhaps he was referring to his own potential $15 million salary, which the Jays had happily extended the previous winter, figuring it was a fair price for the kind of playoff pitching they assumed they'd be needing and getting from Mr. Morris.

"You have to be almost perfect in that situation," he said, referring to Toronto's slim 1-0 lead. Twelve months earlier, one run is all he had needed to stiff these Braves. He had given up just three hits but now one run was nowhere near good enough. "When you have one run to work with, you have to be careful."

Someone obligingly pointed out that his 4-0 World Series record, from his days as a Twin and a Detroit Tiger, was now soiled by the loss. "And look at me. I'm still alive. Isn't that something?" He was not, he insisted, devastated. "I'm not concerned about what people think. I can sleep with myself. I don't have to sleep with the world."

Winning the series debut, and in such diabolical fashion, heartened the Atlanta team and its supporters, all of whom were aware that the betting line favored Toronto as over-all victors. But the betting line was just that — a whim driven by money in a sport that is probably the hardest to predict; a team sport where one man can make the difference. Damon Berryhill proved that in Game One. Ed Sprague was about to prove it in Game Two.

Ed Sprague?

The second game of the series fell on a Sunday night and, earlier in the day, the gospel according to the Atlanta Braves had been preached from pulpits across the city. At the Peachtree Presbyterian church, Rev. W. Frank Harrington delivered a sermon from the mound (so to speak) on the theme of perseverance. "For example, how many of you sitting here today felt the Braves were going to win on Wednesday night?" he thundered, referring to the ninth inning come-from-behind defeat of the Pittsburgh Pirates in Game 7 of the National League playoffs.

Others in Atlanta were praying a different tune. At the Georgia Dome, a five-minute drive from Fulton County Stadium, 40,000 devotees turned out to listen to controversial Nation of Islam minister Louis Farrakhan, whose three-hour "A Torchlight for America" speech, begun two hours late, overlapped with much of the baseball game. It was a hard choice to make for many of the pious who had assembled. Should I stay or should I go? Baseball or religion?

At the ballpark, a U.S. Marine Guard brought the Canadian flag onto the field, marching crisply, eyes straight ahead according to military protocol. Had they looked up instead, they may have noticed that the Canadian flag was upside down. Millions of Canadians watching on TV noticed. Hundreds of them wasted no time phoning newspapers and television stations to complain about this affront to their national dignity. It was an unforgivable misdeed according to some, a deliberate slur according to others. There were even paranoiacs who were convinced it was all part of a sinister American plot to undermine the Canadian team.

Major League Baseball issued an immediate apology. The statement read thus: "Major League Baseball apologizes to the people of Canada and to all baseball fans for the unintentional improper display of the Canadian Flag during the National Anthems prior to the start of tonight's World Series game." In the days to come, President George Bush would offer an *apologia* for the embarrassing foul-up. And the Marines? An inadvertent spy who happened to be on hand when the hapless individual who'd actually carried the standard came off the field, overheard him in a telephone conversation. It was unclear who was on the other end of the line, but according to the snoop's reports, the marine's side of the chat went something like this: "Yes sir...no sir...we'll take whatever's coming to us, sir." In fact, all that happened — for public consumption anyway — is that the same Marines requested and were given another chance to carry the Canadian flag later in the series.

The Canadian flag may have landed on its head but the Toronto Blue Jays landed on their feet.

It was a dramatic ninth inning turnaround that enabled the Jays to escape Atlanta with the World Series tied at one game apiece. But it had been a most peculiar encounter in Game 2. How strange was it? Toronto starter David Cone provided the most offensive clout for the visitors. Singles in both of his at-bats, off Atlanta's John Smoltz, matched the total number of hits that previous American League pitchers had mustered since the designated hitter was introduced to the World Series in 1976.

That's about all that was gratifying for Cone on the night. He lasted only 4 1/3 innings, allowing four runs (three of them earned) on five hits and five walks. His wild pitch in the second inning accounted for Atlanta's first run. In the fourth, Cone walked Sid Bream, who scored on a single. Next frame, Cone had a disastrous inning — a walk, two singles, a stolen base and an error — before Gaston yanked him. It was 4-2 Atlanta after five but Toronto should have been closer than that, had some malodorous officiating not imbued events with a sour smell. In the fourth, Robbie Alomar had walked, moved to second on a wild pitch, taken third on Dave Winfield's ground out and then appeared to score on Stoltz's wild pitch. Home plate umpire Mike Reilly — who had the only opinion that counted — ruled that Smoltz, taking the toss-back from catcher Berryhill, had put the tag on Alomar. The replays showed, clearly, that this was not so. The game could have turned on this questionable call but fortunately it did not.

With Cone gone, the revolving door in the bullpen was spinning. Out came David Wells, out came Todd Stottlemyre, out came Duane Ward, out came Tom Henke. Together, they held Atlanta scoreless for the rest of the match. And in the eighth inning, the Jays finally started to chip away at Smoltz, stringing together three hits for one run. Toronto had a wonderful opportunity to tie the score but reliever Mike Stanton induced John Olerud to pop-up with runners on the corners. Then Jeff Reardon, only baseball's all-time saves leader (he had been acquired from the Boston Red Sox late in the season after Alejandro Pena was sidelined with an elbow injury) came on to fan Kelly Gruber and end the inning. That called strike also brought grumbles from the Toronto contingent. Gruber had gone 0-for-22 in post-season play since homering in Game 2 of the ALCS against Oakland.

Ward held off the Braves in the bottom of the eighth and Reardon ambled back out to the mound in the ninth, prepared to dust-off the Jays. Pat Borders immediately lined out to right. That brought up Derek Bell who was pinch-hitting for Manny Lee. Bell, unusually patient for a rookie in this situation, drew a walk. Gaston, looking down his bench for someone to pinch-hit for Ward, picked Sprague. He would say later, "It was Sprague all the way. You'll be aware of this young man for a long time."

Sprague, a Stanford University grad, economics major and son of a major league pitcher who happened to own the minor league team believed to have been the model for the Mudville

Nine in *Casey At The Bat*, had a brief word with Blue Jay *eminence gris* Rance Mulliniks. The veteran suggested he look for a fastball down.

The spare-part Jay crushed the first offering from Reardon, the ball sailing over the left-field fence. It had been a low fastball. As manager Cox drawled later, "He likes a low fastball and that's what he got." It had been the first World Series at-bat of his life for the sometimes third baseman, sometimes second baseman, sometimes catcher, making him the 17th player to homer in such circumstances. Said Sprague later: "Hopefully, they'll start liking me again."

This was a reference to some of the abuse he had taken earlier in the summer after his wife, Kristen Babb-Sprague, had copped a tarnished gold medal in synchronized swimming at the Barcelona Olympics. Canada's Sylvie Frechette had been jobbed out of her rightful first place finish by a butter-fingered judge who had hit the wrong number on her scoring keyboard. It was a stupid blunder but Babb-Sprague, buoyant over her gold, had never acknowledged that she was not the rightful champion. Her spouse had further infuriated Canadians when he was quoted as saying that he and the missus didn't care what Canucks thought about them. Now, of course, he claimed that he had been "a little bit misquoted" and blamed the media. "They were the ones writing the bad stories about me. I think I was misquoted a little bit in saying that I didn't think or care what the Canadian people thought about my wife winning a gold medal." Kristen Babb-Sprague was in the stands when Sprague connected for the clutch-pinch-homer. Afterwards she gave as many interviews as her husband.

Sprague had been possibly the last person in the ballpark to realize that he had just swatted a two-run shot. "I didn't see it. I looked up right into the lights. I knew I hit it good. By the time I got to first I knew it was gone when I saw (outfielder) Deion's (Sander) back turned. It's exciting. I threw my hands up in the air and I knew we had the lead."

Only once before in post-season history had a pinch-home run taken a team from behind to the lead in the final inning. That was in 1988 when gimpy Kirk Gibson's Game 1 homer off Dennis Eckersley turned things around for the Los Angeles Dodgers against Oakland.

The Jays hugged Sprague in the dugout but the game was not yet over. When the Braves came to bat in the bottom of the ninth, with the score 5-4, they were dazed but not devastated. Closer Tom Henke had taken over from Ward and, as had become his wont, promptly enlivened the Braves by walking one batter and hitting another. "I usually hit one a year," he pointed out. "And I hadn't hit one yet." Henke battled for his three outs but he eventually got 'em — and his fourth post-season save, even if that was a somewhat misleading statistic.

When Gruber put his glove under Terry Pendleton's pop-up behind third base for the final out, he celebrated with two or three tomahawk chops of his own. "I just bubbled and let loose."

The Jays and the Braves flew north to Toronto, the first time in the history of major league baseball that the World Series would be played on foreign soil, and American reporters prattled in print about customs declarations and cross-border shopping. It was a momentous occasion and Torontonians were giddy about their status as hosts. They welcomed the World Series and the world to their house, both within the SkyDome and without. It was not just civic or national pride at stake. In a city which had suffered horribly from the recession, economists predicted that each home game would generate $2.8 million for local businesses just from out-of-towners with disposable income.

There was some concern about how the Toronto fans would react in the wake of the upside-down flag fiasco. Was this payback time? Hardly. Some feelings were indeed bruised by the unintentional slight but most recognized the incident for what it was — an unfortunate accident. The prevailing sentiment decreed that there was enough of a U.S. versus Canada flavor to this series already and for the most part it had been expressed with good humor. Perhaps Gaston put it best when he was asked about this media-driven clash of nations. "I hate it when we're carrying the flag of Canada. We're just a team. Talk to anyone on our club and they'll tell you they love to live in Canada. But they're mostly Americans."

The players had noticed the kerfuffle over the flag blunder. Some shook their heads at the carelessness of it all. During the off-day workout, catcher Pat Borders wandered over to a group of reporters and asked: " So what's happening with this Canadian flag thing? I bet Canadians are mad. I'd sure be pissed." Then he pointed toward the apex of the SkyDome where a giant Maple Leaf had been unfurled across the rafters. "Look at it. How can they get that wrong?"

Dave Winfield suggested that there would have been a greater hue and cry if it was Old Glory that had been mishandled. "If the American flag was sideways or upside down, would there be a mess, would there be a fuss? That's beyond a *faux pas*."

Gruber, who hails from Texas but has a Canadian wife and two children who were born in Toronto, was perturbed by the incident. "There's no excuse for it, no excuse at all," he said, after taking some extra batting practice in what appeared to be his underwear. "But let's not play tit-for-tat. Let's just play the game and get along with each other. People here in Canada have that attitude and that's what sets them apart from most other people." One American reporter, who surely had never been to a baseball game in Toronto over the past 16 years, asked Gruber whether Canadians knew anything about America's game. "This game has not been figured out, even by the greatest of *you* guys."

On game night, the temperature outside was a frosty and wet 2 degrees Celsius and dropping, the coldest ever since they started making official note of such things in 1975. But in the climate-controlled SkyDome, the thermostat held steady at a comfortable 20 degrees Celsius. Hundreds of fans had arrived carrying miniature American flags, topsy-turvy, but the general mood was jovial and bemused. Like one placard at the ballpark said: "Americans invented baseball. Toronto improved it." A few of the more blatantly political signs were ordered removed by the Jays' manager of security. And the U.S. Marine color guard — the same chaps who had inverted the Maple Leaf in Atlanta — got a good-natured cheer when they bore the Canadian flag onto the field. Peace.

On the mound for Toronto was Juan Guzman who had made headlines earlier in Atlanta when he admitted to reporters that he didn't like pressure baseball. This was hardly an earth-shaking revelation but, given the overwrought nature of reporting during the World Series, it was significant news. "I don't like to be in that situation," Guzman had said. "I don't like it, but when I don't have any choice, I just work hard, prepare myself for the game and do my best." Wait a minute. Was Guzman saying he didn't want to pitch in the big games? What heresy was this? "The situations I've been in the last two times — you know I pitched the (pennant) clinching game — you have a lot of pressure on yourself. But when I don't have a choice, I just go hard and do my best." It was an offhand remark but it would bring Guzman some unwelcome notoriety. "I was misunderstood," he would claim later, striving for clarification. "If I can help the team, give me the ball. I feel great, I feel fine."

He did not seem in any way reluctant as he made his way to the hill, in front of 51,813 expectant fans. Impatient to get on with it would have been a better description, as he kicked his toes in the dirt and otherwise customized the mound. At 8.33, he delivered the first World Series pitch on alien artificial turf and somewhere Abner Doubleday must have shuddered. The new world order had begun.

For the next two and a half hours or so, Guzman was ferocious. He threw eight innings of heat, conceding eight hits — three of those to Deion Sanders — but only two runs, just one of them earned. Mostly he stonewalled the Braves, mowing them down with an assortment of fastballs and sliders in the dirt that were efficiently corralled by catcher Pat Borders. "Pat, he gives me confidence. They were swinging at sliders in the dirt and I felt good about throwing them there because he gets them."

The pitching was only the subtext to this story. The histrionics were provided by Kelly Gruber's eighth inning home run to tie the game at two apiece and a *deus ex machina* catch at the outfield wall by Devon White that saved the game in the fourth. This is not hyperbole. White's tendon-straining catch did resemble an Olympian achievement, as if some playful superhuman force had taken an interest in the game and had transposed itself onto the centre fielder.

Sometimes you have to wait till it's all over before you can look back and, with the luxury of hindsight, pick a moment when it all went right. Or wrong. Other times, you can feel it in your guts at the very instant that it occurs. Here it is, your instincts shout, remember this. You may never see such a thing again.

The '92 World Series may very well have been decided at the moment when the ball and Devon White came together, hard up against the centre field wall at the SkyDome, with Braves runners at first and second, Dave Justice poised for his home run trot, and a groan gurgling up from the throats of Blue Jay devotees.

The groan never escaped. For a second, there was no sound at all. It was as if all those who had sat and watched needed time for what they had just seen with their eyes to register with their brains. By the time they began to react — a roar of wonder — White had already released the ball and the extended play was now banging around the infield.

This is a play that should be parsed, like a sentence, divided into subject and object and predicate clauses. There was no score at the time but the Braves were pressing with a brace of Braves on base and nobody out. Then Justice launched the bolt that had, at the very least, extra bases written all over it. But White was scribbling a rewrite to that script. He heard the smack of ash on cowhide, instantly made a mental calculation, turned his back to the plate and sprinted to the warning track in dead centre. Turning only marginally, trusting his instincts and reflexes, he leapt into the air, extended his glove, and hauled in the ball.

Minutes later, panting from exertion, White would look up at the JumboTron to marvel along with everyone else at what he had just done — "I couldn't take my eyes off it" — but for right now the play was still unfolding. White wheeled and threw to second baseman Robbie Alomar. Sanders scrambled back to second base to tag up, passing Terry Pendleton and making him the second out for over-running the lead runner. Alomar threw to first, hoping to nail Pendleton who was already dead. Gruber chased Sanders backwards along the base path and Sanders took off for third but got hung because now Gruber had the ball. Gruber chased Sanders backwards along the basepath.

Perhaps, in retrospect, Gruber should have thrown to second to erase Sanders. Instead, he lunged at his ankles to tag him out, practically tripping him in the process. It was a triple play, except it wasn't. Umpire Bob Davidson called Sanders safe. Later, when Davidson viewed the tapes, he admitted that he had been wrong. Sanders was clearly out. But there was no going back to resurrect the achievement. The World Series history books will continue to maintain that there has been just one triple play turned in the Fall Classic — an unassisted feat executed by Cleveland second baseman Bill Wambsganss in Game 5 against the Dodgers in 1920.

All of this was almost too much to absorb in one sitting. It was a feast of baseball and the leftovers would be savored for months to come. White's spectacular reception had instantly evoked memories of Willie Mays' over-the-shoulder catch on a ball hit by Cleveland's Vic Wertz in the first game of the 1954 Series. The Tribe, with the best record in baseball, never recovered from that kick in the stomach. They lost in four games. The Braves, while expressing grudging respect for White's catch, were not about to pack up their dolls and dishes and go home.

Hall of Famer Ernie Banks, a contemporary of Mays', was at the SkyDome for this game. He flattered White: "It would have been a tough catch for Willie Mays." Added Dave Winfield: "Aaaaa! What can I tell you? It was awesome. It was one of the best catches in World Series history. You don't have to go back to black and white film anymore. That was a thing of beauty." White was uncomfortable about keeping company with such a baseball icon as Mays. "I would never see myself compared to Willie Mays."

He wasn't even prepared to concede that this was the best catch he had ever made, though it was the most timely. "The best catch I've ever made? I don't know, but I made one similar against the Angels. Lance Parrish hit the ball." He did deign to include it in his top 10 list. Did he know, had he been certain, that he would catch it? "There's no wind out there," he shrugged. "Most of the time I know I can get to any baseball. I don't want to be cocky but when the ball has a little hang time, I know I can get to it. I didn't want Deion to score from second base. When I threw the ball in, my job was not finished yet. As a centre fielder, I was still trying to get in to the rundown."

He had bounced off the wall after making the catch, leaving a temporary indentation on the rubber surface, but he said he had hardly felt the impact and hadn't slowed down as he approached the circumference of the field to consider it. "After I was in that car wreck (the previous week) I can't think about no padded wall," he joked. "I wasn't really worried about the wall. I was going full flight when the ball was hit and I couldn't worry about what would happen. You just have to go out there and make the plays."

What he would remember most, he said, was not the catch but the prolonged reaction of the crowd to it. "That's what gave me the chills. I'm not a very emotional person but I got into it."

All these remarks came later, of course, much later. The catch may have been the watershed event of the game, and likely the series, but it still came in just the fourth inning. There were other heroes on this night, waiting to take their turn at bat. And again the propitious contributions came from the most unlikely sources.

When Kelly Gruber stepped into the batter's box in the eighth inning, with the score 2-1 Atlanta, he heard the boos and catcalls from the crowd. In the third frame, he had established a post-season record for futility, going 0-for-23 at the plate, surpassing an 0-for-22 mark that had been co-held by Dave Winfield. As he dug in and waggled his bat, some caterwauler in the stands bellowed: "Bunt ya bum!"

Ignoring the advice, Gruber whacked a 3-2 change-up off starter Steve Avery clear over the left-field fence to tie the game at 2-2. In the bat of an eyelash, or a ball, the jeers had turned to cheers. But Gruber had come to understand how mercurial ball fans can be. "Right now I'm a hero," he said. "I'd be surprised if I didn't hear some boos before my first at-bat."

The shot was "better than any other home run" of his career, he said, including the key dinger from Game 2 of the American League playoffs against the Oakland Athletics, which also put Gruber back in the public's good graces, for a fleeting moment. "I've been feeling pretty good at the plate but I haven't had a lot to show for it. Why, I don't know. When things aren't going too well, it seems that everyone jumps off the bandwagon." His sudden, unexpected clutch homer had at least dissolved some of the anger he had been feeling about the denied triple play. "It was a triple play," he asserted. "I touched him on the back of the heel."

The job of winding up this Game 3 shindig fell to another unheralded Blue Jay. The bases were loaded in the ninth inning when Candy Maldonado came to bat, carting an anemic average. Robbie Alomar had got things rolling by slashing a single by Avery's ankles and into center field. Third base coach Jimy Williams, filling in for Bobby Cox who had been tossed for protesting a called strike, now elected to lift Avery for reliever Mark Wohlers. Alomar promptly stole second, Wohlers intentionally walked Joe Carter and Dave Winfield got down a perfect sacrifice bunt. Wohlers made room for fellow-reliever Mike Stanton although the replacement was required only to issue another intentional walk to Ed Sprague.

Williams, shuffling the reliever deck again, called on closer Jeff Reardon — the goat in Game 2 — to face Maldonado. On an 0-2 pitch, and with the Atlanta field drawn in, Maldonado lined one into centre. Alomar trotted home with the 3-2 winner. In the previous game, Candy had been reduced to just one pinch-hitting at-bat. He'd whiffed. Now he had come through with the game-winning RBI, as the Jays took a 2-1 lead in the Series. Reliever Duane Ward got the W, his third in the Jays' last four post-season victories. "Being part of this is tremendous," said an appreciative Maldonado. "You don't want to be left out. I'm glad this was my chance."

Jimmy Key didn't want to be left out either and he had waited longer than everybody else to be included in.

The veteran lefty, who had been a member of the Jay squads that had three times previously gone to the American League playoffs, had not seen any starters' action in their fourth ALCS encounter against the Oakland Athletics. Gaston had opted for a three-man rotation and Key found himself the odd-man out. He had taken the news like a man but he had clearly been chagrined. "I didn't see any action in the playoffs because Cito thought the right-handers would be better against Oakland."

Gaston had a change of heart in the World Series, figuring that Key's off-speed, lefthanded stuff would be a good weapon to offset the big Atlanta bats. When he got the nod to start Game 4, there were some who worried about Key's long lay-off. He was pitching — apart from a three-inning relief stint in Game 5 of the playoffs — on three weeks rest.

It was evident in the first inning that his pitching arm was strong, too strong. He was hit hard, right off the bat. The first two Braves he faced lashed out singles but lead-off batter Otis Nixon was picked off at first by Key. It was a whippet throw that caught Nixon by a foot. Key had been an unknown quantity for Atlanta. Before the game, Justice had snidely remarked that he knew "absolutely nothing" about the guy, adding: "If he threw a 97-mile fastball, I'm sure we would have heard more about him before now." He, Nixon and the Braves had just learned their first lesson, the hard way.

After those first two hits, Key set down the next 16 Atlanta batters in a row and 20 out of 21 before the Braves managed to remove the cobwebs from their brains, Nixon singling with two out in the sixth. Two frames later, Ron Gant connected with a lead-off double and advanced to third when Brian Hunter beat out a bunt single. Berryhill, without instruction from the bench to do so, popped up on another bunt attempt. Cox was thoroughly

perplexed and supremely unhappy about it. "We were stealing.
I don't know what went through Damon's mind." Then Mark
Lemke slashed a ball off the mound near Key's foot that bounced
in the air and landed behind the pitcher. Gruber raced over,
plucked it out of the air barehanded and threw out Lemke at first
for the second out as Gant scored. Ward replaced Key and struck
out Nixon, but it was a wild pitch and he reached first safely
anyway as Hunter hustled to third. But Jeff Blauser grounded out
to first on what looked like a safe-as-house line drive that John
Olerud managed to spear. "Why Olerud was two feet off the line,
I don't know," Cox said.

Key, exiting after 7 2/3 innings, departed to the sounds of a
standing ovation from the second-largest baseball crowd ever to
squeeze into the SkyDome. His teammates had done the job for
him in the interim, building up a 2-0 lead before the Braves
managed their only run of the game.

Key had got his chance and didn't waste it. Borders had got
his pitch and planted it in the stands in the third frame to open the
scoring. And Kelly Gruber had got the flat of his hand on home
plate, the cleft of his chin in the dirt, and a whole bunch of grime
on the front of his shirt to score the winner. That was in the
seventh when he streaked around from second base on White's
single. It was hardly a routine trip home. The sliding Gruber
knocked himself unconscious for a few moments on the play as
he flung himself headlong towards the plate in a desperate
attempt to beat the throw from left fielder Gant. The boink to the
noggin — actually to the chin — left him with temporary amne-
sia. "I don't remember running the bases or even getting on," a
dazed and bruised Gruber said afterwards. "I saw stars." Nor did
he remember much of what happened after that, including the
fielding gem on Lemke's carom-ball in the eighth. "I just saw it in
here," he added, pointing to the video room. "I didn't know a
thing about it until I saw it on TV."

Details, details. Two hours and 21 minutes after it had begun,
the Toronto Blue Jays had their 2-1 victory over the Atlanta
Braves. Or, as one sign in the stands, tweaking fun at the wife of
Atlanta owner Ted Turner put it: Jane Fonda's Workout — Four
more, Three more, Two more, One more.

Borders' home run in the third helped fatten his World Series
batting average to an obese. 417. He had suddenly turned into a
slugger and a hitting machine. Going back to Game 4 of the ALCS

against the Minnesota Twins in 1991, he was now on a 12-game post-season hitting streak. Those offensive numbers took some of the sting off his inability to throw out base stealers. Toronto had allowed 25 steals in the first nine games of the '92 post-season, 16 against Oakland and nine in the World Series — accounting for the most ever surrendered by one team since the Detroit Tigers in 1907 and 1908. Taken all together, this indicated that Borders was having a most curious post-season experience. "I don't take that to heart much," he said, referring to the base thievery. "The thing I do worry about is throwing the ball away."

That's why he had come to the park early that afternoon, to practice clean throws to second base. In his imagination, he nailed every single Atlanta Brave who was trying to steal on him. But he wasn't dreaming about home runs. He left that for the real thing. "To be honest, I wasn't trying to get a home run. I'm just trying to get my bat on the ball."

Borders' smash and Gruber's crash notwithstanding, this had still been Key's ballgame.

When he had left the mound to a noisy send-off, he'd tipped his cap. Just one tiny, modest gesture. But he was embracing the crowd and the city he had called home since 1984. Everyone in the park knew that this may very well have been the last they saw of Key doing his stuff — his neat, economical, elegant stuff — in a Blue Jay uniform. He would be a free agent at the end of the year and this five-hit, one-run performance was his swan song.

He said, afterwards, that he hadn't been thinking of that, not while he was taking care of business on the mound. But he did mull on it as he departed. "That's probably the reason I tipped my hat," he said. "I usually don't do that. But it was a special moment and I wanted to remember it."

How ironic that this likely final start for the Jays had come against a team that was managed by Bobby Cox, the man who had given Key his opportunity when Cox was the skipper of the Toronto contingent. "I had some rough times back then. Coxie stuck with me. He gave me my confidence when I needed it most and whatever I've accomplished in the major leagues, it's because of him."

Key had been here through all the hopeful seasons that had fallen too short, ended too soon. It would be fitting for him to ride out a world champion. "It would be extra special to the city and to the country after what everyone's been through," he said.

On this night, beneath his Blue Jay jersey, Key had worn a Clemson University T-shirt — the South Carolina school is his alma mater — just as he had been doing since September 1, when he had begun to turn around what had been a frustrating season personally. He wound up the year on a five-game winning streak, only to lose his place in the starting rotation during the playoffs. That's why he wanted this night. "It meant more to me than I can ever describe. And I won't ever forget it."

At the other end of the emotional spectrum, Jack Morris was trying to forget — his three post-season starts of 1992. But there was no escape from the probing questions of reporters and the accusing looks of fans. What's up, Jack? How could you, Jack? What's the problem, Jack?

Jack just gritted his teeth and offered a pinched smile. He was even quizzed about that smile. If you keep losing, howcum you keep smiling? "If I was swearing at 'em, you'd be writing the same crap," Morris chided the media. "So now I grin." Sometimes he looked like a grinning fool. "You can never be perfect although you strive to be," he sighed. "I have said all along that if I was a robot, I would go out there and throw perfect games every time and at the end of the year, when I was 37-0, or however many starts I had, I'd quit because I'd be bored to death."

Whatever had gone awry with Jack Morris, at the tail-end of a season in which he had won 21 games and lost only six, surely his personal travails were about to end? *Hubris* is one thing but humiliation was another. As the patrons began pushing through the turnstiles at the SkyDome for Game 5, there was a sense of destiny to the evening. Jack Morris on the mound, the World Series championship on the line, how could he and they be denied?

Gaston never for a moment considered altering his rotation. Morris had brought them here and he was entitled to the last dance, even if the bullpen ended up cutting in. Now, if only his teammates would come through with some hits. "I think it's time that the other guys picked up Jack a bit," Gaston said, noting the lack of run support in Game 1. "These guys have picked him up (in the past) when he's had a hard time." No kidding. How about an average of 5.44 Toronto runs in Morris' 34 regular season games? Or, as Morris himself once put it: "Score me 10 runs boys, and I can beat anybody."

We thought he was kidding.

Ten runs is damn near what it would have taken for the Jays to win Game 5 and the championship title in front of their primed-for-a-party supporters. Morris not only lost the game, he lost it with a bullet — a resounding grand slam home run by Lonnie Smith, the 16th such creature in the history of World Series but the first since Jose Canseco did it for Oakland in 1988. And did we mention this was also the first-ever grand slam by a designated hitter in the WS annals?

It was a harmonic convergence of elements for Smith, who had been the stooge in the '91 World Series, when his baserunning mistake in the eighth inning of Game 7 may have cost the Braves the championship. He still hadn't lived it down. "Individuals have brought it up all year."

Morris had started the game with smoke coming out of his nostrils. But there was no smoke in his fingertips. A crowd of 52,268, second only to the '91 All-Star game in Toronto, fidgeted and fretted as Morris got himself in and out of trouble through the front four. They had gathered expecting a whoop-de-doo ritual of celebration in their own park — the local papers that day had even published the route map for the expected World Series parade. Dumb, not to mention arrogant. The Braves saw it and were not amused. And the festivities? Well, not tonight dear. Jack Morris was about to give the fans a headache.

Nixon led off the game with a ground-rule double into the left field seats on the very first pitch. That stilled the crowd right there and an unsettling feeling began to calcify in the pit of the stomach. Deion Sanders struck out but Nixon stole third, then scored on Terry Pendleton's double to right. The Jays were lucky to get out of the shaky first inning down by just one.

Toronto tied it in the bottom of the second when Pat Borders' double off starter John Smoltz cashed in John Olerud. It remained tied until the fourth when Dave Justice tagged Morris for a lone-run homer. The Jays fought back in their half when Borders, with a single through the box, again cashed Olerud. But that would be it for Blue Jay scoring in Game 5.

In the fifth, Damon Berryhill fanned and Mark Lemke bounced out to second. But with two outs, Morris dug himself into a hole. First he gave up a single to Nixon who stole second and scored on Sanders' single to centre. The crowd barely had time to calibrate this before the table was thoroughly set for Smith: Pendleton had smashed a ground-rule double to right, forcing

Sanders to halt at third, and Justice was walked deliberately to load 'em up. Gaston made no move to hoist Morris. Smith, on a 1-2 count, smashed the ball towards right field. It just carried and carried and carried. Good golly Mr. Lonnie! "I saw Joe Carter drifting back and back on the ball, and I started screaming 'get outta here.' When I saw it go, it was a tremendous relief."

Now, when it was far too late, Gaston promenaded to the mound as a crescendo of boos rained down from the stands. It was unclear whether the disgruntled fans were booing Gaston or Morris. "Let's hope it was the situation but it could have been for me," Gaston conceded. He called for reliever David Wells to mop up, followed by Mike Timlin and Mark Eichhorn — the Toronto bullpen now boasted 13.1 scoreless innings in the Series. With a bullpen like that, why wait for the roof to cave in? Why dither with a struggling starter?

Morris was responsible for giving up all the runs in Atlanta's 7-2 victory, the first ever for a visiting team indoors in a Series game. Had Gaston put loyalty to his pitcher over common baseball sense by leaving him in too long? "I guess the results show that perhaps I did. As I said earlier this week, I believe in Jack a lot. Without Jack, we wouldn't be here. It just didn't work out. Of course I feel bad for him. He made some pitches I know he'd like to have back. Most of the hits off Jack have been home runs, something Jack didn't do a whole lot of this season. I feel bad for him because I know he's out there giving it his all. And we really would have liked to wrap this thing up at home. Jack's a battler and a survivor. I know he'll be okay."

When he trudged off the field, wiping his brow with his forearm, Morris had been derided by those in attendance. He was now 0-3 in 1992 post-season games with one no-decision. The big money pitcher had been all nickels 'n' dimes for Toronto in the playoffs and the World Series.

In the clubhouse, Morris was swarmed by reporters and television cameras and microphones. He was his usual, mildly smirking self. But there was something else there, too. A hint of sadness, of something lost, and not just a baseball game either. Jack Morris would never again be the man who couldn't lose when it counted the most.

"It's not easy to stand here right now because the results were not what I have accomplished in the past," he said, as the reporters measured him for a hair-shirt. "But I can honestly say

I tried the best I could." In his locker, on a shelf, a bottle of champagne had been tucked between the mail and the other personal effects. Gathering dust.

"You've got to find the positive in something like this," he continued, the positive being that the Jays still held a 3-2 lead in the Series. On only five occasions had a team trailing 3-1 rebounded to win the whole enchilada in October. "I did my best," he kept repeating. "It wasn't good enough tonight but I did my best. I can think of 24 other ball clubs who would really like to be in our position." Whatever his hurts on this evening, Morris was keeping them to himself. It was enough that he'd shown his fallibility on the mound, for everybody to see. "If you're asking me to lay down here and cry, I'm not going to do it."

He had now been reduced to the role of spectator, relegated to the sidelines. Whatever the Blue Jays' fortunes, he was no longer a factor. "I'll be out there doing what I can do and that's being a cheerleader. I'll be pulling for my teammates." Or, as he also described his role: "Pompons and skirts." He did point out, however, that he had tried to keep his team in the game, as the Jays twice battled back to tie the Braves, mostly on the efforts of Pat Borders who had continued his hitting streak with a double and a single and two runs batted in.

"Again, I can't tell you how humbling this game can be," said Morris. "You've got to suck it up and accept it." Twelve months earlier he had blockaded the Braves. This year, they had breached the ramparts and bayoneted Morris. "I don't know how to describe it. I think it's just a case of pitching against the same team two World Series in a row. They've seen me five times now. Sometimes, the advantage goes over to the other side. Tonight, they got me."

In the end, Jack was still Jack. He was confident the Jays would take it in Atlanta. "The Atlanta Braves have won two games and I've pitched them both. They're in trouble, they're in serious trouble, because I don't pitch again."

Atlanta, a city that knows all about lost causes, had fought back with all their muskets blasting. Jay revelers replaced the cork in the champagne and the action shifted again to the capital of Georgia.

The locals (seriously, how many expected the World Series to return to Fulton County Stadium after the Braves lost Game 5?)

were in fine spirits (Wild Turkey? Peach daiquiris?) A mob of 5,000 fans turned out to cheer the team at the airport in the wee hours of the morning. Such a spontaneous gesture of public affection should not have been unexpected. This was the city that had held a World Series parade in 1991 — after their team *lost*. The size of the civic welcoming committee was larger than some of the crowds the Braves used to play for at the park only two years earlier, when the franchise was a bottom feeder in the National League West. There were even "Lonnie For President" signs at the airport.

The Jays arrived in town several hours later and they too were confronted with some message-bearing banners. Such as: "Go Back Home Jays." Or this one, aimed at Kelly Gruber, who had last been seen around these parts tomahawking the fans. "In Tyrone, Georgia, We Eat Grubers."

The Braves had been revitalized. After Game 4 in Toronto, Dave Justice and Sid Bream had knocked their teammates for a lack of intensity but Cox dismissed the rumors of dissension on the team as "a crock of crap." Nevertheless, Atlanta had played inspired baseball in Game 5. Would it continue? Would there be a Game 7? Could Toronto be counted on to do what they had always done before in the clutch — choke? Their club history was Atlanta's wild card and everybody knew it even as they pooh-poohed it.

David Cone had nothing to do with Toronto's past. He would probably have nothing to do with Toronto's future either — he was generally regarded as a short-term acquisition by general manager Pat Gillick. It was clear that he longed for the razzle-dazzle of New York, from which he had come. But for the moment he was a Blue Jay and he was pitching Game 6.

Cone, scheduled to face Atlanta's lefty Steve Avery, had something to prove. He had left Game 2 trailing in the fifth and escaped with a no-decision thanks to Ed Sprague's pinch homer. But he had not been forceful in that encounter, not the strikeout power of recent repute. "I was very timid," he admitted, "especially with runners on third base and less than two outs. I walked some guys (five actually) which I shouldn't have because I didn't come in with my pitches. I have to start going after people like I'm capable of doing. That's something I'm planning on doing to-night."

He wanted very much to atone. In fact, he had started his mental preparations for Game 6 at the very moment that Lonnie Smith struck his death-blow in Game 5. "When that home run was hit, in my mind I started preparing. Sure, we were still in the game after Lonnie's grand slam but I knew I had to be ready to pitch." Cone, like everybody else in Toronto, dreaded the thought of a Game 7. "We don't want this series to be tied 3-3. Anything can happen in Game 7, anything at all. We'd rather get it over with."

Getting it over with would take four hours and seven minutes.

It felt at times like the end would never come; at other times that it would come too soon. It was not a thing of beauty but it was a beautiful thing.

Robbie Alomar's elbow was sore, but it didn't matter. The Blue Jays, denied their designated hitter again in the National League park, had to juggle their line-up to accommodate Dave Winfield's bat, and that mattered. Henke slipped the Braves a whiff of a miracle but, in the end, that mattered not either. It only drew out the entertainment for 11 breathless innings.

The evening had begun with some playful shenanigans. Atlanta general manager John Schuerholtz ordered mellow music to be played as the Jays took batting practice: opera and Mario Lanza's rendition of Over The Rainbow. When the Braves took the field for BP, the sound system pounded out energetic rap. Psychological warfare?

The real warfare got underway at precisely 8.43 Eastern Standard Time. Too late for a lot of kids coast-to-coast in two nations but TV was calling the shots. As well, presidential candidate Ross Perot had bought airtime that evening, thereby reducing the pre-game coverage in the States. America's national pastime can wait when a media-fabricated demigod is prepared to throw around that kind of money.

Back in Toronto, 45,551 dyed-in-the-blue-wool Jay devotees assembled in the SkyDome to watch the game on the JumboTron. They had come together to share whatever fate the evening held. This had to be a communal experience, it demanded the intimacy of a united crowd, even if the action was taking place hundreds of miles away.

Should we recount it from the beginning or from the end? From the middle then.

Cone lasted for six occasionally wobbly but always gritty innings, departing with a 2-1 lead. For the Jays, Devon White had scored in the first after singling, stealing second and advancing to third on a sac fly by Carter. Justice missed the catch anyway. The Braves tied it in the third after Sanders doubled down the right field line. With Pendleton batting, Sanders stole third and then scored on Pendleton's sacrifice fly.

Next inning, Maldonado homered to left-centre on a 1-0 count. After Gruber grounded out, the unstoppable Pat Borders doubled down the left-field line, extending his post-season hitting streak to 14 games, the third longest in history. Manny Lee struck out looking, Cone walked, White singled to left. But Borders was tagged out at the plate by Sanders' throw to Berryhill.

With the pitching duties now turned over to Toronto's stingy bullpen, it appeared that a 2-1 score could be enough for the Jays to clinch their first World championship. The innings wore on, one scoreless frame after another, and suddenly it was the bottom of the ninth. Tom Henke — who had taken over from Ward, who had taken over from Wells who had taken over from Stottlemyre, who had taken over from Cone — gave up a lead-off single to Jeff Blauser. Berryhill tried a sacrifice bunt, but Henke fielded it and threw to Alomar, who was covering first. Blauser took second on the play. Pinch-hitter Smith walked. National League playoff hero Francisco Cabrera pinch-hit for reliever Wohlers and lined out to left. Nixon singled to the same area, scoring Blauser.

The game was tied. The Terminator had blown the save. The corpse twitched. And all of Atlanta, maybe all of the U.S., rejoiced.

Extra innings now. The hard-luck Charlie Leibrandt came in to pitch for the Braves but, apart from Gruber's single to centre, the Jays couldn't put anything together. In the bottom of the inning, Key came out of the bullpen to pitch in emergency relief — his second swan song as a Blue Jay — after Pendleton had grounded out. Justice and Bream followed suit.

In the 11th, Key hit for himself and popped to Bream in foul territory. Liebrandt bonked White with a pitch. He advanced to second when Alomar singled to right-centre. Carter flied out to Nixon. That brought up Dave Winfield, the heart of the order for the Jays throughout 1992. He had only four singles to show for his 21 trips to the plate in the series but all that mattered was this moment, this situation. Gaston could have lifted Winfield, who had been playing right field so he could contribute with his bat, and gone to the bench for Olerud, who had been left idle when the repositioned Joe Carter started at first. But the Toronto manager, playing his own hunches, didn't do that.

In the other dugout, Cox could have lifted Leibrandt for Jeff Reardon who had warmed up. But Cox had quickly lost faith in his star acquisition. It would be Liebrandt and roll the dice.

Winfield wiggled his hips, slapped his palm against his batting helmet and stroked a double down the left field line. White scored. Alomar scored. And all the oomph went out of the crowd.

The Braves tried to engineer another rally in the bottom of the 11th. They even got one of those runs back when Blauser, who had singled and reached third on another misplay by Alfredo Griffin, made it home on Hunter's ground out. Key was finally done for the night and young Mike Timlin — he and Mark Eichhorn were the only arms left in the pen — made his way to the mound to face Nixon. "Game 6 of the World Series, two out and the tying run on third," Timlin recapped later. "I dreamt and dreamt of this day, this situation. I always wanted to be in it." Gaston's last words to Timlin were: "Watch out, this guy might bunt."

That was precisely what Nixon did — straight back to the pitcher. Timlin fielded the ball and tossed it gently to Carter for the final out. Carter sprang into the air. He jumped and he jumped and he jumped until the rest of his teammates joined him for a round of mass pogo jubilation.

Game over, series over. Hail the new champions.

It seemed to have happened in slow motion, that last out in the 4-3 final. "When he bunted and Mike picked it up, I wondered if he was ever going to throw that ball," said Gaston. Marveled Timlin, still agog with his tiny but pivotal role in the affair: "Tonight, I came through, just like I always came through in my dreams."

O Canada! O joy! Oh boy oh boy oh boy.

The Jays were running crazy on the field, piling into a tangled heap of arms and legs and bobbing heads gasping for air. At the SkyDome, thousands of fans shrieked with abandon, grabbing strangers to hug and kiss. Then they spilled onto the streets to hug and kiss some more in an all-night victory orgy — half a million of them strong and nobody got hurt. Canadianas don't overturn cars and set fires when they're happy. In 36 hours, the country was supposed to vote on a new constitution in a national referendum. For months, Canadians had been scolded about unity and threatened by politicians who predicted dire consequences for the nation if voters said no to the new deal. Baseball had been a release from all that. Here was unity, here was a lovely distraction from everything that ailed a country.

The team, the city, the whole blessed nation had been swept away by the bliss of it all, riding on a crest of World Series diamonds. A bunch of honorary Canadians — American or Dominican or Puerto Rican or even Jamaican-born — had captured the President's Trophy four games to two. The gallant Atlanta Braves had been southern fried. And chop-phooey to you too.

Pat Borders, the tow-headed catcher who had hit close to .500 in the series, with a single and a double in Game 6 alone, was named the Most Valuable Player. He was near speechless with shock. "I can't believe they really gave the award to me." In the tumult of the clubhouse merriment, Borders looked completely bewildered. He had taken off his jersey by then, had stripped down to the cut-off T-shirt that he preferred, the one that showed off the muscles in his upper arms. He'd undone his pants too, like guys do when they've finished their labors for the day. Wife Kathy, pregnant with the couple's second child, was pushed forward by relatives. "Go on, go get your picture taken with your husband," one of the women kinfolk urged. But Kathy Borders was shy and tried to hang back "Get up there girl," the other lady persisted. "You're even having a good hair day." So Mr. and Mrs. Borders clasped each other for the cameras and Pat planted a self-conscious kiss on his wife's lips, then slid his hand down her back. She giggled and tossed her long blonde mane.

Everybody wanted words from Borders, who had risen so graciously and unexpectedly to the occasion. Except Borders is a man of few words and all of those are uttered in a sometimes incomprehensible hillbilly twang. He mumbled a few sentences, then raised his palms in a what-can-I-say gesture, before scurrying off to fill his batting helmet with cans of beer.

Security officials outside the dressing room had thrown up their hands too as media, wives, children, friends and strangers jammed into the champagne-sodden clubhouse. At this party, everybody was invited and nobody needed an invitation. "Man, I just gotta get up and dance," shouted a flush-cheeked Ward as he grabbed Timlin, the two of them hopping on to a table where they boogied and bopped to the thumpa-thumpa of rock music.

Tom Henke planted a big wet one on his wife, who said: "It's been a long time coming, hasn't it honey?" In another corner, White broke away from a cluster of gladhanders for a few words with an elderly blind man who kept clutching at the sleeve of the player's jersey, saying "Devo, Devo, Devo." White, wearing a World Series championship cap — the tag still dangling over his right ear — paid tribute to Gaston. "Ah man. All year he's been talked about and dragged through the mud. He deserved this more than anyone else. When I came to Toronto, he showed me the kind of respect all players want. He's a friend before he's a manager. The whole organization is like that. It's five years ahead of any organization in baseball."

Meanwhile, the wives broke out in a spontaneous chant of We Stopped The Chop. Jack Morris held hands with his girl-friend, Gruber hugged his mom, game-winner Key put a headlock on Dave Stieb, Alomar babbled in Spanish and English. Carter smooched with his missus and whispered, "Were you a little nervous up there honey?" She buried her face in his shoulder. Timlin talked about the final out, after he had tossed the ball to first. "I didn't know what to do. I just wanted to give everybody on the field a hug."

That was the general idea.

Winfield had to deal with a media scrum before he was allowed to join his mates in the clubhouse. "This is the most fun I've had playing professional baseball," he told the scribblers. "It's a culmination of a good year, a tough year. This year, we set some goals and we reached them. I'm almost speechless. I can't even think of words to describe it. These guys deserve every-thing. This is a consummate team. This is the best team I've ever played for."

Then, smooth public speaker that he is, he paid tribute to the citizens of Atlanta. "I'm going to give the people of Atlanta, the fans, a lot of credit. Some of the cities you go to, the people are really rude and nasty. But they treated everybody in our families and our entourages really well, they were first-class. We really didn't want to come back here because we knew it would be really tough. We're just glad to escape here with a win and go back to Canada. They deserve it. America's game is now going to Canada for a while."

In the clubhouse, awash with the bubbly stuff, Winfield continued the monologue. "I didn't do a whole lot but I did it at the right time. I'll tell you, I'm the oldest man in the room, the longest waiting for a world championship, but also the happiest man here."

Hard to quantify that sort of thing. Who was the happiest man there? Paul Beeston pumped hands, flitting from one player to another. Pat Gillick was in tears, so was Gaston. "Can't tell you what it means to me right now," the manager apologized. "Maybe tomorrow. I guess I'm thinking of what it means to other people, our fans, our families. It's been a hard struggle to get here. A lot of people stuck by us. I'm kind of lost for words. I'm not thinking too clearly now."

The merrymaking in Toronto, and in one small corner of Atlanta, went on throughout the night. The Jays, once they were finally dressed and out of the stadium, had a club party in the basement of their hotel. Their flight home was scheduled for early the next morning but nobody wanted to say goodnight. They clung to the moment, to the feeling.

It couldn't go on forever. By dawn, most had staggered back to their rooms. But not all.

In one of the hotel corridors, a media straggler happened upon Pat Borders. He was sitting on the floor, leaning against the wall, his wife nestled in his lap. Arranged in a protective semi-circle around the couple, members of the Borders clan sat cross-legged.

Talking baseball as the sun came up in Atlanta.

# Gl⊛ry Jays

## *Farewells* 18

All good things must end. But surely not this quickly?

It had taken 16 years to get the formula right and the Toronto Blue Jays were, finally, the best team in baseball. Yet the winning combination stayed intact for less than 48 hours.

On the day after the club's return to Toronto, the city staged a lovin' feast through the downtown streets attended by at least a quarter-of-a-million revelers. Kids skipped school, adults slipped away from their offices, young mothers pushed infants in prams bedecked with Blue Jay regalia. The victory parade, through the drizzle and the pandemonium, inched its way in a cavalcade of champions from the train station to the SkyDome. Celebrants chased after the players, who rode on the back of convertibles. The pursuers stretched out their arms to touch their heroes. It was a rhapsody in blue.

With police sirens blaring and a band playing, the players entered the stadium to a prolonged standing ovation. Some in designer suits, some in faded jeans, they waved like royalty to the capacity crowd. Hundreds of fans had been turned away from the SkyDome which had filled up hours before the team was scheduled to arrive. As the athletes made their way onto the stage, their wives and girlfriends peeled off towards a reserved section of seating that had been set apart for family and friends. The ladies, outfitted in leather Blue Jay jackets, twittered like exotic birds as the men took their bows.

"We're all Number One," Joe Carter reminded the fans, as he shouted to be overheard over the din, the amorous ovation. It was baseball erotica, a convivial and touching and curiously intimate gathering, even in this concrete ballpark, with plyboards laid over the artificial turf and the pitcher's mound sunk back into its subterranean lair.

And Carter did have it right. Because, while this event was supposed to be about Toronto saluting the Jays, it also turned into the Jays saluting Toronto. They wanted to thank their fans for filling the SkyDome night after night, and for embracing them as fellow citizens even though they had all come from someplace else and were all going home to someplace else. Some of the players would leave shortly — a few not even waiting until the day's festivities were over. Some would linger for a day or two. Too many would not be coming back at all.

Only hours after the last fans had filed out of the SkyDome, the Blue Jays announced they had released Dave Stieb, Mike Maksudian had been picked up on waivers by the Minnesota Twins, Dave Winfield would not be offered arbitration and neither would Candy Maldondo.

The news about Winfield was not too troubling because nobody believed that it meant anything. The fans had been warned about this eventuality but assured by reporters that it was a mere technicality. Denying Winfield arbitration made him a free agent, which meant he could negotiate with any team he chose, including the Jays. Had he been extended arbitration, the Jays would have been compelled to put him on their protected 15-man roster, with the expansion draft coming up. It was a luxury the franchise could not afford. Still, on this day of rapture and warm feelings, the impatient moves brought a jarring note of baseball reality to the proceedings.

"I'm gone," said Stieb, after meeting with the team's braintrust. "They bought me out. That's it." That, too, was baseball. The heartless part of baseball. The business of baseball.

Earlier, an emotional Stieb had thanked the crowd "for supporting me when I was down and out." Later, he described the sensations of the day to reporters. "Seeing all those people on the sidewalk, in the streets, hanging from the trees, it was a great feeling to be perched on that car, taking it all in. God, what a feeling." It was one final kindness. That Stieb, after 14 seasons as a Blue Jay — his entire major league career — had been given the chance to know that feeling.

And Winfield? He had waited two decades. "Let's hear noise!" he demanded of the audience. "Winfield wants noise! All right...all right...all right." He was 41 years old and this marked the first time he would be measured for a World Series ring. "As you can see, age doesn't mean a thing," he crowed.

It was Winfield who directed the crowd to look up, way up, as the World Series Championship banner was unfurled and the fireworks display lit up the cavernous interior of the SkyDome. "I love you," he said, simply.

Afterwards, Winfield lingered for a while in the clubhouse, came out to talk with the media. It was as if he did not want this tremor of happiness to end. "When you're right in the middle of it, it's hard to describe. I have to see it again in order to put it in perspective. I just saw these waves and waves of people. The way the crowd supported us, especially through the last part of the season, it's the best I've ever seen. That's something to be proud of." Then he added: "The first time is the best." Forty-one years old and he was still talking about the first time, still looking forward to the next time.

It was obvious on that afternoon that some players were saying goodbye. Candy Maldonado...maybe Tom Henke...possibly Jimmy Key...perhaps David Cone.

Cone had passed this way briefly and many observers felt he would not tarry long, that he was headed for the New York Yankees as a free agent. They hadn't been given enough time to know him well in Toronto but they liked what they saw. And on this day, they liked what they heard. Cone was poetic in his farewell. "It was like I was hitchhiking on the side of the road and I got a ride to the World Series," he said. Then, sweeping his arm towards his teammates: "It may be true that we're all Americans or Latin Americans on this stage. But we still feel the pride of Canada. We see the flags. You don't have to be Canadian to feel that pride.

"Don't ever change."

Pat Borders, sweet Pat Borders, had finally shaved off the billygoat stubble he had sported throughout the World Series. Offstage, he popped a wad of tobacco, masticated contentedly, and talked about the pleasures of the civic reception. "That was one of the happiest days of my life. To see that many people going wild. I just couldn't have imagined it. I could not stop smiling." Yet already there was talk that the Jays were prepared to trade him. "So you guys keep telling me," Borders said to the reporters.

The Blue Jays had a heavy representation of free agents who were looking to negotiate a profitable future, if not with Toronto, then somewhere else: Jimmy Key, David Cone, Tom Henke, Joe Carter, Manny Lee, Alfredo Griffin, Pat Tabler and Rance Mulliniks. "I hope they sign a few guys," said Robbie Alomar, safely locked up for the next few years. "Some of the guys will stay and some will go. But we'll be back at it next year with a bunch of new guys."

No World Series champs had repeated since the Yankees in 1977 and 1978. Toronto devotees had braced themselves for changes and losses. But nobody expected the mass exodus that would shortly ensue. Some jumped, others were pushed. A few left with a sour taste in their mouths and insults on their tongues.

Stieb, who had been cut loose but extended an invitation to spring training as a non-roster invitee, found greener pastures with more security in Chicago. Within weeks he had signed with the White Sox for $300,000 guaranteed, $750,000 if he made the team in the spring. He did not go quietly. "I never envisioned it being like this," he told Bill Lankhof of the *Toronto Sun*. "It isn't a pretty ending. At least I have the World Series ring. But the real hurt came when they put me in the bullpen. I mean, what was I going to do there? I felt I wasn't given a fair shake."

When the winter baseball meetings opened in Louisville, Kentucky, in early December, chroniclers of the sport weren't expecting much action on the Blue Jay front. The Toronto brass had made it known they intended to toe the line and hold the payroll at $45 million. With voracious free agency shunting salaries into the stratosphere — in spite of the general blathering from major league owners that this financial madness had to stop — it was clear the Jays could re-sign only a handful of their own desperately-seeking-raises free agents. General manager Pat Gillick had hinted he was hoping to sign three mercenaries, and not necessarily from within his own shop.

But the Blue Jays quickly made headlines out of Louisville. The first shockwaves occurred when Toronto traded Kelly Gruber, and his $4 million salary, to the California Angels for...Luis Sojo? The same back-up infielder they had shipped to the Angels just two years earlier as a throw-in to the Devon White swap? It was even worse than it looked on paper since the Jays agreed to pick up a sizable chunk of Gruber's salary in the process, more than $1 million. Gillick gently described the transaction as a "salary reallocation" but it was also evident that Gruber had taxed the Jays' patience with his assortment of baffling maladies in 1991 and 1992.

The third baseman was devastated. "I don't like it," he told his biographer Kevin Boland. "It's definitely not my choice. I'm leaving a great ballclub. I'm leaving family. I'm leaving friends. It really hurts. I'm in shock, I guess. I wanted to finish my career in Toronto. I didn't want to be known as anything but a Blue Jay. There was nothing more important to me in the game. Not saying anything untoward about Luis but am I that bad a player to where they just traded for one guy? What were they thinking?"

It must have wounded him deeply too when a couple of his recent teammates stepped forward to make disparaging remarks about Gruber. Devon White, in town for a card show, suggested that Gruber hadn't been dedicated enough to the team and to his job. "As far as Kelly goes, not because he's gone now, he was in a way a bad influence for the younger players," he told the *Toronto Star*. "He wasn't really a leader. And you need leaders on the Blue Jays team." Added Rance Mulliniks, who would shortly announce his own retirement from baseball: "He wasn't missing anything but his work habits really fell off the last couple of years, especially this year. There was no extra batting practice, no nothing. I think that's one of the reasons his performance has fallen off. You can't be consistent in this game if you don't work hard every day."

The Jays, with their liberated stash of cash, immediately turned around and signed old nemesis Dave Stewart to a two-year $8.5 million contract. Now the writing was on the wall for Jimmy Key. The southpaw, whose wife acted as his agent, told reporters he thought there had been an offer on the table from the Jays before he set out on a Caribbean cruise. He claimed he had been offered three years with a one-year option — by fax. But when his financial adviser tried to contact the Jays for further discussion, there was nobody around to take the call. That was Key's version of events anyway. Gillick wouldn't comment. Key comforted himself by accepting $17 million over four years from the Yankees. Jimmy Key in pinstripes? What was happening here?

Events were moving at a dizzying pace. The sly Gillick snatched free agent Paul Molitor away from the Milwaukee Brewers for a potential $16 million on three years plus an option for a fourth. But the veteran Molitor was an obvious DH addition, so what did that do to Winfield? What it did was make him expendable if, indeed, he had ever been part of the Blue Jays' plans for '93. Immediate speculation was that Winfield's agent, Jeff Klein, had pressed too hard and demanded too much from Toronto. He had bargained Winfield right out of the picture.

The fans were appalled. Winfield's legion of supporters lit up switchboards at the SkyDome and Toronto radio call-in shows. There was talk of a fan boycott. How could the Jays do such a thing, they moaned? Was there no loyalty in baseball? None at all, at all, at all? In town for a promotional gig — he was having his cleats inducted into a local shoe museum — the always public relations-conscious Winfield held a press conference. He said he was "flabbergasted" by what had happened and he steadfastly maintained that he had not made excessive contract demands. "There were some communications things that didn't work out. At this point in my career, people who know Dave Winfield know he doesn't demand multi-year contracts or money. This was not personal. It was business. The Jays wanted to move in another direction."

He had always planned on coming back to Toronto, he said, and was disappointed that it was not going to happen. But he wasn't bitter and he would always remember what he and this team and this city had accomplished together. "I can say I lived out a dream, winning the World Series," he told reporters. "I visualized it. Whenever the young guys griped during the season, I'd tell them that things were a lot worse elsewhere around the league. I know. I've been there. They'll miss some of the intangibles I feel I brought but they'll still have a very good team here. To the fans, I can only say that in one year we became great friends, almost like family. One of the greatest things that ever happened to me was when they sang Happy Birthday to me. You don't forget things like that. You won't forget me and I won't forget you."

A short time later, Winfield became a Minnesota Twin. He was going home.

Dave Cone left too, but not for the Yankees. He accepted $18 million — including an unprecedented $9 million signing bonus up front (who's afraid of no lockout?) — to return to his own hometown and the Kansas City Royals. Candy Maldonado said yes to $3.5 million from the Chicago Cubs. Manny Lee took $3.4

million guaranteed and two years from the Texas Rangers. At least he had some Blue Jay company in Arlington — Tom Henke signed on with the Rangers as well, for $8 million over two years. But he was the most reluctant to leave, shuffling his feet and waiting for a Toronto offer that never came. "I'd have loved to have had the chance to come back to Toronto. But it was never up to me."

The Toronto Blue Jays had been gutted.

Only one big fish had been reeled back in from the stormy waters of free agency. Joe Carter, who had been seriously courted by the Kansas City Royals, opted to remain a Blue Jay. The Jays had made re-signing their big RBI man their top priority and had staved off all other suitors with a four-year contract (the final year an option only by the merest technicality, incumbent on Carter reaching 400 plate appearances in the first three seasons) worth up to $25 million. The 32-year-old outfielder told reporters that he'd had this dream, see, a sign from God, the way he figured it. "I had a vision of playing beside Devon White. I had a vision of having a press conference in Toronto. Everything just sort of came together."

God moves in mysterious ways. So does Pat Gillick.

This Toronto Blue Jay season in the sun had lasted 202 days, from the first at-bat in Detroit to the last out in Atlanta.

Game over. Fade to blue.

*Marge Schott...Unleashed!*: Explores the controversial tenure of Marge Schott as owner of the Cincinnati Reds, and what really led to her suspension. Available June 1993.

*Pittsburgh Pirates: Still Walking Tall*: Takes an exciting look at the team that won the last three National League East division crowns, and is picked by many experts to do it again this year. Available April 1993.

*Lady in the Locker Room: Uncovering the Oakland Athletics*: Follow the career of Susan Fornoff, one of the few female reporters to cover a major league baseball team on a daily basis. Find out what a female reporter "sees" in the locker room. Available April 1993.

*Lou Boudreau: Covering All the Bases*: Boudreau tells the story of his exciting career in this autobiography. His years as a player manager with the Cleveland Indians, and his nearly three decades of announcing for the Chicago Cubs. Available June 1993.

*Phil Rizzuto: A Yankee Tradition*: Tells the story of Rizzuto's rise to baseball stardom, including his years in the minors, four All-Star appearances, and 1950 MVP performance. Available June 1993.

*Down for the Count: Investigating the Mike Tyson Rape Trial*: This controversial new title gives an in-depth description of the trial of the year; including the numerous miscalculations by Tyson's defense team, the testimony of Desiree Washington and of Mike Tyson himself. Available May 1993.

**Please call Sagamore at (217) 359-5940 to order any of our spring sports titles or to receive a free catalog of the best fall sports titles.**

| | |
|---|---|
| *Against the World: A Behind-the-Scenes Look at the Portland Trail Blazers' Chase for the NBA Championship* ISBN 0-915611-67-8 $19.95 | *Metivier On: Saratoga, Glens Falls, Lake George, and the Adirondacks* ISBN 0-915611-60-0 $19.95 |
| *Best in the Game: The Turbulent Story of the Pittsburgh Penguins' Rise to Stanley Cup Champions* ISBN 0-915611-66-x $19.95 | *Stormin' Back: Missouri Coach Norm Stewart's Battles On and Off the Court* ISBN 0-915611-47-3 $19.95 |
| *Blue Fire: A Season Inside the St. Louis Blues* ISBN 0-915611-55-4 $22.95 | *Take Charge! A How-to Approach for Solving Everyday Problems* ISBN 0-915611-46-5 $9.95 |
| *The Fighting Irish Football Encyclopedia* ISBN 0-915611-54-6 $44.95 | *Undue Process: The NCAA's Injustice for All* ISBN 0-915611-34-1 $19.95 |
| *Hail to the Orange and Blue* ISBN 0-915611-31-7 $29.95 | *William Warfield: My Music & My Life* ISBN 0-915611-40-6 $19.95 |
| *Lady Magic: The Autobiography of Nancy Lieberman-Cline* ISBN 0-915611-43-0 $19.95 | *Winning Styles for Winning Coaches: Creating the Environment for Victory* ISBN 0-915611-49-x $12.95 |
| *Lou: Winning at Illinois* ISBN 0-915611-24-4 $18.95 | *Woody Hayes: A Reflection* ISBN 0-915611-42-2 $19.95 |